FORTY FATHOMS DEEP

PEARL DIVERS & SEA ROVERS
IN AUSTRALIAN SEAS

ION IDRIESS

ETT IMPRINT

Exile Bay

This 23nd edition published in Imprint Classics in 2025.

This book is copyright. Apart from any fair dealing for the purposes of private study, research, criticism or review, as permitted under the Copyright Act, no par t may be reproduced by any process without written permission. Inquiries should be addressed to the publishers.

ETT IMPRINT
PO Box R1906
Royal Exchange NSW 1225
Australia

First published by Angus & Robertson 1937. Reprinted 1937 (four), 1938 (twice), 1939, 1941, 1942, 1943, 1945, 1947, 1950, 1951, 1952.
Reprinted in paperback 1968, 1973, 1979, 1990, 1991.
First electronic edition ETT Imprint 2017.
First published by ETT Imprint 2020.

Copyright © Idriess Enterprises Pty Ltd, 2017, 2020.

ISBN 978-1-923205-94-9 (paper)
ISBN 978-1-922384-81-2 (ebook)

Cover design by Tom Thompson

Cover image: Japanese pearl divers off Broome, early 1920s

AUTHOR'S NOTE

Forty Fathoms Deep is part of the story of the pearl seas of north-western Australia. In all but a few instances, I have used names well known in the pearl world of Broome, but have taken care not to hurt susceptibilities. I am conscious I have only gleaned in a field rich with romance. There is material for many books in the adventurous lives of the men who have built up the history and industry of Broome. It is to be hoped that someone more persuasive than I will induce them to sit down and write, or, failing that, sit and talk for the enlightenment and entertainment of fellow Australians.

I am greatly indebted to numerous friends in Broome who have helped me with material and who went to such pains to get for me authentic data.

Hail and farewell, with a warm heart, to Con and old Sebaro, and to all the divers and tenders and seamen who were so patient at explaining the many things I desired to see and know.

To all, a fair wind and a hungry market when the fleets put to sea!

ION L. IDRIESS.

Commander A. G. Goldie's fleet getting ready for sea.

ETT IMPRINT has the following ION IDRIESS books in print in 2025:

Prospecting for Gold (1931)
Lasseter's Last Ride (1931)
Flynn of the Inland (1932)
The Desert Column (1932)
Men of the Jungle (1932)
Drums of Mer (1933)
Gold-Dust and Ashes (1933)
The Yellow Joss (1934)
Man Tracks (1935)
Over the Range (1937)
Forty Fathoms Deep (1937)
Madman's Island (1938)
Headhunters of the Coral Sea (1940)
Lightning Ridge (1940)
Nemarluk (1941)
Shoot to Kill (1942)
Sniping (1942)
Guerrilla Tactics (1942)
Trapping the Jap (1942)
Lurking Death (1942)
The Scout (1943)
Horrie the Wog Dog (1945)
In Crocodile Land (1946)
The Opium Smugglers (1948)
The Wild White Man of Badu (1950)
Outlaws of the Leopolds (1952)
The Red Chief (1953)
The Silver City (1956)
Coral Sea Calling (1957)
Back O' Cairns (1958)
The Wild North (1960)
Tracks of Destiny (1961)
Gouger of the Bulletin (2013)
Ion Idriess: The Last Interview (2020)
Ion Idriess Letters (2023)
Walkabout (2024)
Our Flying Aces (2025)

CONTENTS

I. LOVE AND PEARLS	7
II. CON THE BOSUN	13
III. THE PEARL	21
IV. THE THIEF	28
V. THE CONSPIRACY	32
VI. MURDER	39
VII. THE ARREST	48
VIII. THE DIVER AND THE HERRINGS	56
IX. TIME AND LIFE AND DEATH	63
X. DOWN WHERE THE DEAD SHIPS LIE	71
XI. THE WRECK OF THE "KELANDER BUX"	77
XII. THE SWIM OF CAPTAIN GREGORY	85
XIII. CON MAKES LOVE	92
XIV. A SLEEPER IN THE NIGHT	99
XV. MEN AND FATE AND DESTINY	106
XVI. HAZARDS OF THE SEA	110
XVII. THE "KOOMBANA"	119
XVIII. A QUIET NIGHT AT SEA	126
XIX. LOST ON THE BOTTOM OF THE SEA	135
XX. BLACK MAGIC	141
XXI. THE WHALE	148
XXII. THE SHELL-OPENER ON THE "DONNA MATILDA"	155
XXIII. PROSPECTING THE OCEAN FLOOR	163
XXIV. THE JAPANESE RIOTS	172
XXV. AT THE BOTTOM OF THE SEA	178
XXVI. THE MONKEY-FISH	187
XXVII. MONKEY AND THE DIVER	193
XXVIII. DEPTHS OF THE SEA	198
XXIX. TIGERS OF THE SEA	206
XXX. THE BABY DEVIL-FISH	212
XXXI. LEVIATHANS OF THE DEEP	217
XXXII. THE RAIN-MAKER	225
XXXIII. BROOME DAYS	229
XXXIV. THE "BISHOP'S GHOST"	235
XXXV. SEA WEALTH	242

Japanese pearl divers ready to go down off Broome.

CHAPTER I
Love and Pearls

Castilla Toledo was in love. He liked being in love. But his adored was white, and he was a Manilaman diver. Still, Castilla's burning ambition was to marry a white woman. His opportunities were limited for few girls in Broome would speak with a coloured diver, much less encourage friendship. Another thing: misgivings whispered that his beloved was not really a nice girl. And Castilla believed he was worthy of the best.

This woman was young and buxom with a smiling friendliness that disguised a sharp temper. Well, her white skin, in Toledo's eyes, covered various shortcomings. His suspicions were lulled in the joy of a promised attainment. Their lovemaking was discreet of course; unknown to the white community and most of the coloured, despite their uncanny intuition in affairs of the heart.

Toledo first had to gain money. with which to buy a home and set up in fashion as befitted the girl he adored. Naturally she insisted on that. Then Toledo dreamed of a pearl. Only a pearl could bring the realization of his dreams. Sudden wealth to any in Broome meant one thing—a pearl.

The girl in each stolen meeting was gaily anxious that he should win a pearl. Always her first smiling greeting was: "Oh, Castilla, how well you look. Is it meeting me that makes you smile so, or is it that you have found a pearl?" Toledo was familiar with this failing of the rare girl willing to become friendly with a coloured diver; always so pleasantly coquettish that he should one night show her a pearl—a good pearl. But then every soul in Broome found pleasure in admiring a good pearl.

Toledo was a handsome Manilaman, a "flash" diver. Not a first-class diver, though when on shore his appearance proclaimed this envied reputation. Tall and lithely built, his youthful, light brown skin allied to speaking brown eyes, coal-black hair and flashing teeth made him almost an Adonis. He was strong too, his well-knit frame active with a cat-like grace. At sea, dressed only in a sarong, he was sulky or savage or merry just as his mercurial temper dictated. But at Broome, with his bright shore smile, and smartly dressed in the flash Manila way, he was laughing, hail-fellow-well-met, pleasant company. In the starlit evenings on the foreshore he would strum the guitar while his soft, melodious voice was plaintively expressive in the love-songs of old Manila.

Toledo was working diver on Bernard Bardwell's *Phyllis*. A tight little craft, she had so far dodged the perils that wait for ships at sea. Bardwell sailed for Lagrange Bay, eighty-five miles south-west of Broome, then south past Cape Bossut, lying towards the northern end of the Eighty Mile Beach. Diving operations commenced and time drifted by.

Now, aboard a pearling lugger the diver generally sleeps in the starboard bunk in the master's cabin aft, should a master be aboard. And in that narrow space, during those months at sea confidences ooze out. It is the monotonous sameness. Lying in bunk in the evenings staring up at the cabin roof while smoking thoughtfully, subconsciously aware of the whispering tide, the comforting creak of the chain, the music of the wind passing through the rigging, a man is apt to lose perspective; the world seems a lonely place shared by the companion in the bunk opposite. As the months drift by even a secret clamours to be discussed, while colour and caste and racial antipathies become blurred. The town life of Broome where these things necessarily count so much recedes into the future of the next lay-up season.

So to his white master and companion Toledo eventually poured out the longings of his heart.

"I love her," he declared. And his eyes shone, his voice sighed to the cabin roof. "She like me and I like she! Suppose I get enough money I marry him and him promise marry me! He got good heart! I like him, I *love* him!" His voice would sigh away, he would stare at the roof only to sigh again. "I love she very much more, she loves me! I only want money and she will marry me!"

As Toledo gradually forgot discretion in the loneliness of sea life he revealed to Bardwell his heart and soul. Bardwell warned him—not of trespassing against the whites, but of the woman.

He explained that she was not a *real* white woman; she was an adventuress who had drifted up from the cities in the south. Her antecedents were unknown; she was after "what she could get". Even if he won a pearl, it would not be his. If he stole it, then the woman would wheedle it from him and disappear in the first steamer south. And he would not dare say a word.

The diver laughed. His woman was not like that!

Bardwell captained the *Phyllis* and did his own shell-opening. He made sure that none of the crew knew whether he was getting pearl or not, and that no unopened shell remained on deck after sundown. This slick Manila diver would get no opportunity of stealing a pearl from him.

Day after day, away from those miles upon miles of gleaming white beach, Bardwell fished for the pearl-shell oyster, with moderate success, until his provisions and water ran low. Then he sailed north for Cape Bossut and anchored in Lagrange Bay. A lively bay on a lonely coast. Sandy, with occasional scrub patches, low hillocks, small flats, grass covered.

Here, amidst virgin bush, were the primitive shacks of a large camp. It was a base camp of the Chamberlain brothers and several others, swelled now by the crews of several fleets and individual vessels congregating on the arrival of several supply schooners from Broome. Scattered over the bay were the luggers at anchor, the schooners haughtily riding among them.

Chamberlains' *Alma* was there, with the saturnine Conard Gill, the West Indiaman bosun, leaning over the rail. With a lazy wave of the hand he welcomed the *Phyllis*. Toledo scowled, while the crew waved greeting in reply. Among the coloured crews of the fleets this dark-visaged, suave-voiced Con was feared as the hoodoo man, worker of pourri-pourri and the more dreaded black magic. But Chamberlain did not care, for Con was a capable bosun and above all a trusted man.

Loaded dinghies were leaving the luggers to dump their shell aboard the schooners ready for the shell-opener's knife, returning with stores and water for the luggers. Other dinghies were rowing to the shore where from the rough timbers of a foreshore camp rang bursts of riotous laughter. A rousing hail came out to Bardwell. Instructing Toledo to start the crew at filling the water-tanks Bardwell rowed ashore to meet the masters, the captains, and white shell-openers. There would be news here of Broome, and months-late news of the outside world. And there would be discussions on pearls, and a heart-burning examining of pearls recently found by the lucky ones.

A lusty crowd, the Chamberlains, the Macdonalds, the Jameses, in fact the especially "lively" white population of the fleets. "Gentleman James the Pirate" with his ready wit, his perfect manners hiding a lurking devilry. There were here too "Long" James and Jimmy James, the Chamberlain brothers, "Black Jack" Macdonald with his Blackbeard's beard, "Red Jack" Macdonald with his shaggy head of red, "White Jack" and "Pretty Mac" — and others of the clan. The "Pirates" of the fleets these, unaware of fear. Except Gentleman James. He admitted to just one fear — that in years to come he might go blind. He swore he would shoot himself if he did.

He kept his word, in a very lonely place.

Bardwell plunged into the rough gaiety of this devil-may-care camp. After months at sea the companionship of white men all obsessed by the lure of pearls was pleasure indeed.

At sundown came quietness over shore and bay, and the welcome evening meal.

Then suddenly it was night with the stars shining coldly. Fires crimsoned the shore-edge while riding lights twinkled from mast-heads; a smell of the bush rose from the shore, smell of the sea from the waters.

Upon favourite luggers groups squatted around some Malay story-teller. In a listening silence they were all eyes and ears, punctuating each point with an applausive "Wah! Wah!". Should, however, that coloured Kipling make one mistake his reputation would be laughed to scorn.

From the *Phyllis* came the twang of a guitar, then Toledo's silvery voice. Around him dusky Manilamen, dreaming with the song centuries of racial antipathy separating them from the Malays. The Japanese among the fleets talked in groups apart. These were only beginning to engage in that ruthless competition against the Malays and Manilamen in which they were to achieve almost supreme mastery in the diving profession throughout the pearling-waters of Australia. The Koepangers and the Amboinese mixed in friendly fashion with the Malays.

At the foreshore camp a concertina was mixing it with a fiddle to a chorus of lusty song, as the white men made the most of time ashore. By and by, dinghies came gliding back to lugger and schooner for the refreshment of sleep.

Under the starlight the deck of the schooner *Alma* was patched in shadows. The soft lap of the tide against the bows, the ghostly creak of a block, an occasional rumbling snore from the fo'c'sle forrard, and over all, that peculiar odour of shellfish, curry, and blatchan (fermented fish in paste). On the deck lay separate heaps of pearl-shell oysters, on each heap a stick upon which was scratched the number of the lugger that had brought the shell. But the shell-opener was ashore and the oysters must wait. Each pile of shell represented a separate diver's take; some piles were larger than others. At the end of the season each diver would be paid so much for the "lay", and extra for the extra shell he had won. One heap was wretchedly small. If it was to remain so, this diver's money would be paltry indeed.

A shadow appeared up forrard near the fo'c'sle.

Crouching back aft, Con the bosun glanced at the sky. It showed no floating cloud that might throw a shadow across the deck. Con's eyes glared forrard. Curious eyes, glowing almost like a cat's. By day they were eyes of smoky brown, the iris encircled by a bluish ring. Men feared the eyes of the bosun of the *Alma*.

He smiled; the crouch eased from his shoulders as the shadow reached the heaps of pearl-shell. Stealthily it took a shell from a big heap and placed it on the tiny one. Noiselessly it took shells from the larger heaps and piled them on the tiny heap until it was nearly as big as the largest. Then it drew back and vanished down the fo'c'sle.

Con chuckled noiselessly. He alone had watched the joke all through this season.

That once tiny heap was the take of Ahmat the "Poor Diver", ill these years past from the effects of diver's paralysis. His season's take was consequently very small. Yet, all through last lay-up season in Broome from his meagre money he had spared four-and-sixpence per week to a sick Malay. Now the Malay was a crew-hand aboard the *Alma.* The Poor Diver was signed on aboard one of the Chamberlains' luggers. And whenever the lugger was near enough to load her shell aboard the schooner, the Malay thieved shell from the big heaps to add to the little heap of the Poor Diver.

Con chuckled. What a happy surprise awaited the Poor Diver! His money now would keep him in luxury throughout the lay-up season. He need not worry at all.

What if a valuable pearl should one day be found in the Poor Diver's heap! That would mean a rich commission for him. But where would that pearl really have come from? From a shell fished by the Poor Diver or from one stolen from another diver's heap!

Con chuckled. No one would ever know. Even Conard Gill would never know.

These enigmas in life Con loved. He loved to know what was going on among the whites, the Japanese, and the coloured men individually and collectively. And, except in sheer mischief, he loved to keep that knowledge to himself.

Suddenly Con crouched down, his eyes flaming. Again a shadow moved up forrard! Presently that shadow appeared near the heaps of pearl-shell. Con's eyes narrowed, his lip sneered as the shadow neared heap number seven. Ah! So this man knew that number seven lugger was fishing rich shell carrying baroque. Only Chamberlain, the shell-opener, and Con the bosun, were supposed to know that! For a certainty this shadow was a pearl-thief. Con began worming his way around the side of the scuttle, a marlin spike in his hand.

Now, that shadow thief made not the slightest sound or vibration. If he had made vibration the pearl-oysters would have closed their "mouths".

The two shells of the bivalve open and close upon a gristly hinge. On deck the fish soon begins to sweat and suffocate within its close-shut home. When merciful night comes it opens its shell to gasp. The hotter the day, the warmer the night, the wider the fish inside opens its shell. Many die that way, gasping out their life.

And upon number seven heap were numerous shells with mouths wide open. But at a touch or vibration these would immediately close. Rats aboard ship are occasionally caught that way; they bite into the oyster and it closes its shell.

The thief wormed his naked body nearer inch by inch, unaware of the bosun now crouching behind him. When close enough, the thief peered at the shells within the dull heaps. In the shadows among that pile of big shells it required keen eyes to distinguish any with mouth open.

His hand reached slowly out toward the heap. Between his fingers he held a cork. With a delicate, quick movement he thrust this cork into the mouth of a shell. The shell closed tight-on the cork.

For an instant the thief's teeth gleamed. He squatted there, took the shell and thrust his finger inside. With rapt expression he probed all round the flesh of the oyster, running his finger around top and bottom shell and in and under and all around the fish, seeking a hardness that would betray a pearl. Disappointment showed in his crouching attitude. His finger was not long enough to reach right into the oyster so from behind his ear he took a wire; its end was twisted into a small hook. He inserted this probe and manoeuvred it to detect what his finger might not feel.

Con the bosun had seen enough. The cork was new to him, they generally used a stick or flicked in a pinch of salt. Con reached out his hand. With hot finger-tips he touched the man on the bare back, then crashed the marlin spike between those horror-stricken eyes.

Broome: Along the foreshore, Dampier Creek.

CHAPTER II
Con the Bosun

At dawn the bay awoke to the splash of buckets as all hands bathed, then came the click of rowlocks and the sound of voices over water and shore. On occasions like this, the crews might visit some favourite ship if they wished.

The *Alma* was one. In the absence of the white masters, Con presided here, but unobtrusively. His was the authority that delights in letting others do the talking, boasting, and planning. The *Alma* was brown with men sipping steaming mugs of coffee. Francis Paddy, the bluff-faced Koepanger, joked in his deep, harsh voice. Nearly black was Francis Paddy, shrewder than most of his race, an excellent diver too. Little Sebaro the diver, another friend of Con's, smilingly sipped coffee while his quick eyes noted everything. A Manilaman was Sebaro, quick of body, square of face. His air of watchful alertness was in marked contrast to the calm of Bin Mahomet, the "quiet Malay" who sat beside them. Castilla Toledo was there, bright and cheery, monopolizing conversation.

Pablo Marquez and Simeon Espada arrived the evening before on a lugger whose master was a freelance pearler, lounged there too. The presence of these two brought a curious restraint, somewhat similar to the wariness that might be noticeable should gunmen mix in a modern party. Yellow-brown men whose thin lips and shifty eyes belied their smile, both were of ordinary stature, wiry, strong, and cat-footed. Both born in Manila of Filipino and Chinese parentage, they had drifted to Hong Kong as small boys, where Pablo obtained a "government job" which he could not hold. Besides Malay they spoke pidgin-English. Each had graduated in the shady life of Singapore; and both were members of a Chinese secret tong which enforced its decrees by the knife, the cord, and the gun. Pablo's sullenness of temper forced him, when obsessed by a fixed idea, to cling to it with ruthless persistence. Simeon was slightly darker than the swarthy yellow of Pablo; and Pablo was bulldog in temperament, whereas Simeon would go mad in a flash. When inflamed by drink it simply needed the suggestion "Savage that man!" and he would attack a perfect stranger; knife him, strike him with a bottle—anything. Apart from the cultured variety, they were two of the shrewdest, most dangerous coloured men in or out of Broome.

There came a lull in the conversation. Then a low, suave voice carrying clearly the length of the schooner—a lazy, insulting voice, a friendly voice, according to how a listener chose to take it:

"So she falls to the white master R— —, da Golden Queen of Broome!"

All hushed. Toledo gaped with parted lips. The "Golden Queen" — the white woman he loved!

"She marry him too," went on the laughing voice. "All legal tied up before da parson. An' they say a diver's heart be sore!" Toledo flushed. Involuntarily he snatched for a knife. Every eye was upon him. The *Alma* had brought news from port since the *Phyllis* left Broome! Not only was the woman false, but his heart's secret was known to all! He daren't think lest he shriek among them like a mad Malay. That cursed bosun was humming a ditty as if he had never spoken. Conversation broke out accompanied by winks and twisted smiles.

Toledo stood it until he had command over his limbs. Then he walked to the stern, cast off his dinghy and rowed back to the *Phyllis*.

From the deck above there followed him the mocking laughter of Francis Paddy, the chuckle of Sebaro, the jokes of Pablo and Simeon. There is none so merciless as the coloured man against his fellow who has aspired to a white woman and failed.

Later in the morning, when Bardwell came aboard, Toledo greeted him in tense entreaty:

"The woman! True that one white man marry him?"

"Yes."

Toledo saw red. He raved. Demanded to sail immediately to Broome so that he might bury his knife in her heart.

During the day Chamberlain came aboard the *Alma*.

"How's things, Con?"

"All's well, Master Alec." The bosun never mentioned the Malay down forrard nursing a cracked head. That was a personal thing between Con and the individual — just another man under his silent influence. Whenever that man saw Con, every time he thought of him, he would feel the master-hand. Con would never tell, just he and the man would always *know*.

Provisioned and watered, all vessels sailed again from Lagrange and separated at sea to north and south as captain or diver desired. Each sought its pearling-ground as eagerly and jealously as mining parties seek auriferous country. Bardwell sailed south knowing well that little profit would be won from the sea until his brooding diver abandoned his rage for revenge.

Toledo got over it during the following months at sea. Why should Castilla Toledo place his neck in a noose for such a worthless one as that? He was proud of his neck when adorned in a soft silk short ashore. He shivered at what a hempen collar would do to that statuesque neck. Besides, it was impossible to win out against the whites. Recently, two coloured men had tried the justice of the knife against the justice of the whites! And died.

Yes, it was as well he had not learnt the facts ashore.

By lay-up time in early December when the fleets returned to Broome he was almost resigned. There was a clear three months ashore now. Some among the crews would be paid off; others would be kept on to work in the sheds packing shell, and to clean and recondition the vessels ready for sea, probably in April. Toledo would be free until the signing on of the crews.

Quickly he cast about seeking a new love—a white girl. Thwarted ambition had become an obsession. His black hair shone to the desire in his eyes. Never before had he washed so often, shaved so often, worn such flash clothes. Certainly he had never sung so well, expressed such longing in such melting words.

One night in the big Chinese gambling-den while marking Chefah tickets Francis Paddy spat in disgust. "That Hash coon Toledo get shock one day," he growled to Sebaro. "He look out longa 'nother white girl. He catch him bullet by em by! More better he look out black gin." The fact that Francis Paddy was black while Toledo was brown did not occur to Paddy.

Con the bosun laughed. He was dressed nattily, his head of tiny black curls a picture.

"Where you come from, eh?" growled Paddy suspiciously. "I no see you come! Make love to some young girl, eh! One fine night you wake up with your throat cut too!"

Con smiled, marked a Chefah ticket on the signs that portray success in love and vengeance against enemies, then slipped out of the stilling, smoke-filled room. The bosun was transformed; his small, well-knit figure brimmed with energy. There was an eagerness of face, a light in the queer brownish eyes, a purposeful quickness of step.

Con conducted his love-affairs subtly—as he avenged his private feuds. His time on shore when not on duty by day was occupied in warding off charms made against him by enemies, and in planning amorous adventures. In both he was adept.

This business of the feminine allure occupied much of the thoughts and time of the crews while ashore. Love, and dreams of love, gambling, intrigue, rivalry, jealousy, business legitimate and questionable, fights and racial antipathies, marked the life ashore leavened by a slack time in work.

In the hectic days of Broome, girls came out from Japan. Schooners arriving from the South Seas, from the Coral Sea, from Dutch East India waters, all attracted by pearls, now and again brought girls of different races. The local aborigines came to the white man's developing town as moths to the flame. So was started, not a half-caste, but an inextricably tangled hybrid question. The immigration restriction act came too late. Into this melting-pot of the East and the tropics were mixed white men, Japanese, South Sea men, Torres Strait islanders, Rotumah men, Manilamen, Cingalese, Javanese, Amboinese, Koepangers, Chinese, aborigines, and other races. From this experiment in humanity an entirely new people was destined to arise. Luckily, in point of numbers they are not noticeable nationally.

There was always jealousy, sometimes bitter rivalry, among the Asiatics for the charms of the coloured sirens. And the man who often settled these quarrels and who kept the simmering intrigues as much as possible from coming under the notice of white authority, was Brahim Sa Maidin the Imman, the Mohammedan priest. A tall, lithe Indian from Jahore: his short-cropped hair, small black moustache, pronounced cheekbones and rather wide mouth made a mask for filmy brown eyes that could blaze into fury. His quick, intelligent brain had engineered many a scheme, though he was one of those men who always kept out of the limelight. He ruled his unruly followers not only by the Koran but by his own personality. His was the job too of quelling racial outbreaks, particularly religious, amongst the Buddhists and Mohammedans. He is· another of those in Broome who could tell a wonderful story—if he would only talk!

The white people, except for the usual flotsam, held themselves apart from the coloured life of the town. Their job was that of the master. They had pioneered this industry, and through many vicissitudes along a wild and uninhabited coast had built it to its present flourishing state. The coloured people had been introduced because they were willing, even eager, to do certain labour; otherwise they lived their own lives. The whites were occupied in building and organizing their fleets, in managing them at sea and on shore, in prospecting for new pearling-grounds, in winning oversea markets for the pearls and pearl-shell produced, and in establishing various pearling-towns.

This story reflects certain incidents and certain phases of life around Broome, the main pearling port.

To tell the romance of the Western Australian pearl-shelling industry would occupy volumes. It goes back to 1861. In that year Tays the Sailor discovered pearl-shell in Nickol Bay. From then the tiny craft of the earliest sea pioneers crept up from the south and discovered shell ever farther north. First was the period of "dry shelling" along the coasts with "skin" (naked) divers; then came the diving-dress followed by more systematic diving in deeper water and the establishment of freelance base depots at Shark's Bay, Onslow, Roebourne, Cossack, Port Hedland, Condon, until finally as the industry grew and spread the sea roamers established a base in Dampier's Roebuck Bay. Almost it seems as if Fate had decreed that the greatest buccaneer navigator of all time should have given name to that portion of the coast destined to yield such wealth and romance.

For then came the era of the pearling fleets and the supply schooners, the "mother ships", and Broome was born. A tiny place, yet the richest and greatest pearling-port that the world has even known.

Lay-up season for all hands, though a busy time in some respects, was a well-earned rest after eight to nine months at sea. Some among the whites lived on their schooners. Among these were a few married men whose wives went to sea with them. Game women: game as they can possibly make them. Along the coast, by inland tidal creeks generally, such as Barred Creek and Beagle Bay, isolated camps were formed by some of the pearlers. In these lonely places that offered shelter from the sea large camps were built for the laying-up and reconditioning of vessels. But the majority of the fleets laid-up in Broome.

The luggers, generally in trenches, were nearly all drawn up along a mile of foreshore to be reconditioned. Near them were the foreshore camps where owners and shell-openers lived. And close to each camp was the big shell-packing shed near where the vessels were repaired and refitted and provisioned.

The married whites built the large and pretty bungalows whose gardens these many years past have been a delight to Broome. These bungalows, standing well back from the foreshore and behind the sand-dunes and among the native trees, very widely spaced and spread out for over a mile, comprised the distinct "white" portion of Broome.

With the advent of the diving-dress white men did the diving, but it was soon found that some, Malays and Manilamen in particular, could be trained to be capable divers. This chance was seized upon, for almost every white diver was ambitious to own his own vessel and as soon as he did so he wanted to "build up into a fleet". So the diving-dress was handed over to coloured men. Years went by; and then the Japanese took to this diving, as a duck to water.

The Japanese, with shrewd intrigue and dogged purpose, set out to control the diving entirely. And this created a problem that the whites are up against today.

The various coloured divers were individualists, good men too. Nature has been extraordinarily kind to the Japanese so far as diving capabilities go, for, when diving in dress with equipment, they are almost immune from otitis, otorrhagia, and epistaxis while working under pressures greater than two atmospheres, that is ten fathoms (sixty feet) or over. (Two atmospheres equal ten fathoms approximately.)

Otitis is inflammation of the ears, otorrhagia is bleeding from the ears, epistaxis is bleeding from the nose. Divers, due to pressure, are prone to all three.

Immunity is enjoyed individually by others, but the Japanese are naturally immune, or rather almost so. Being collective too, they were gradually and efficiently organized. In addition they were ambitious, painstaking, quick to learn, patient, ready to take any risks, fatalistic.

So equipped, they were destined not only to win control of the diving in *all* pearling-seas, but to tender almost every vessel, and to form the majority of the crew. In one important locality to-day they take the fleets to sea. The white man goes to sea no more. In those particular waters the Japanese receive their money, commission on the shell won, and *all* the pearls. Now these men, who years ago came to Broome, Thursday Island, and Darwin as humble seamen, are building their own fleets to compete against the Australian pearlers.

This condition of things is just evolving when this story opens.

Running out from the low, mangrove-fringed shore of the bay at Broome is the jetty, and the rise and fall of the tide (over twenty feet) necessitates a jetty nearly a mile long. Along the shore, midway between the white and coloured towns, stands up Buccaneer Rock upon which on hazy nights, the coloured people say the ghost of Dampier has been seen gazing out to sea. On a sand-dune back from the water's edge is the Ghost Light, guiding beacon for vessels entering the bay at night. That light sometimes mists over when there are no mists—when the night is clear.

Just back of the foreshore dunes is the pretty Residency, and opposite it the Bishop's Palace. From here to the town proper, a mile away, stretch the white bungalows. The town is right on the foreshore, thickly hedged here by mangroves. This is the business portion of the town, its few streets and tiny Asiatic smelling lanes densely hedged by wooden buildings. Surrounding a few large white stores are the Japanese and Chinese quarters; and surrounding all are the hives of the coloured people.

Scattered here and there are the cottages or offices of the resident and visiting pearl-buyers. Occasionally a visiting buyer has his quarters in one of the few hotels. Like the town, the buyers are a hundred per cent cosmopolitan; generally men familiar with most gem-buying or producing quarters of the globe. To be successful, each has to be adventurous yet cautious, while imbued with the spirit of a gambler. Knowing when to hold his tongue, a buyer must be ever wideawake, and to be a really big man he must be personally familiar with the pearl markets of the world. In the lives of those pearl-buyers are fascinating stories—if they would only speak. Such men as Mark Rubin, Schaumer, Bauer, Davis, Haffiz, the buyers for the great house of Rosenthal and Freres, and others. Mark Rubin was actually the man who put the Australian pearl definitely on the market; he *made* the market. In youthful days, essentially a battler, he pushed a barrow as a hawker. He made a crust in various ways. A small man and apparently not physically strong, he did not hesitate to lump coal at Newcastle. Uncultured, forcing bluster when necessary to cover his lack of knowledge, his assets were courage and a determined will.

Fortune guided Rubin to the White Cliffs opal-fields, in the north-western corner of New South Wales. It was really destiny; he was to be a famous buyer of gems. He swung his pick as an opal-gouger, but was soon buying small parcels of stones in the rough; facing them; then selling them at a profit. In a month he learnt more about opals than the majority of men would learn in a year. In a very short time he rose to be a recognized buyer.

Later, Rubin noticed that one of the big buyers made trips of long duration from the field. Rubin, with the genius of a Sherlock Holmes, tabulated this man's time. He traced him to Sydney and Melbourne, to Paris, Vienna, Berlin, London, and New York. The man would be selling his opals there of course. But again and again occurred lapses of time which Rubin could not localize. He asked the man point-blank where he regularly spent so much valuable time. A shrug was the answer. Rubin tracked him by coach, train, and sea for nearly four thousand miles. The man visited practically unknown tiny places on the north-western Australian coast and finally stayed at a wild and woolly meeting-place of motley craft called Broome.

There Rubin started buying pearls; he knew no more about pearls than he had known about opals. A man would bring him a pearl and ask five hundred pounds. Rubin would examine the gem with the air of a connoisseur, then gruffly offer two hundred and fifty. Probably he would buy for three hundred or three hundred and fifty pounds. He got together a big parcel of selected pearls, took them to London and sold them at a handsome profit. This so impressed his bankers that they concluded he knew all about pearls.

"I knew nothing about pearls when I went to London," he chuckled to Long Jimmy James. "But when I returned to Broome I knew more than the pearlers did. When I went to London the second time I knew more than the pearl-buyers did."

On his third trip to London he made a big deal. He returned in delight. Long Jimmy James called on business and congratulated him.

"I've got a valet now, Jimmy," Rubin chuckled. "I'll show him to you. Charles! Charles!" he called. James made himself comfortable on an easy chair as the man appeared.

"Whisky and soda!" promptly ordered James. That rather took Rubin's breath away.

Bankers gained great confidence in Rubin's shrewdness and judgment. Although much of it was bluffing, their confidence was not misplaced for he began to rise toward the millionaire class.

And among all this mixture of passion and commerce and ambition and adventure in high and low and mixed degree Castilla Toledo was still seeking his dream girl.

Old Con.

CHAPTER III
The Pearl

One glorious day Toledo found the girl. She was a nice young thing at a treacherously impressionable age. Toledo fell passionately in love. He worshipped at a distance before seeking her with the caution of a cat stalking a fledgeling in a nest of hawks. Should the fathers or brothers find out then Castilla Toledo would disappear one night-with a weight round his neck.

As to the girl—she must not comprehend his fascinating wiles until suddenly she realized she liked him. After that father and brothers would find too late—a secret marriage.

Thus he planned, and smiled in his dreams.

During the three months lay-up, Toledo progressed flatteringly well. No one guessed his schemes. Indeed, the very people he wished to delude unconsciously helped him. The family was struggling to win a living with one small lugger, and the flash Manila diver was welcome enough when he strolled along to their foreshore camp for a yarn. There was ample opportunity and excuse while they were refitting the vessel, painting her, overhauling ship and diving-gear to have all shipshape preparatory to the next season. He was not even debarred the private home whenever he found excuse to dawdle for a yarn.

A diver had some interesting gossip and possibly information when he was willing to talk, a sly hint as to a profitable shelling-ground off some point on the coast, a slip of the tongue as to some patch of shell, some boastful allusion to a reef where the shell carries a percentage of baroque. Possibly, by working on his vanity, this flash diver might at any time be decoyed into dropping a hint that could be profitably taken. So he was treated with the familiarity that sometimes exists between the white man and coloured while still adhering to the unspoken line of demarcation.

But it was enough for Toledo. He saw the girl more and more frequently at her work at her father's bungalow. As to the rest, well—there was the message of the eyes, the intriguing lure of the smile! And there was night-time, and the trees and gardens that shadowed every widely spaced bungalow.

As the love-making gradually developed towards possible reciprocity, so the everlasting question returned with heartbreaking persistence. Money! He must have money to make a home for this girl who had now become as life to him. Bardwell knew his diver was no longer to be trusted, so he paid him off.

This was of small consequence to Toledo for even moderately successful divers were not over plentiful. The Japanese divers were only just beginning to be engaged in force; they had not yet proved superior to others. Toledo signed on with a pearler captaining his own lugger. When the fleet sailed at the opening of the new season Toledo sailed too. And as he watched Cape Riddell vanishing astern his heart beat fast. Fiercely he determined that when he. saw those red headlands again he would possess a pearl—his pearl.

Among the crew were Pablo Marquez and Simeon Espada. Toledo tolerated them as acquaintances holding merely the job of crew-men while he was the diver. There is a sharp distinction. Both Pablo and Simeon returned his instinctive dislike, but not too openly, for aboard a lugger the diver can make life unpleasant should he decide to do so.

The owner of the lugger was soon well pleased with his new diver. Why, he was a *good* diver! He might be as flash as they make them ashore, but at sea he was a demon to work; the tender had almost to force him to come up for a breathing spell. As the weeks slipped by into months, the lugger's hold became almost full of shell. The pearler was pleased indeed. Some baroque and a pearl or two had been found, but small stuff and of little consequence. To the owner this mattered but little in comparison with the take of shell.

But to Toledo it meant tragedy; it did not give him a chance. Yet still he worked as he had never worked before.

Now the crew resented this, for the diver who stays down below overlong puts a strain on the men at the air-pump. When Toledo was working in shallow water he stayed down so long that the pump-crew became wellnigh exhausted. One day they remedied this. Each vessel carries dried chillies which the crew mix with the blatchan to produce an appetizing condiment for flavouring the curry. This condiment has the reputation of making a dead man eat if put on his tongue. So one day, while Pablo and a Koepanger were toiling at the pump, the crew ground a dried chilli into powder and placed it in a little brass pan by the air-pump where the suction would carry the powder down the air-pipe.

Down on the sea bottom, Toledo was groping about seeking shell when suddenly he sneezed; he sneezed and gasped as his eyes and nose began to run; he choked; he was inhaling asphyxiating, red-hot air.

At his violent signal "Haul up!" the little pan of chilli powder was instantly hidden. Toledo shot to the surface waving helpless arms. When the tender unscrewed the face-glass he was screaming with rage; blindly he attempted to plunge upon the innocent pump-crew. For ten minutes he wheezed and gasped and sneezed, helplessly wiping the water from his eyes.

The master of the lugger was as angry as the tender. But nothing could be done. It was just one of those little things that happen at sea.

Occasionally the fleets fished in company; one day when fishing off the First Wash about two hundred miles south-west of Broome, they saw in the distance the sails of Captain Talboys's and Hughie Biddles's fleets, the schooner *Isabel* gracefully drifting along. Aboard that schooner, both Talboys and Biddles were opening shell; they lived upon her and each controlled his own fleet from the one mother schooner, the luggers bringing their shell to the schooner and each master opening his own shell. A fair sea was running, the schooner lazily rising and falling. Talboys opened a shell, and stared. In a little pocket, a slimy sac in the oyster, was a fine round pearl, about eighty grains in weight. In quiet delight Talboys laid the shell down and went on opening others. When finished, he crossed the deck to where Biddles was opening his shell.

"What do you think of this, Hughie?" laughed Talboys and showed the pearl still in its slimy sac.

"Phew!" exclaimed Biddles. "It looks like a couple of thousand pounds' worth!"

"It's a beauty!" said Talboys. His fingers squeezed the pearl and the sac burst, the pearl slipped out on to the deck just as the schooner heaved and rolled. Talboys snatched at the pearl but it slipped through a scupper and was overboard. In an instant Talboys leapt for the leadline and heaved it overboard, making the end fast to a watertight tin to mark the spot. The men stared at one another; the crew gaped.

"Hard luck!" whispered Biddies. Talboys signalled the nearest lugger. She came sailing up and Talboys shouted the situation to the diver.

The lugger sailed for the little tin bobbing upon the waves. The diver went down and-found the pearl!

A tiny speck of nacre, a tear from the eye of a god lost on the bottom of the sea. The chance of ever again finding it was one in a million.

In the lay-up season coming due that pearl was to be sold in Broome for eighteen hundred pounds.

But neither Toledo nor his master knew the dramatic meaning of the manoeuvring of the *Isabel* and the lugger several miles away. In due course Toledo's master sailed farther north and in a prospecting drift his luck still held good, and he found more shell. But not a decent pearl.

Towards the close of the season a sail hove in sight. She anchored a mile away, and next day was fishing on a parallel course. Frowningly the master surveyed her. No captain likes an interloper to come cruising upon his own payable drift. The stranger fished for several days. Not a Broome vessel; apparently she hailed from south down the coast. Then one afternoon a dinghy came off from her and raced towards the lugger. A white man jumped on deck, feverishly excited. The pearler immediately knew—he held up a warning hand and took the man below. He had found a pearl, a beauty! He was a stranger from the south, new to the pearl cunning of Broome; he was eager to show this pearl; he could hardly contain himself. Toledo's master cordially congratulated the stranger. He examined the pearl with the love that pearlers lavish on these gems of the sea. He had never had the luck to win one like this himself. It was the most exquisite gem he had ever seen. Almost reverently he laid it upon its cotton-wool on the little cabin table. He sighed; this wondrous thing meant a fortune for him who owned it. He weighed it under the fascinated eyes of the stranger.

"Sixty-five grains!" he murmured. "You are lucky, mate. This stone will take very little cleaning, judging by the eye. There are several spots on it; a skin or two will remove them. Suppose it loses ten grains in the cleaning, its weight would be fifty-five grains—a beauty. I wish I had half your luck."

"What should it be worth?" the man almost whispered.

"Impossible to estimate until it is cleaned. Depends mostly on the depth and lustre. Judging by looks, it will be rosae tint which is the most prized. Its shape is a perfect round. Should it clean as it promises, a big buyer would pay you anything from one hundred pounds per grain."

"Phew! Five thousand five hundred pounds."

"Yes, easily. Mind, if it was mine I would demand more. You could ask what you liked for a gem of this class."

"Heavens! I wonder what the buyer will get for it?"

The pearler laughed. "He will sell it as a gem of all the seas," he sighed. "He can approach the rich men of the world as buyers. He will make a fortune out of it, far more than you will."

They heard a heavy scraping on the deck; the click-clack of the air-pump ceased.

"That's my diver come up. Do you mind if I show him the pearl? It will spur him on to find a pearl for me."

"By all means show him."

Toledo, just come up from below, was sitting on deck in his diving-dress. As the tender unscrewed his helmet Toledo heard a whisper of "pearl" from the cabin below. He listened. The pearler's head appeared from the scuttle and nodded meaningly.

"Toledo, never mind about going below again to-day, sun nearly set. Come down cabin, we have drink."

Hurriedly Toledo got out of the diving-dress while willingly the tender and crew prepared to make all shipshape for the night.

When Toledo slipped down into the cabin the master greeted him in low tones, a warning in his eyes lest the crew should hear. He whispered that he wanted Toledo to see a pearl—a real pearl, and to wish good luck to the diver who had found it, and the man who owned it. A wonderful diver he must be, to find such a pearl! And such a big commission he would receive too!

Toledo's heart leapt at sight of the pearl, the world stood still for him. Then he smiled, graciously he admired the gem, congratulated the owner.

"Oh that lovely pearl, number one good!" he enthused with shining eyes. "I wish you luck."

Toledo's fingers trembled as he examined it; the smile trembling on his face seemed inlaid. As he turned the pearl around and around his eyes outshone its hidden glow.

A bottle of square-face was produced in honour of the occasion. They drank and smoked and admired the pearl, then talked of other finds, of famous pearls; then drank again and admired the pearl again. Late afternoon rapidly faded into evening. The new-comer stayed aboard for dinner. Toledo lit the hurricane lamp and another bottle was produced. While drinking sparingly himself, Toledo kept the glasses of the others constantly filled. Gin is a quick worker, Toledo an unobtrusive one. After a hearty dinner he cleared the table, reaching the empty dishes up out through the scuttle for the crew to wash up.

The white men filled their pipes, Toledo rolled a cigarette, the pearl was produced again, examined for the tenth time. They bent over the table watching the play of the beautiful thing in the palm of the hand. They enthused on its weight; admired its shape; guessed at its lustre. On Toledo's darker hand the pearl seemed to tremble. The owner would put it back in his pocket, only to produce it and display it again. He would drape it in fine Japanese skivvy paper, place it lovingly in the little tin match-box and bury it deep down in his pocket. As evening drew on into night his voice grew hoarser, he could not keep from fingering that box.

"Some woman will wear this pearl," he growled, "some beautiful woman. It will grace the neck of a queen."

"It will see Vienna," prophesied Toledo's master, "London, Paris, Berlin, New York! They will not know it came out of the belly of an oyster off the Eighty Mile Beach on the Western Australian coast."

By ten o'clock the white men were hopelessly muddled, Toledo's master almost asleep. The owner of the pearl would have been so, only his excited brain persisted in fighting against the gin fumes to talk of pearls, pearls, pearls! As he rose unsteadily to go, he lurched back against Toledo's bunk.

"By gum!" he muttered. "A sea has sprung up, the cabin is rolling like a rocking-horse! I'll have to get aboard my lugger before the wind freshens."

"You get aboard all right," assured Toledo soothingly.

"Of course I'll get aboard, me an' the pearl. It's a lovely pearl, diver, isn't it! I'll bet a thousand pound you've never seen one like it before!" he challenged.

Toledo truthfully admitted that he had never seen such a gem, then smilingly suggested a final drink and one last look at the pearl.

Gratified, the owner smiled owlishly, fumbled for the match-box, and after clumsy delay held the pearl between his fingers, swaying there in the tobacco smoke. Toledo poured out three drinks, two were stiff gins, one was water. He handed each their drink then lifted his glass. The glasses tinkled to "The Pearl! Good luck." They drank solemnly. Then Toledo gazed quite a while at the pearl, holding it to the light of the hurricane lamp, admiring it most flatteringly.

"This pearl bring you good luck. I please you gottem good luck. Very, please." He smiled as lingeringly he wrapped the pearl in the soft paper, bedded it in the match-box and closed the lid. The owner with drunken gravity put it carefully away deep down in his pocket murmuring:

"Good night, diver. Good luck! I hope you find one too."

"I hope so; I wish I could gettem good luck," murmured Toledo as he took the man's arm and helped him up the scuttle; guided his clumsy steps across the deck; almost lifted him overside and down into his dinghy. He smiled farewell to the visitor's drunken "Good night. Good luck!" as he cast off and started to row away towards his riding light.

But the pearl was in Toledo's pocket, the empty match-box in the pocket of the other.

CHAPTER IV
The Thief

Toledo dropped softly down the scuttle, tapped his snoring master, then lifted him into bunk. Breathing quickly, he glared down a moment; except for the man's heavy breathing there. was silence throughout the lugger, all hands were asleep. Then a cockroach leapt on to the table and rattled across a paper. Toledo shook his master.

"Master! Master!"

"Ugh!" grunted the man. "Go to hell." Toledo shook him again.

"Master, more better we go Broome. Spring long valve in helmet won't work good."

"What's that?" growled the pearler.

"We go Broome, more better. Suppose you want me to work good, must fixem valve!"

The pearler sat up and rubbed his eyes. "Spare valves!" he snarled.

"No more," replied Toledo humbly. "Forgot 'em."

"What!" roared the pearler. "I told you especially not to forget those springs! Well, then, you damn well repair the one you have!" and he rolled over.

"No good, master," insisted Toledo urgently. "He broke proper! S'pose those springs you no puttem new one in, I no more go down. I no can work."

The pearler sat up grumbling sharply at this waste of time and lack of forethought in not bringing an extra set of valves. Toledo took it humbly, insisting that the sooner they sailed for Broome the sooner the springs would be replaced and they back on the fishing-grounds again.

"Heave up then and damn it!" snapped the master. "And you look out tiller too!" he added bellicosely. "Then you might remember next time!"

Toledo leapt up the scuttle and hurried forrard. "Ha! below! Wake up! Heave up!" he called urgently. "We got to go Broome. Quick feller all hands heave up!"

Sleepily they tumbled from bunk to come naked on deck, yawningly manned the windlass with Toledo actively helping. But his concern was to get the chain in with as little noise as possible. Apprehensively he glanced towards the tiny riding light just visible in the darkness to starboard.

"Up mains'l!" he called and sprang to the tiller.

"Up fores'l!"

"Up jib!" And they were gliding quietly to sea, bound for Broome under a gentle breeze. When once under way Toledo ordered the crew turn in. "You all fellow can go down and sleep now. I look out tiller. By em by, two hour time, Pablo he look out tiller."

Alone with the night, Toledo laughed noiselessly to the skies. He had the pearl of his desire; a gem even above his dreams. It only remained now to sell it quickly; he knew plenty of "snide" buyers.

He glanced at that riding light fast dimming astern. But there was no sign of pursuit. There would be if that drunken white man looked in his match-box for the pearl. He might look at any moment...

Toledo gazed at the sky, praying for the breeze to freshen. Such a beautiful sky, cloudless and velvety, its deep blue set with stars. Only the gurgling from the gently moving bows, a homely whispering in the cordage broke the quietness. The sweetness of the air overcame that odour of shellfish and Asiatic food inseparable from a pearling lugger at sea. Anxiously he gazed around the deck seeking a hiding-place for the pearl. He *must* hide it. Knowing the vagaries of wind, and although the lugger had a few hours' start, it was still possible for the robbed one to reach Broome before him.

But he could neither see nor think of a safe hiding-place should the lugger be searched. Searchers had grown so devilishly cunning. For an hour he stood in growing anxiety, his nervous hand automatically steering the lugger.

Now, whites and coloured people are all inquisitive; "coloureds" particularly so, and, concerning another's business, perhaps craftier and more dangerous than either whites or Japanese.

No wonder then, that Pablo Marquez, invisible forrard, was stealthily watching Toledo. Pablo's body was down below the hatch; but the top of his head was pressed against the hatch combing. Below his swarthy forehead only the gleam of cunning eyes was visible had any one been capable of detecting them. An alert aboriginal could perhaps have done so—no other man. Certainly not Toledo, his mind filled with anxious uncertainty. Suddenly he smiled with joy. Lying by the starboard bow was a bulky coil of four-inch anchor rope, a rope thicker than a man's wrist. It was made as are all coir ropes, of big thick strands twisted round and round one another.

Toledo lashed the tiller so that the lugger would steer herself for the time being and tiptoed forrard. As he did so, Pablo crouched down in the hatch. Toledo knelt by the rope and, with hands and a steadying knee, twisted open a section until he could force a finger deep under a strand. As he felt for the pearl the eyes of Pablo came up on a level with the hatch. Pablo could not see what that bent back was doing, but the intuitive cunning of his hybrid race was aroused. Toledo gently but firmly poked the pearl deep in the crevice, then gazed around in frowning thought. A thread of cotton from a ragged Malay sarong was between his very toes; he must have caught it up while walking across the deck. Smiling with intense delight, he took the thread and carefully poked it down towards the pearl. Then he unloosed his grip and the elastic strand immediately bit back into place with its fellow rope. Just the tiniest end of the thread was visible should a keen eye know where to look for it.

With a sigh of relief Toledo stepped back to the tiller. He wanted to sing; he felt indescribably happy; he hummed his favourite love-song while smiling at the stars. Even if the lugger was now searched no man would ever dream of such a hiding-place. He did an hour more than his watch; at any other time he would have roused Pablo should he be a minute overdue. At last he did call; it would not look well if he stayed up there all night. "Pablo! you get up and come," he called down forrard. "Look out tiller now. I sleep; I tired."

Pablo required a lot of rousing; eventually he appeared up the hatch, rubbing his eyes, yawning. In blink-eyed sullenness he took the wrath the diver showered upon him. With a final admonitory threat, Toledo disappeared down the scuttle.

Immediately Pablo was wide awake, eyes and ears alert towards the cabin scuttle before him. He heard Toledo turning into bunk; heard him humming to himself; saw the cabin darken as he turned low the hurricane lamp. Presently there was silence except for the snores of the master down there below, the gurgle of water from the bows, the faint creaking of cordage.

Even after Toledo's regular breathing joined the murmurings of the night Pablo was patient for another hour. Then he lashed the tiller and stepped softly as a breath past the scuttle, past the hatch, and on up forrard. As he knelt by the coiled rope his eyes gleamed. He searched along and around the strands that formed the topmost coil. Carefully he lifted that coil and examined the coil beneath until he espied a tell-tale end of thread. A wolfish grin spread from ear to ear. No man would ever have found that end of cotton had he not known where to look for-something!

With a tigerish glance aft he bent over the rope. He thumbed the cotton end to the strand, then bent and gripped the strand with his teeth, gently levering it back, his eyes following the cotton down. He inserted stubby fingers between the strands and gently but strongly pushed and pulled them one apart from the other. The gleam of pearl was reflected in his eyes, the breath hissed from between his teeth. He pulled with hands and jaw, his face wolfish as his brown fingers squeezed down for the pearl. Carefully he allowed the strands to relax back into place while holding the cotton exactly as it was. Slipping the pearl into his mouth he darted back to the tiller.

In mid-afternoon the following day they cast anchor in Roebuck Bay. Broome was enjoying its afternoon siesta under a warm sun. "You go up town and get those valve springs quick!" ordered the pearler to Toledo. "Send the crew ashore for stores from the foreshore camp and see they do. their job. We sail with the tide to-morrow. And don't forget anything this time!" He scowled at the crew, for his head felt wretchedly thick. He was rowed ashore to make the best of his few hours at his home. His dinghy had hardly cast off when Toledo turned to the crew:

"You take big dinghy and go along foreshore camp. We get more tucker." He could barely conceal his excitement. The crew had hardly reached shore when he was on his knees beside the coil of rope. His eyes immediately sought the pin-point of thread. Trembling, he used hands and knee to unwind the strands. The pearl was gone.

Coming up.

CHAPTER V
The Conspiracy

If he had had the strength of a hundred men Toledo would have torn that rope to shreds. Certain at last the pearl was gone, he raced screaming along the deck. Both dinghies were ashore; the smaller should have returned but the master had ordered the boy to run a message. Toledo rushed to the windlass, but to heave up that anchor alone was beyond even a madman's strength. When the crew at last returned he raved among them, frenzied in that he dared not form articulate words. He wanted to shriek:

"Who stole my pearl? Who stole my pearl?"

But he dared not accuse them of stealing what he had stolen himself. He leapt into a dinghy, rowed ashore, raced across the beach through the town and on to the master's bungalow. He gibbered at the pearler; gibbered to him to discharge the crew. He spluttered formless charges, but made direct accusation only with his eyes. The pearler frowned, mystified. His diver must have got a touch of the sun or a twinge of diver's paralysis or something. He advised him to return to the lugger and lie down and rest.

Slowly Toledo walked back towards the foreshore with murder in his heart. Sunset had come. The water rippled in silver out on the shadowed bay; dull lights were appearing in coloured town. Toledo stepped into the dinghy, berserk misery in his heart. Who was the thief that had stolen his pearl! Who could be the accursed dog who had ruined his great joy? Rowing out to the lugger, he leapt aboard and glared at the crew with convulsive fear, his fingers twitching. He snarled at them each in turn.

The crew in a body went ashore. They complained bitterly to the master. There was hell to pay aboard the lugger and they did not know why. Pablo in a low-browed surliness was spokesman:

"Boss, you better come. We don't know what's matter! Diver he all the time growl, humbug long we fellow. No good that one! Make him trouble! By em by fight! By em by we kill him! What's matter that diver make him trouble?"

Furiously the pearler strode to the beach and hailed the lugger. He was troubled now. Dissension among the crew would probably mean the lugger would not sail, while if his diver really had a bad touch of the sun he would not be able to dive. He determined to take Toledo ashore to see the doctor. Toledo sulkily refused. And the crew as stubbornly would not board the lugger. They would camp in the foreshore camp until the lugger was ready for sea.

That night, Pablo suddenly seized Simeon's arm. No words; just a gleam of eyes, an expressive glance. Instinctively their footsteps quickened. They were passing down the narrow, crowded John Chi Lane with its Japanese and Chinese, its Javanese, its Malays and Manilamen, its trousered women-folk and children squatting upon the little verandas and doorsteps and tiny balconies. The packed buildings faced each other hardly a cart width apart. Through open windows dim lamps glowed, momentarily showing dark-haired women in sandalled feet passing, talking in the rooms. Black-haired Japanese, smart in snow-white singlet and clean shorts that showed their muscular brown legs, sat in groups telling tales of the sea. Chinese with shuffling gait talked in sing-song voice or stared motionless at nothing. Koepangers, almost black of skin, lightly built and excitable, disappearing towards the gambling places brushed shoulders with stocky brown Malays ready to laugh or fly into fury according to the gesture of the moment. A crowd of half- and quarter-castes adoringly listened to an Adonis listlessly singing to his mandolin. Pretty coloured girls sought excuse to smile, mischief lurking ever in their dark brown eyes. A confused hum of talk, of laughter, of squeaky music, came from small, poorly ventilated rooms. The smell of the East was over all.

With nods to acquaintances Pablo and Simeon turned up Carnarvon Street, turned again up the higher ground into the narrow smelliness of Sheba Lane. The low, double-storied houses nearly touched across the lane; chinks of light came through closed shutters. There was a sinister atmosphere in this laneway of ill repute. As if uneasy Pablo suddenly wheeled around and they turned up Napier Terrace, then across the dusty road and out on to the dark water-front.

In the blackness of the mangrove shadows Pablo showed Simeon the pearl! Pablo could not have held the secret a moment longer.

Simeon gasped. He exclaimed in astonished Chinese; he stared with parted lips, while his eyes fairly danced. In incoherent whispers they talked and laughed and stared and smiled at one another. They decided it must be sold. That was obvious. Simeon's hands trembled; his husky voice could hardly form words. Between sidelong glances into the night, in whispers they cast about for a likely snide-buyer, one with a closed mouth, yet one who would not assess two innocent coloured men too cheaply.

For there are degrees in snide-buyers, just as there are in illicit diamond-buyers. And there are degrees in the cunning of coloured rogues too. All work in proportion to their cunning.

Simeon suggested that they take a white man into their confidence. "Snide-buyer not dare cheat us then," he whispered, "not so much. This is big pearl, it pay us to get white man sell for us."

Pablo hesitated.

"Yes," whispered Simeon urgently. "White man more better! He sell to big white snide-buyer! Japanese man and Chinaman he buy him pearl too damn cheap—make us damn fool! He give little bit money; he sell it himself plenty money. He tell we feller 'pearl no good; it got hole; it no proper good one!' More better we look longa white feller. He sell it for more money; we give him share money."

"S'pose we sellem that pearl longa white feller," frowned Pablo. "He might steal that pearl from we fellow; might callem policeman!"

Mention of police startled Simeon, but he laughed in protest. "Oh, we feller not stealem! We never steal him pearl longa white man, Toledo steal him! Toledo get trouble; he go jail. They feller no savvy we got him pearl!"

Pablo grinned and nodded evilly.

"True! More better that way. S'pose Toledo get jail, more better for we!"

"I know one white feller," urged Simeon. "He keepem quiet; he won't say nothing; he sellem pearl. He true feller; he good feller; he talk longa me all time friend."

"What name that one?"

"Oh, he name Hagen. You know. He live longa that Manilaman house."

Pablo nodded. All the coloured life of the port knew Hagen the billiard-man; he who was on confidential terms with so many divers and crews of the fleets. This could be for only one reason as the whites knew full well. But Hagen laughed at their undisguised dislike. He was a seller of snides to the snide-buyers and he did not care who knew, so long as they could not prove it. And he would see that they never did.

"You wait. Me bring him here," whispered Simeon. "You no frighten; he come. He go hell for pearl."

"We go together," growled Pablo.

"Arright. When we go see him now, you savvy keep quiet; me talk."

They turned back towards the dim lights of the town, their bare feet noiseless on the sand. Furtively they approached the Manila house where Hagen had his billiard saloon. The smoke-wreathed place smelt unpleasantly of hot humanity; it was crowded with coloured people, their brows and arms and chests gleaming with sweat beads.

Just one glance, and Hagen understood. They followed him outside and merged among the shadows of the ·night. He took them into his cottage, locked the door and lit the lamp. As he slowly turned up the wick the gathering flame illumined his harsh, cynical face. He sat opposite them, his sinewy arms upon the table.

"Now what?" he smiled.

Pablo showed him the pearl. He gasped. "How you get this?" he exclaimed. "Who give you? You find him?"

He checked his obvious excitement. The pearl lay in the palm of Pablo's hand; the brown fingers cautiously closed upon it as he growled, "Me and Simeon two feller find him."

"Never mind, I don't want to know. It is a beauty, but you two feller know it not cleaned yet. I think it got him flaw!"

"No got flaw," answered Pablo stolidly, and frowned towards Simeon.

"Flaw hell!" burst out Simeon. "That one no flaw I tell you true!"

"Show it me then. I must examine it first time."

With reluctance Pablo laid the pearl upon the table. Hagen critically examined the beautiful thing but his frowning brows failed to shade the delight in his eyes. His fingertips tingled from its silky touch; this lovely gem already was growing on him as it would grow into the mind of any who handled it. He weighed it carefully and estimated its uncleaned value at easily six thousand pounds, it was apparently flawless and would be easy to clean. This might prove to be the most beautiful pearl taken from the sea in the memory of man. His heart beat exultantly; he pictured himself watching an expert skinning the gem and bringing its loveliness to light. If this pearl cleaned as wonderfully as it gave promise there was no estimating its value. He leaned back with a sigh.

"You want me to sell him for you feller?" he inquired.

"Oh, yes, you sell him," replied Simeon. "You savvy sell him more better. We want big money!"

"I can certainly get you a much better price than you could get yourselves," smiled Hagen. "I sell him all right."

He took out the keys of his safe but Pablo reached across the table and took the pearl.

"Arright. More better you bring him pearl-buyer here, I keep him pearl until you bring him money."

Hagen glared across the table into those crafty eyes. After a moment's silence he grinned tigerishly.

"Oh, that is easy; I sell him easy. But I must keep the pearl, I must have it to show to the man before he will buy it."

"You bring man here, we show him pearl together!" growled Pablo.

"Who you think will buy him?" broke in Simeon. Hagen hid his chagrin in frowning thought.

"Liebglid," he replied.

"Ah!" grinned Simeon.

Liebglid was the commercial traveller who had been seen flashing large rolls of money. Certainly this Liebglid would have plenty of money to buy a pearl.

"Arright," agreed Pablo. "We three feller go together! We three sell him."

"You don't trust me!" leered Hagen.

"Arright," smiled Pablo with narrowed eyes. "I believe you," and his smile broadened. "But we three feller go all together and sell him! Then I give you some money, me some, Simeon some! We share him money alla same, all together!"

Hagen frowned. His revolver was in the table drawer while Pablo's lean brown hand ... If he shot these men dead for attempting to rob his safe it would serve them right but ... Pablo's hand slid to his knife-hilt.

Hagen had never dealt with such suspicious coloured men before. The others had all been easy. He would just love to put a bullet into this Pablo's twisty smile. And he wanted that pearl, had made up his mind to get it; but realized that craft alone would secure it.

"All right," he agreed. "Suppose we sell like that, all right. Suppose to-morrow night we three feller go together, we sell him pearl. I see Liebglid to-morrow, make arrangements. You two feller meet me here same time to-morrow night. Bring that pearl same time, then we three feller meet Liebglid, sell pearl, divide money!"

"How much he give?" demanded Simeon.

"How much you want?"

"Plenty!" answered Simeon craftily. "One hundred pounds gold money each man not enough. This plenty good pearl. We no fool! How much?"

"Five hundred pounds," answered Hagen, and noted the delight in their eyes. To a coloured man a hundred sovereigns was a fortune but Hagen dared not risk losing the pearl through a false offer to two such crafty ones as these.

They parted, Hagen back to his saloon, Pablo and Simeon to walk the dark foreshore far into the night. Once Simeon snatched Pablo's arm and wheeled abruptly as at the slither of naked feet. But the night was utterly still; just the shadows, and the breath of cool sea-air, and the pervading smell of mangroves and water.

The lugger did not sail next day. Pablo and Simeon simply refused to sail with the "mad diver" even though now the diver himself refused to sail. The owner had to replace them from men ashore. He sailed with the tide at night, roundly cursing the ingratitude and vagaries of coloured seamen.

Hagen met Liebglid and confidentially told him two coloured men had approached him with a wonderful pearl for sale, a gem probably worth twenty thousand pounds in London. The price was five hundred pounds cash. Five hundred to be paid in the presence of the sellers, "And," he added with his leering smile, "five hundred commission to be handed to me-later."

Liebglid laughed at the price. But Hagen shrugged: "When you see the gem you won't haggle," he sneered.

"And if you don't want to see it—you needn't. There are plenty of other buyers."

Then when Liebglid's curiosity was aroused Hagen grew indifferent about giving details. In fact, he seemed to coo] off and abruptly parted saying that he would see him to-morrow and arrange a meeting.

The pearl had grown on Hagen. He dearly wished to see it cleaned; to possess the glowing beauty he knew waited there within its covering film of nacre. But he understood coloured people well enough to realize he was now dealing with two tigers.

That night, the three men met as agreed at Hagen's cottage. To Pablo's questioning eyes Hagen replied:

"It's all right; Liebglid could not draw all that money in time for to-night. He will meet us on the foreshore at the back of the Residency to-morrow night at eight o'clock. You bring the pearl. He will bring five hundred pounds. Everything must be secret, not a soul will know. It is all arranged."

The three looked at one another.

"Five hundred pounds!" whispered Pablo. "He bring it sure?"

"Yes."

"Arright. That big money. Arright that one. More better than sell him pearl along those—Chows."

Simeon chuckled. "I told you we know proper white man," he smiled. "That one arright! That are plenty money."

"Not much when divided into three!" murmured Hagen.

They looked at one another; the cottage grew silent as the grave.

"Show me the pearl," whispered Hagen.

Pablo reluctantly placed it on the table. It lay there glowing like a marble dropped from the bright moon. Five hundred pounds, it's snide value—five hundred pounds! What must its real value be if only it could be sold as a beautiful pearl! Shame—that men should taint this wondrous thing with thievery even while it was hardly dry of the sea.

"True he bring that money?" whispered Simeon. From under lowered brows his eyes glared up. "True he bring it?"

"True," assured Hagen.

"Nobody don't know?" whispered Pablo. "You not tell nobody. Nobody don't know?"

"Not a soul will know!" emphasized Hagen. Uneasily their glances fell.

Brooding silence possessed the room. Hagen examined the pearl, turning it between his finger-tips, staring at it; the others felt he would stare thus until they said something.

Simeon's brown hands fidgeted nervously. He reached across the table and his long thin fingers idly tapped an empty lemonade bottle. The stopper rattled.

In shocked silence they stared at the bottle. The round glass marble inside gleamed in the lamplight. "That one alla same pearl!" whispered Pablo.

"Little bit more bigger than belong me and you!" hissed Simeon.

"Close up the same size," whispered Hagen. "Nearly same shape—round—nearly same weight too."

They arranged to murder Liebglid; to take his five hundred pounds, and to keep the pearl. They would tie the lemonade stopper in a handkerchief and hand it to him as the pearl. When he was untying the handkerchief they would kill him.

Without another word, with just the silent compact in their eyes, they crept from the cottage.

And a shadow followed them.

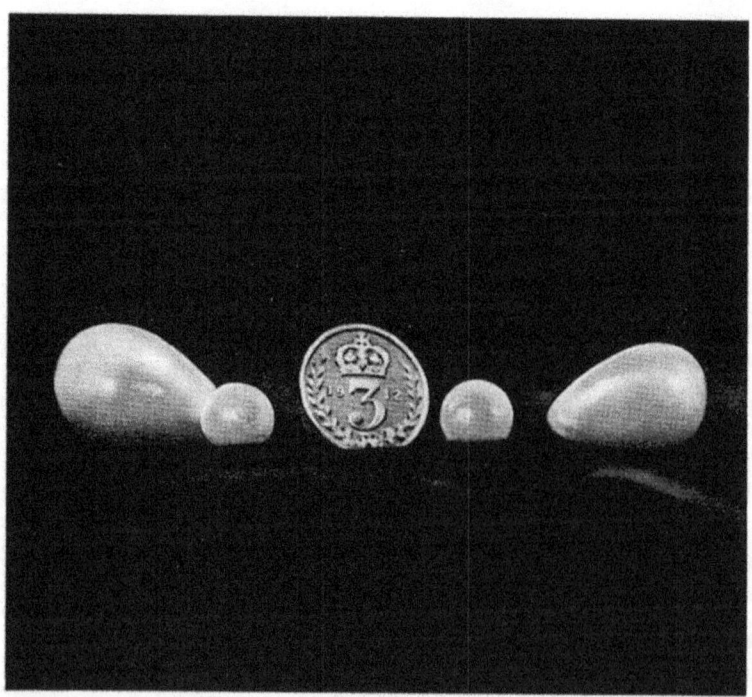

Pearls worth £6000.

CHAPTER VI
Murder

The following night Pablo and Simeon met Liebglid as arranged on the foreshore behind the Residency.

"Where is Mr Hagen?" inquired Liebglid suspiciously.

"He no come yet," answered Pablo uneasily. They glanced round at the shadowed sand-dunes. Distant laughter came from the pearlers' bungalows; a fish plopped close by. Otherwise a dreamy silence under the stars. The black mass of Buccaneer Rock lay cold and still. Upon its sand-dune the Ghost Light steadily burned.

"Mr Hagen promised he would be here!" whispered Liebglid. Uneasily they stood there, listening for soft footsteps in the sand.

At that moment Hagen was walking into the Governor Broome Hotel not far away, whistling as he strode into the billiard room to play far into the night, with joke and laugh, ensuring for himself a perfect alibi.

"Well, did you bring the pearl?" demanded Liebglid at last.

"Yes."

"Show me then."

Reluctantly Pablo pulled the handkerchief from his pocket. Liebglid took it wonderingly, his fingers tingling as he felt the supposed pearl. It must be extraordinarily large, and felt perfectly round. But Pablo roughly claimed the handkerchief.

"You got him that money?" he growled.

"Yes," answered Liebglid testily. "But I must examine the pearl first!"

"You let me see money first time! You show me that one money."

"How much you want?"

"Five hundred pound!"

"Let me see pearl first."

Hesitatingly, Pablo let him just feel the handkerchief again. Liebglid grew excited. "If the pearl is as good as it feels," he whispered, "I'll give you the money now. But you must let me examine it."

"You count him out that money. Let me see how much you got first time! I want look see that money," demanded Pablo.

Liebglid shrugged, then slowly counted out the money—four hundred and fifty pounds. He imagined that sight of all that wealth would turn these two coloured men into greedy children.

"Five hundred pound!" demanded Pablo sulkily and thrust the handkerchief back in his pocket.

"I can easily get the remaining fifty pounds to-morrow!" protested Liebglid. "You can take the four-fifty now and I'll pay you or Mr Hagen the remainder to-morrow."

"Que boonoo!" (kill him!), hissed Simeon in Malay.

"No!" snarled Pablo in Chinese. "Hagen is not here! Speak in Chinese, you fool!"

Liebglid waited beside them, thinking they were arguing as to whether to sell or not. He listened uneasily, sensing the menace in their whispers.

"Kill now," hissed Simeon in Chinese. "He is only a snide man!"

"No," growled Pablo with the rising anger of the Manila blood at disappointment. "If we kill him now we must share with Hagen or he will send us to jail for murder! He could take the pearl and the money too and we dare not say a word. No, we will kill him when we are all together!"

"Do you think Hagen would sell us to the police?" snarled Simeon.

"If not, then why is he not here to share alike in risk and profit?" shrugged Pablo. He turned to Liebglid and growled in pidgin-English, "We sell you pearl to-morrow night-time. You bring him five hundred pound-gold money!"

"Show me the pearl and take the money now. It is good money," persisted Liebglid. "Maybe to-morrow I have other business."

"You bring him gold money—five hundred pound!" growled Pablo. "Paper money no good—policemen tell him that one! You ask Mr Hagen morning time where we altogether meet. Come!" he grunted to Simeon and they walked away.

And their shadow crept after them, a shadow that had heard Simeon's urge: "Quee boonoo!"

It was not until well into the small hours that Hagen returned to his cottage. As he unlocked the door Pablo and Simeon stood beside him. "Hell!" he shuddered, "why didn't you say something!" He glanced once at their faces.

"Come inside," he whispered. He lit the lamp before speaking, turning the wick low.

"What happened?" he inquired.

"You no more come!" growled Pablo menacingly.

Hagen affected not to hear the accusation; not to notice the eyes of Simeon.

"I no come because big business turn up," he answered. "We all three together make much money. But tell me what happen; then we talk."

"Suppose we two feller kill Liebglid to-night," hissed Simeon, "*then* what happen?"

"I knew you would not kill him," exclaimed Hagen impatiently, "because me no there. I know you wait longa me; we kill him; we share altogether. What he say to-night?"

Still suspicious, they told him. "Good!" he murmured. "Could not be better. Now listen!" he leaned towards them, excitement in his voice. "Listen! and only whisper. We three be rich men—in one night! I think it out to-night. That's why I no more come.

"To-morrow night the steamer due—for Singapore! She sail again, early morning time! You two men have your discharges; you are not working now. You go Singapore longa holiday. All your countrymen go home too when lay-up time come! Now, to-morrow night we kill Liebglid. Take him money; take him pearl; take him keys! Rob him sample-room safe, money, pearls, jewellery there! Then quick we go longa Ted Hunter's. Kill him; open safe with keys belonga him. Plenty pearls, always big money in Ted Hunter's safe! Then we hurry to Smythe, manager Union Bank. Rob his safe too! In one night we three be rich men! We share 'em pearls, money, jewellery, quick feller. You two men sail for Singapore next morning. No one suspicious longa you two; you go home for holiday! Me stay longa billiard saloon. No one suspicious that way either! What you say?"

They stared in breathless silence, absorbing the scheme. That steamer sailing to Singapore! Such a quick getaway, so natural they should board her to spend the coming lay-up season in their home town. Liebglid's keys! His sample-room, his safe—so sure to hold pearls that he had bought. Ted Hunter! One of the richest pearlers, living in his lonely bungalow. They would open his safe with his own keys. He always held large sums of money in his safe. He lodged the pearls won by his pearling fleet there too. Smythe of the Union Bank! What might they not find in *his* safe! Untold money, gems of pearls entrusted to his keeping by the pearlers. And all to be got in a night! They nodded assent. Hagen laughed noiselessly.

"We work quick to-morrow night," he whispered. "Listen carefully; you must be aboard Singapore steamer by sun-rise."

Details were planned. They would meet Liebglid on the foreshore in front of the Roebuck Hotel and row him out to the old *Mist*. She was a hulk belonging to Robison and Norman, lying out in Dampier Creek in the mud of the mangroves barely a hundred yards from the shore. Everything had long since been stripped from her, and she had been abandoned, to rot. A fitting scene for such a deed. No one would ever think of her, though she was plain to every eye in the town by day. Not a soul ever visited her and there would be no tracks for trackers to find, no accusing body to raise a hue and cry. They would throw the body down the hold where it would rot in the mud with the *Mist*. Speed was to be their watchword. It sounded so simple; loot seemed so certain. They looked on the triple deed as good as done. Still, Pablo would not hand over the pearl to Hagen even though it was not but one pearl among many.

"Ah, no, I keep it. I no get drunk. You believe me."

But later that day he took the pearl to old Sulu, an old, old Filipino who gained his daily bread by being wood and rubbish man at the Rio de Janeiro, Gomez's rambling boarding-house. Sulu existed in a den behind the wash-house and apparently here to the odour of sour suds he would end his days, dreaming of Manila, but dreaming most of Jolo and the beloved isles of Sulu. He had been Pablo's father's friend in the good days of Sultan Jamal Kiriam II, and with the wild Moros from the hills had fought against Spaniard and American alike. Pablo showed him the pearl, then whispered in Malay:

"I am in peril, Sulu. Enemies seek this pearl. Not a soul knows that I hand it to you. Guard it with your life! I may want it again quickly; but if plans miscarry I may not want it for a long time. No matter what happens to me, I will come again and demand the pearl. If you have lost it, then I will slit your throat."

Old Sulu nodded to the finality in Pablo's eyes. Thus Pablo made him guardian of the pearl throughout anything that might happen. By the most solemn oath of Manila the old man promised to guard the pearl with his life.

"Where shall I hide it?" he mumbled.

"That is for you to decide! If you bury it where a thief will find it, then you dig your grave."

"I want my bones to rest in Jolo," mumbled the old man.

"I will give you steamer fare to Manila when I sell the pearl," promised Pablo, "and money to live with, besides. If you lose the pearl, you need not bother any more. So think wisely, and when you have chosen a hiding-place, whisper me quietly."

Old Sulu promised by his mother's spirit.

Pablo nodded, and walked away, his mind at ease. He feared neither Simeon now, nor Hagen. Full well he knew that the man who carried that pearl could never believe his life his own. He grinned at thought of old Sulu. What a load had been lifted to *his* mind.

Early that morning Hagen called on Liebglid and shammed anger at him for not having kept strictly to his word on the previous night.

"I promised them faithfully that you would bring the whole five hundred pounds!" he protested. "And you arrive fifty pounds short!"

"You were not there!" parried Liebglid sullenly.

"There was no need for me to be there! All you wanted was the pearl; all they wanted was the five hundred. We could have finalized our own private arrangement here now, and all would have been over. As it is, you have made them uneasy and given them time to demand sovereigns. You should have changed those notes into gold anyway. You know notes may be traced. These coloured men are not fools!"

"Five hundred sovereigns is a weight to carry about," mumbled Liebglid.

"You only had to carry it down to the foreshore! Anyway, bring the full five hundred to-night. If we don't finalize to-night, those two coons will get suspicious and sell to someone else. Then you'll lose the pearl and I'll lose my commission. You know how touchy coloured people are when once their distrust has been aroused. I have been arguing with them half the night as it is, persuading them to stick to the bargain."

"What are the arrangements then?"

"Meet the three of us on the foreshore tonight at eight-thirty, right opposite the Roebuck Hotel. We'll have a dinghy handy and row out to a schooner; on shore there are always coloured people prowling about even in the quietest places. Besides, it would only need a whisper to the pearlers that Hagen and Liebglid had been seen talking to coloured seamen in a suspicious place, and our movements in future would be closely watched."

"I've a wretched feeling that I've been watched already."

"What!" Hagen was on his feet, his eyes blazing.

"Oh, it's only nerves," Liebglid reassured him.

"Have you seen anyone?"

"Not a sign. It was just an uneasy feeling; I cannot explain it; I suppose it is the strain."

"Not a soul can know," said Hagen. "Both those men have cunning above the ordinary coloured men. I am positive not a word has slipped from either of them. And neither has had a drink since he came ashore. There is no talk anywhere of a big stolen pearl, no rumours of any kind."

"They will drink immediately they get the money," sneered Liebglid. "They will not be able to hold it."

"They will not be here to drink," answered Hagen. Liebglid stared. But before he could think too much Hagen added: "They will be on the steamer bound for Singapore in the morning."

"Ha! That is good!" laughed Liebglid. "I never thought of that."

"It pays a man to think in our line: to think and to keep a quiet tongue. Don't forget! Eight-thirty to-night on the foreshore opposite the Roebuck. And don't forget that money either. I want to see those two coons bound for Singapore to-morrow morning."

"I shall be there!" nodded Liebglid.

Liebglid sat long and thoughtfully after Hagen's departure. It was hardly premonition, but he felt mentally uneasy. He could define no reason; he was running no more risk in this instance than is generally associated with the illicit buying of a pearl. But just now, when he had looked into Hagen's eyes as once last night when that man Simeon's eyes blazed upon him, he felt like death. For the moment that feeling had been horrible.

Presently he picked up his pen. He had a vague idea of leaving a sealed letter to be opened should he not appear to-morrow. He wrote slowly, with thoughtful pauses. What if the letter by mischance or design was opened before he could claim it! It would contain his name, and particulars of the transaction. That might mean arrest—disgrace—jail. He sat back, frowning. Finally he wrote a short account of his recent meetings and his appointment for to-night, but mentioned no particulars, and no names. He intended to leave this letter with George Stapp, to be called for by himself in the morning.

Still wondering whether he would leave the letter or not, he took his hat and strolled thoughtfully into town. He walked into a large Japanese store and in the office sought Murakami. "Would you cash a cheque for fifty pounds for. me, Mr Murakami? I would like sovereigns."

As Murakami took the cheque, a faint smile enlivened his alert face. "Gold money?" he murmured.

Liebglid nodded. Both men understood.

Murakami was destined to own this large business. A tall Japanese, his clever face did not belie his head. He was to grow into a rich man, and a leader among the Japanese. Time was to play pitch and toss with his fortunes. To-day in Broome he is a poor man again. Still—a very clever man is Murakami, he could tell of intrigues that would interest both East and West—if he would only talk.

He counted out the fifty sovereigns. Liebglid accepted them with a nod of thanks and walked thoughtfully away. He now determined not to change the four hundred and fifty pounds into gold money; something whispered to him that five hundred sovereigns gold money might prove a fatal temptation.

Meanwhile, Hagen strolled into town, with a glance across the foreshore at the old hulk lying by the mangroves. Though fronting the business portion of Broome, and within a stone's throw of the shore, an ideal place for a murder. It is doubtful if Hagen seriously intended to attempt the murder of Hunter and Smythe. There would hardly be time, while the trebled risks would be frightful. But he could visualize one clear and safe murder. Liebglid's body would never be found. It would be days, perhaps weeks, before the robbery of his sample-room was discovered. By then, Pablo and Simeon would be well away. Liebglid would simply have disappeared or else cleared out, as others had drifted from the pearling-port. That five hundred pounds would be easy money ... and the pearl!

He quickened his pace at thought of the gem. He was determined to possess it. He could easily bluff it from Pablo and Simeon after they had killed Liebglid. They would have their share of the loot: of the five hundred and of the proceeds of Liebglid's safe. After which, there would be the steamer at the wharf to take them to the safety of their own land. They would be wild to get aboard. Hagen would have then the overpowering moral mastery of the white man knowing the coloured had committed murder in a white man's land. He would dangle the threat of a noose over their heads, and they would give him the pearl. They would have to.

He nodded to acquaintances as he walked down the road that there runs parallel with the foreshore. Only a few luggers were in the bay. He noted the *Rosa* lying fairly near the old *Mist*; the *Rosa* was owned by the Chinaman Lee Sing. And there was Robert Annear's *New South Moon* lying only a few cables' length away. The crews, hardly without exception, would be ashore in early night.

Coming with long easy strides down the street was Long Jimmy James, of James and Piggott. Hagen stopped him: "I may have some business to put through with you soon, Mr James."

"Yes. What is it?" replied James ungraciously.

"I would not tell my own father that—at present."

"Well, what is the good of mentioning it to me—now!" snapped James. "Good morning." And he walked on. Later in the day he noticed Hagen walking out of Gould the solicitor's office. James walked over:

"Pardon me, Gould—but that fellow Hagen! I just saw him walking out of your office. If it is not breaking any confidences, I'm curious to know if his business concerns me. He mentioned this morning that he may have business with me in a day or two. Forewarned is forearmed. I don't like the fellow."

"Oh, there's no harm in telling you," said Gould with a smile, "as you will have to be approached. He is thinking of taking a lease of the *Star*."

"Where would *he* get the money to take a lease of the *Star*?"

Gould shrugged.

"He's got jolly confident all of a sudden," added James.. "He'll be blossoming into a pearler next. Anyway, why couldn't he have asked me for a lease straight out?"

"Business," smiled Gould.

"I don't like his business," replied James. And he walked on.

That evening came peacefully; the night so dark that the stars shone like polished gold. Except for roisterers at the Roebuck, the squeak of a Chinese fiddle, twang of a guitar from some lantern-lit veranda, the town was quiet. Distantly, from among the pearlers' bungalows came a chorus of song. Some gay party just starting. The foreshore fronting the town was black as night, the water without a ripple. Out there gleamed a solitary ray from the masthead light of a lugger. Liebglid shivered by the mangrove shadows, staring alternately out on the bay then back across the street towards the town. He could distinguish shadow forms disappearing up the dark lanes, hear faint laughter from invisible groups, a burst of revelry from the Roebuck. From the bay behind him came a cool breath of air. He shivered—then jumped.

"Why—why d-didn't you speak!' he stuttered angrily. "You scared the life out of me!"

"Hssh!" hissed Simeon. "No more talk! Here Hagen—we ready now."

"Come!" whispered Hagen. "We've got a dinghy ready on the beach." They silently crossed the sand, stepped into a dinghy and quietly rowed away. Hagen glanced back—once. Dim lights were streaming out on to the veranda of the Roebuck; noisy figures were emerging; some began to dance to a chorus of song and fiddle. Liebglid looked ahead, trying to peer over the shoulders of Pablo who was pulling with noiseless strokes. Like a wraith the skeleton of the *Mist* loomed up. Pablo pulled the dinghy beside it and reached out towards the slimy side. A shiver of apprehension ran through Liebglid.

"But this is not a schooner!" he whispered.

"Yes it is—what remains of one," whispered Hagen. "Come, I'll help you board. The pearl is hidden here. You don't think Pablo keeps it on him all day, do you?"

Liebglid breathed easier; this hulk was really a perfect hiding-place. He stared up at the black timbers; the hulk was leaning well over, the rotting deck at an abrupt angle. No one would dream that a pearl was hidden in this beastly shell.

"And there is no crew aboard this ship to put the show away either," growled Hagen as he clambered up the sides. "No spying eyes to watch Pablo hide his pearl; it would be safe here until Doomsday. Here, I'll lend you a hand, the old deck slopes right down to the water. Don't make any noise—and watch out for splinters!"

Stooping in the climb against the steeply sloping deck, Liebglid was glad to reach out and grasp the hatch combing. He drew back momentarily for before him was the open blackness of the hold, the smell of mangrove ooze down there. He sat upon the hatch edge, Hagen beside him, Pablo standing close by while Simeon vanished.

"He's gone to the old galley," whispered Hagen. "You could not imagine a safer hiding-place than the galley of the *Mist*, eh!"

"Unless it was down this dark hold!" Liebglid shivered.

Hagen chuckled. "No one will ever look down there," he whispered, "not for anything! Here comes Simeon."

Simeon handed the handkerchief to Liebglid who smiled in relief as he felt the supposed pearl.

"This is a good one!" he whispered. "If it is only as good as it feels!"

With trembling fingers he undid the knots and peered. "This is no good—Ah!" ... The sling shot thudded on his head. He slumped to the deck and they wolfed him. There was the chink of gold, the jingle of keys—he struck out and kicked and screamed, then slid straight down the deck overside and thumped into the dinghy. As he saw their faces coming he screamed "Murder!" and struggled over into the water. But he could not swim. He snatched at the dinghy and screamed "Murder!" to the thud of the sling shot. He sank like a stone.

"The money!" panted Simeon. "He's taken it with him!"

"Shut up!" hissed Hagen.

The night was listening ... Not the sound of a laugh, not the murmur of a voice, not one squeak of a fiddle ... The unblinking lights ashore seemed listening. The three stared towards where dim lights showed on the *New South Moon* and the *Rosa*. But they, too, seemed listening.

Then a shout from the shore; then other shouts: "What was that?"

"Did you hear that?"

"Someone screamed!"

"Someone called 'Murder'!"

"Where was it?"

"Down on the foreshore ... Sounded like out on the bay!"

"Come on," hissed Hagen. "To the shore for your lives—and keep to the mangrove shadows away from the beach—Quick!"

CHAPTER VII
The Arrest

"Murder!"

Constable Trebilcock, patrolling John Chi Lane, had wheeled around at that terrified shriek. Old John Chi came pattering out of his store carrying a hurricane lamp. Along the lane coloured people stood listening.

"Murder!"

The constable ran back towards the waterfront with old John Chi shuffling after him; there came the quick click-clock click-cluck of sandals, the pattering of feet; white diver Neale hurried out of the Pearler's Rest with a lantern. Men were hurrying to the foreshore. The constable heard the agitated click of rowlocks. He shouted to the unseen rower to stop, then ran along the water's edge keeping pace with the sound until it dimmed apparently towards the *Rosa*. With Japanese Taro and Jiro he launched a dinghy and rowing out into the night boarded the *New South Moon* and the *Rosa*. But his inquiry was met by non-committal answers from the few coloured men aboard. He learnt nothing; eventually he rowed ashore. After fruitless inquiries it seemed that the trouble had probably been one of the disturbances that were of frequent occurrence there.

Meanwhile Simeon, during that panicky row to shore, lost his nerve, jumped from the dinghy when near shore, and began to swim. Pablo followed him.

"You fools!" called Hagen urgently. "Separate! and wait for me at the cottage."

As the dinghy grounded, Hagen leapt ashore and, with one glance towards the groups streaming along the shore, sped across the road and disappeared among the dark, hushed buildings.

It was only minutes later when Castilla Toledo suddenly appeared in a crowded gambling-den.

"Murder!" he shouted. "Some man call 'Murder!' out on bay. Police there! Big mob there!" The den emptied with a rush. Pressing out with the crowd Toledo edged up against Francis Paddy and whispered: "I see Simeon Espada in bath-room of Rio de Janeiro—shivering! Pablo Marquez run there too! Their clothes all wet!"

The bleary eyes of Francis Paddy stared at Toledo. Francis had been drinking heavily; had been smoking the poppy too.

"We go there," he muttered. But when they arrived, the bath-room was empty. They stood out in the shadows near the unrailed veranda that jutted on to the lane, whispering for a long while. A jumble of wood and iron buildings surrounded them; the dark veranda of the ramshackle boarding-house was occupied only by a cat. Every soul seemed to have rushed down to the waterfront. "Ssh!" hissed Toledo.

A chink of light suggested a door opening noiselessly. Out on to the veranda stepped Gomez the Manilaman boarding-house keeper. Clad as usual in silk pants, shirt, and slippers, his lined, swarthy face was frowning as he listened. He was uneasy; suspicious at being left alone by the crowd. He listened awhile, then stepped back into the room. The closing door blotted out the light.

"Men they do something here!" declared Francis Paddy.

"Not that one!" whispered Toledo. "He don't know yet, I think. You wait!"

A hum of voices grew louder. Crowds were collecting at the Roebuck and the Pearler's Rest to discuss the incident of the night. Suddenly Toledo gripped Francis's arm ... Only old Lucas the coloured night man doing his rounds earlier than usual. He commenced his work among the garbage round by the kitchen.

They stood there a long time. Then a shadow came from out the lane and stood by the veranda, breathing heavily. He placed a bag on the veranda. Toledo and Francis heard a chink as of coins, a tinkle as of jewellery. Two shadows joined him a moment later. As they did so old Lucas on bare feet came around the side of the veranda. He was right amongst them, staring stupidly down at the bag.

In an instant Pablo had reached up and pulled him down; had stretched out his neck; a knife gleamed.

"Wait!" whispered Hagen. He glared down into the bulging eyes of the terrified coloured man, then—"He won't dare say a word. He too much fright. Let him go."

"More better we kill him!" growled Pablo. "He see too much!"

"No," growled Hagen, "too risky now. We have made a mess of things as it is—if we slit his throat here we'll swing!" Bending close to Lucas he hissed, "Suppose you speak—*any* time—we cut your throat!"

The terrified man could barely breathe.

"Let him up," ordered Hagen.

Pablo drew back with a nasty growl. The old man sat up, slobbering from fear. Hagen gripped him:

"Tonight, you see nothing! You hear nothing! You know nothing!"

Lucas nodded dumbly.

"Go."

On trembling feet old Lucas shuffled away.

"He safe!" whispered Hagen urgently. "He will never breathe one word. You wait here, Simeon, while we fetch the rest."

They vanished, leaving Simeon with his nerves on edge. He stared to right and left, he knelt down and peered under the veranda. Standing up again he peered all around, clutching the bag. Slow, silent minutes dragged by.

An urgent "Hiss!" came warningly. Instantly Simeon ducked under the veranda. He stayed there too, his heart thumping madly, until presently he saw the legs of Hagen and Pablo before him. He crawled from the veranda.

"Where's the bag?" whispered Hagen. Simeon nodded at the veranda ... The bag was gone!

They stood speechless.

"Lucas?" snarled Pablo.

"No, no," answered Hagen agitatedly. "He would not dare. He is frightened out of his life. No, no. Someone is watching us!" They stared in a stricken silence. "Come!" whispered Hagen. They disappeared up the lane.

"Who took that feller bag?" whispered Francis Paddy. "He damn quiet; damn quick! I never see him!"

Toledo smiled in the dark.

"He too quick for me!" he answered. "We see no more tonight. You better go longa your friends; I go visit mine."

Francis Paddy nodded.

"An' we better be like that one Lucas!" he whispered warningly. "We see nothing; hear nothing; *know* nothing."

Toledo nodded. Silently they separated. But Toledo hurried straight to Hagen's cottage. On bare feet he crept to listen at the door. He could only hear a murmur of voices. Hagen was in a rage made crazy by fear.

"We have messed up everything!" he snarled. "Placed our necks in a noose! Now listen, if you two feller don't want to hang! Say nothing. Go about your work to-morrow as if nothing happen ..."

"But we go longa Singapore boat soon now!" broke in Pablo.

"Fool! They will find Liebglid's body in the morning! Suppose you two feller run away on board steamer—then they know you kill him!"

In startled fear they realized this.

"Stay here! Mix with your friends all same every day. No one know we kill him! What you do that pearl?" he demanded of Pablo.

"I hide him," answered Pablo sulkily.

"Where?"

"Me no tell!"

"Well, don't tell any one else either," snarled Hagen. "And don't try sell pearl. If you do they find out then why we killed Liebglid! We sell him pearl together—after next lay-up time. Never let no man ever know we have pearl. Understand? Suppose police never find out we have pearl, they never know then why we should kill Liebglid. Suppose they never know, they never can prove."

They nodded dubiously.

"What about that man stealem bag?" inquired Simeon uneasily.

"He keep quiet. He keep sovereigns, keep jewellery, he never say nothing because if he do police arrest *him*!"

They nodded. Then the three uneasy murderers separated.

Next morning, 31 August 1905, Robert Loten Annear of the lugger *New South Moon* reported to the police that the body of a man was lying in Dampier Creek near the old schooner *Mist*. Sergeant Byrne sent Constables Trebilcock and Nelson to investigate. They brought ashore the body of Liebglid. On him was found four hundred and fifty pounds in notes.

That same morning a crowd was drinking at the bar of the Roebuck, discussing the news. Toledo and Francis Paddy were among them. Paddy had again been drinking and indulging in the poppy and the fumes had deadened his native caution; the alcohol had given him false courage. Hagen tramped in and with loud sociability ordered drinks for his cronies. Presently, the grunts of Francis Paddy disturbed the conversation.

"What's a-matter, Paddy?" a Malay called from down the bar.

"H'm! If I was pleece!" grunted Paddy.

"What name you Francis?" laughed the Malay. "Suppose you pleece, what then you do?"

"If I was pleeceman I'd catch murderer!"

They laughed. Jeering sallies brought a snarl to the face of Francis Paddy.

"By hell!" he growled and clenched his hands, "if I was a pleece I'd catch him now. He's here, the——murderer ... he's here now!"

Hagen caught his breath. Silence chilled the bar. The faces of Pablo and Simeon turned sickly yellow. Then laughter broke out, and Francis was challenged to point out the man. He wheeled around and looked full into the fiendish eyes of Pablo. He gaped—then slouched out of the bar, cursing at the laughter that followed.

Hagen presently slipped away; Pablo left soon after. As Simeon was leaving, the voice of Toledo hissed in his ear: "Come outside along passage, Simeon. I want talk longa you!"

Uneasily, Simeon followed. Toledo wheeled upon him: "Where my pearl?"

Simeon stared, then a mocking smile brought colour into his face:

"I no got pearl. I don't know what you talk about."

"You lie! You steal my pearl!"

Simeon shook his head with a slow, malicious smile.

"Who steal him then? Pablo?"

"Pablo no steal him. I don't know what you mean. Suppose someone steal a pearl belong you, where you get him that one pearl first time?"

"You think me— —fool!" sneered Toledo. "Never mind, you find out different soon! First time, suppose you tell me who steal my pearl I no tell police you murder Liebglid."

"You lie!"

"Where pearl?"

"Don't know!"

"Liebglid got him?"

"No."

"Ah," grinned Toledo, "you no more sell him, eh! P'raps you sell him; then you kill Liebglid; then you take him pearl back again, eh! You or Pablo got him that one pearl!"

"We no got him."

"I tell police!"

"You know nothing."

"Me know *everything*! Me hear you say 'Quee boonoo'. Me see you row out longa *Mist*. Hear Liebglid scream. See you three feller row ashore. You steal him money, jewellery, in bag. Me tell police you kill Liebglid."

Simeon drew a long breath. Toledo watched him with dilated eyes. Then Simeon hissed:

"Suppose you tell police, you never get him pearl! You steal him that one feller pearl yourself first time. Police claim him pearl. Suppose you say nothing, we sell him pearl by em by, we give you share!" And he hurried away.

So did Toledo—to the police station.

But he only told sufficient for the arrest of Simeon on suspicion. Simeon acted the part of the injured innocent perfectly. Even after the coroner's inquiry the police were not certain that he had taken part in the murder.

To Francis Paddy's disgust *he* came within an ace of being arrested for complicity. It was believed that he knew who rowed the dinghy back towards the *Rosa*. Possibly he did. When the *Rosa* slipped away, a police patrol went after her; then ensued a long chase along the wild coast of the far north.

Old Sulu, as poor as a church mouse, was the guardian of a fortune. A fortune beyond his dreams of avarice, for in the Philippines he could have lived out his life on a hundred pounds. But this fortune weighed him down.

Though not his own fortune he knew that to lose it meant losing what of life and hope remained.

He dared not sell the pearl and take the first steamer to the East, for Pablo would follow as certainly as the rising of the sun. While if the pearl were stolen from him ...

Penniless, yet with a fortune, and worried to distraction. During the hot afternoon siestas he lay motionless on his ragged pallet, his watery old eyes staring up at the hot iron roof. The dingy shed was really an oven. Except for a plank table, several boxes and his pallet, it was bare, smelling of suds from the wash-house adjoining, and with the taint of damp firewood stacked in the corner where the centipedes were. Through the open door came a business-like buzz as a large black-and-yellow hornet flew in and buzzed up to its mud nest in the roof corner among the cobwebs. The old man lay there, watching the hornet modelling a little clay ball upon its nearly built nest. Subconsciously he stared, his mind aching under its hopeless job of solving a safe hiding-place for the pearl. Suddenly he gasped; stared; and his eyes slowly closed. In a moment or two he was breathing as if in sleep.

That night, when Broome was asleep, Sulu crawled from his pallet and across the floor to the boxes. In the pitch darkness he knew exactly where to place them one on top of the other. Then he stood upon the topmost box, his head touching the corner of the shed. With his fingers he sought and found the hornet's nest. Softly he began boring into the nest with a thin-bladed knife. He worked silently, regulating his breathing to the softest, catching the dust from the nest in his hand and transferring it to his hair. He stopped, listening. Then again worked softly and carefully.

When he had a hole bored deep enough he took the pearl from his pocket. It was wrapped in a small piece of black silk soaked in liquid poisonous to insects. Carefully he poked the pearl into the hole. Then stepped down; noiselessly replaced the boxes, and crept to his pallet.

First thing in the morning, the hornet would discover the hole in the wall of its home, and would work angrily and busily to fill that hole up ·with fresh mud.

In the slow days following Simeon's arrest Hagen and Pablo lived in a hell of fears. Wires had flashed to Perth and Detective Mann was *en route* for Broome. Toledo, too, spent sleepless nights—lest he should not recover the pearl. He dared not tell the police all, for he had stolen the pearl himself. Besides which, if he told all and Pablo and Hagen were arrested in possession of the pearl, then the Crown would seek the rightful owner. But he could not understand that a man, knowing the whereabouts of the pearl, would not tell when threatened by arrest for murder. He had been convinced that Simeon had the pearl, but it must be Pablo. Not Hagen, because if he had bought or sold it then both Simeon and Pablo would have been flashing their money long ago. But how to force Pablo to tell the whereabouts of the pearl?

At last he feared the police were rapidly piecing the truth together.

If so, then the arrest of Hagen and Pablo would take the last weapon from his hand, and the police might seize the pearl. Cunningly he worked. Choosing just after middle afternoon when most people in Broome were well in their afternoon siesta, he walked up the sunlit lane to the boarding-house. Men were asleep inside; others asleep on the veranda. Among these was Pablo—only he was not asleep; he was all tense nervousness. Gomez was there too, asleep in his light silk clothes on an easy chair, Gomez who generally took his siesta in his office inside.

Toledo sidled up to Pablo. "Pablo," he whispered, "I want him that one pearl!"

Pablo stared.

"You steal him from me!" insisted Toledo in an agitated whisper. "You kill Liebglid. I know! I follow you to Hagen cottage; I listen. I follow you behind Residency; I hear Simeon say 'Quee boonoo'! I follow you Hagen cottage again. I listen alla time! I follow you three fellow that night; watch you meet Liebglid longa shore; see you altogether row out longa *Mist*. I know!"

Pablo drew a deep breath.

"No chance you knife me," sneered Toledo. "I ready; too many men here. Suppose you tell me where pearl. I no tell police."

"But Simeon?" breathed Pablo.

"Simeon say nothing! He too fright. Police by em by let him go. No one say nothing against him! No one know—only me! Suppose you no tell me where my pearl is, then you swing!"

Toledo had almost gained his point—he could see it in the drawn face of Pablo. In tremulous excitement he spoiled everything by his next answer to Pablo's question.

"But," whispered Pablo, "suppose I give you pearl, and then Simeon talk! Perhaps Hagen talk too! Suppose pleece arrest me, then I lose pearl and hang too."

"No, no," whispered Toledo urgently. "You no more hang—you turn King's evidence!"

"What name that one?"

"You tell truth about kill Liebglid. Then Simeon and Hagen they two fellow hang. That law. But when man turn King's evidence *he* no more hang. That English law."

A startled expression lit the face of Pablo. "I hear that same way long time before!" he whispered eagerly. "You sure that King's evidence one true?"

"True," assured Toledo.

A cunning smile creased the face of Pablo. Fear was replaced by a malevolent grin.

"Toledo!" he whispered. "I never tell you where pearl is—now!"

They breathed into one another's faces, the devil in their eyes. Toledo drew back with a snarl:

"Then I send you longa hell, Pablo. Police arrest Hagen."

"What!" cried Pablo.

"Police take Hagen. They come for you now." He leapt out into the lane. "Yes," he cried. "Here come sergeant and policeman now!"

Pablo was beside him on the instant. Around the distant corner and into the lane appeared Sergeant Byrne and a constable, walking quickly. Pablo leapt back to the veranda and dashed around the corner of the house. Toledo followed ... And behind Toledo came Gomez. Pablo had run straight to the garret where old Sulu lay sleeping. Pablo awoke him, whispering rapidly, a terrible threat in his eyes. Dumbly the old man nodded; he understood. Then his eyes warned.

Pablo stared around—into the fiendish face of Toledo. With a cry he whipped out his knife, then saw Gomez standing there. He trembled on his toes at the sound of heavy footsteps coming along the veranda. He sheathed his knife, glaring at Toledo; then snarled down at Sulu. The old man nodded.

Toledo knew now who knew where the pearl was but—Toledo did not know that hiding-place.

Pablo was arrested.

CHAPTER VIII
The Diver and the Herrings

While being taken to the police station Pablo thought cunningly. He must act quickly or Hagen might act. As neither Hagen nor Simeon knew the whereabouts of the pearl, they would have less inducement to talk. But fear for their necks might make them turn King's evidence.

He grinned at the thought of how Toledo had let him out. He would tell all. Simeon and Hagen would hang; he would be allowed to go free. And he would have the pearl!

At the station he had hardly been cautioned when he walked up to Sergeant Byrne who was entering the arrest in the Occurrence Book. He took the sergeant's hand in his and said:

"Sergeant, I tell everything, I tell you true!" He then asked for Mr Martin and Father Russel to be present and witness his statement. These gentlemen were sent for and Pablo made a statement but becoming uneasy left it incomplete. That evening he called the sergeant, stating that he wanted to say more. He then guided Constable Nelson to the lane near his house where he had buried some jewellery. He stated that Hagen had given it to him. But next afternoon, quite convinced that by betraying his accomplices he would be allowed to go free, he told all, only omitting the existence of a real pearl. He asked again for Mr Martin and Father Russel to witness this.

The case excited keen attention. The attempt to sell as a huge pearl a lemonade stopper wrapped in a handkerchief was unique. But among the twenty-eight witnesses called there were many who evidently were afraid of saying too much. Never throughout the inquiry did the existence of the true pearl come out publicly. Though a few men knew of it now, each kept quiet for personal reasons. The coroner's jury returned a verdict of wilful murder against Charles Hagen, Simeon Espada, and Pablo Marquez. When this news spread around the town old Sulu crept to his shed, tears of joy coursing down his withered cheeks. He was almost overcome: his heart was thumping so, he thought he might die.

If Pablo should hang, swing by the neck until he was dead, the pearl would be Sulu's! He would own a pearl of fabulous value. Why, he would be as wealthy as the Sultan of Sulu!

Sulu gasped; he rolled his head and closed his eyes to steady his throbbing heart, his skinny hands clutching his chest. If Pablo should swing, he could sell the pearl to Gomez ...

Ah! Gomez. His heart beat normally. He stared at the roof, anywhere but at the hornet's nest. Gomez had been so considerate to him lately. So thoughtful. Had mentioned his kindness in giving Sulu a home for so many years. Had even come and sat with him one quiet evening and in low tones boasted of the great price he gave for pearls, a price bigger far and fairer than any given by Rubin, or Davis, or Schaumer, or Bauer, or by any of the white buyers of the town. And Sulu recollected how narrowly Gomez had watched him as he talked in that low, persuasive voice.

Sulu smiled. Though not certain, he could feel an eye watching him through a nail-hole in the wash-house wall. The wash-house was built right against the boarding-house. For days past, he had had the feeling that an eye was watching him at night, and by day whenever he was in his shed. But never once had he even glanced towards the hornet's nest, he only rolled over softly and gazed there after he put out his light at night.

But—if Pablo should swing!

Meanwhile, farther north among the tiny, picturesque islands of King Sound the scattered pearling fleets were at work. Tiny sails, dotted throughout the Buccaneer Archipelago and among the green tipped islets of the Sound. Treacherous tides, and currents, and whirlpools flow and swirl through the rock-walled passes of the great Sound.

A few more burial posts had been added to the forlorn forest that marks the Graveyard: just a few more divers dead of paralysis, or misadventure, or inexperience. But less and less now was the toll taken by the dreaded beriberi since the white masters had learnt that plentiful fresh foods would keep it away. They were overcoming other problems, too, by bold and successful organization. This season shelling had been good, a fair number of pearls also had been won. But now almost daily the sky blackened as cock-eye bobs shrieked upon them, to lash them in sheets of rain. Twenty minutes after in the brilliant sunlight, as the blow howled away, the crews would say:

"Willy-willy season he come soon now. Close up lay-up time."

Down south too, down past the Eighty Mile Beach, past Condon, Port Hedland, Cossack, Onslow, right down to Shark Bay, the little sails of pearling luggers dotted the sea.

It was far down south that the muddled owner of the pearl had run when he awoke to find his treasure gone—chasing a phantom lugger south when the real lugger had sailed north. He was to be caught in the cyclone season at Shark Bay. When the lay-up was over and he sailed for Broome the fleets were all at sea again. It was to be more than a year later before he would locate the lugger, and long before then he was hazy himself as to where he had really lost the pearl. When eventually he did locate and question Toledo's one-time master that mariner was caustic and indignant indeed. In mutual distrust they parted, very bad friends.

Several vessels were sheltering near one another in the Sound. Con the bosun was shell-opening, cleaning up the last of the day's shell. Con had an awful cold. Only dogged determination and pride held him at work so late. It was near sundown and all the crew excepting young Assan were already rowing to nearby vessels for evening coffee and yarn-time, while all the white people had boarded a just arrived schooner eager for mails and news. That day all of Con's cunning had been needed to prevent the crew of his lugger from learning that the shell was carrying an occasional small pearl, for he kept coughing. He dare not hide the baroque in his mouth lest he cough! So now he was opening the last of the shell while fortune favoured.

And that vey last shell contained a fair-sized pearl. With greasy fingers he examined it while young Assan sang and boiled coffee at the galley. Con was well pleased with the pearl, it would be a nice little "round" to show the master. He popped it in his mouth for he could easily take it out now if he must cough. He straightened his back, thankful that the long day's toil was at last over. His hands were slimy, ropy with fish slime. He bent down overside to wash them and—coughed! On the instant he plunged straight in after the pearl; he could see it like faint silver fast slipping away.

Now, a flattish object goes to the bottom in zigzags, redoubling its speed when half-way down. A pearl or similar shaped object travels on the slant, also redoubling its speed. Con sped down trying to swim past the pearl so that he could hold up his palms and it would then glide into them. He knew that to grab with his hand would be but to push it farther down. But the world quickly darkened until he could only just see that vanishing silvery point. He was beaten, he could not hold his breath long enough, the cold had him beaten. He struggled to the surface; Assan was leaning overside, he reached down and grabbed Con's clutching hands.

"You lose him pearl?" Assan demanded.

Con collapsed on the deck, his teeth chattering, utterly exhausted. He shook his head. "No—lose—him—pearl!" he gasped. "No pearl. I swim—try and beat—this, cold."

Assan smiled. Con staggered below for dry clothes. "Dinner he cook!" called Assan.

Con reappeared on deck with a spoon and sugar and bottle of eucalyptus oil. A cool sunset helped the food smell tempting. Con carefully measured a few drops of eucalyptus on a spoonful of sugar and swallowed it. It was a fairly strong dose and made him cough a bit.

"Me got cold sick too. Bad one!" said Assan eagerly. "What about you give me some one that white man medicine?"

"You take him, suppose you like," answered Con wearily. "Only little drop. Suppose you take too much you go longa hell quick time!"

Eagerly the young Malay took the spoon and some sugar. He tipped up the eucalyptus bottle until the spoon brimmed over. At Con's warning cry he tilted back his head and tipped the contents down. He looked startled; his eyes bulged; he coughed violently; he choked. He writhed, fighting for breath; he beat at his throat; foamed at the mouth. Con lost his head. He leapt at Assan, thumping him on the chest, calling wildly:

"A-san! A-san! What's up? What's up? A-san, A-san, what you done!" He ran for water; Assan was choking. Con pulled him down on his back shouting: "Hs! A-san you dead!" He tried to blow into his nostrils, he saw the whites of his eyes. "He'll die! He'll die!" wailed Con. "They'll hang me for murder like they'll hang Pablo!"

But young Assan did not die, though he wished he could. When he began to recover, he swore violently in Malay. This made him cough, which eased him a lot. An hour later the crew came singing back, with Francis Paddy and Sebaro the diver and Bin Mahomet the quiet Malay and others of several crews eager for a yarn. Assan was lying on the deck, still gasping. Francis Paddy laughed hoarsely:

"Young man all same fool," he growled contemptuously. "You tell him one thing, he do another, alla time he know better."

Sebaro laughed too but not with the cynicism of Francis Paddy. That cynic should have been more considerate, for he himself had had a fright not so very long ago in Broome. He had been called upon to explain why his dinghy, tied up at the *Rosa's* stern, was stained with something looking particularly like blood-stains. He had used the dinghy to bring in a supply of red mangrove bark for tanning, and the stains did resemble dried blood. There may have been real blood-stains among the tan. And the police had as good as proved that it was the dinghy used by Hagen, Pablo, and Simeon.

The diver had had no little trouble in proving his innocence. The schooner just arrived had brought news that Hagen, Pablo, and Simeon had been taken away under escort in the steamer for Fremantle jail. Some of the men on board now had not heard full details of the case, so Francis Paddy took the deck in oratorical explanation. Con listened closely.

It was an interesting yarn-time, with just a whisper of the great pearl stolen by Castilla Toledo and eager speculation as to where that pearl was now. Then followed gossip of the hidden life of Asiatic town, and a résumé of the white men's activities in matters of which the coloureds were supposed to know nothing at all. From stories of home-life in Malayan villages, of bloody raids of the Moros against the Americans in the Philippines, to stories of Samal pirates and the tough krismen of the Sultan's Royal Guard, and terrible tales then of the hell-mad Juramentado. From stories of the Dutch and of Koepang, the yarns naturally turned to diving and the wondrous things the diver sees beneath the sea.

With lowered voices then came stories of the "ghost ships", those eerie vessels under transparent sail that glide the seas at night with ghostly skipper at the helm, ghostly crew upon the deck. Then stories of those dead hulks at the bottom of the sea that come to life at night, the captain coming from his bones below to take the ghostly bridge. Tales too of those "other sort" sea ghosts that prowl the ocean bottom by day, melting into the water before the diver's eyes.

Then tales of living sea maids that the divers constantly see, laughing sirens these, from the depths of sea-gardens luring divers to doom. Old Sebaro, his voice sinking to a droning murmur, told a weird story of sea maids taking a diver in the water-worn depths of the Pass. The dress was hauled up but there was no diver in it, only a little round hole. He told them of the phantom divers that ever and again greet him while at work, shadow divers who without air-pipe or life-line emerge in the water haze to wave a greeting then melt back into water tremors. In hushed whispers other divers told of queer spirit things that glide across the trackless ocean floor and melt right through the bodies of shoals of fish.

Both listeners and tellers believed every word spoken. Uncanny indeed are many of these stories of the older divers, and as fantastic as have ever appeared in any storybook. No doubt their life in the underwater world and the varying pressures of air and water upon the brain, are responsible for these fantastic imaginings.

Before the first blush of dawn, the tender on each tiny vessel, hearing the cook at the galley, roused the crew. Tiny wisps of smoke rose from the luggers while yet they were but shadows against headland, or upon the sea. Patter of feet, buckets overside for the morning bath, then the chatter of early morning coffee-time. Cleaning of teeth followed, and the tenders got busy at the coils of life-line and air-pipe while the diver was dressing. Anchor chains creaked; blocks rattled as mainsail and jib were hoisted; and sails murmured as vessels stood out to work. The sun had not quite chased the early shadows from the shore-line cliffs when all the divers were overside. The crews would snatch breakfast as they could while their vessel was sailing back to start on a new drift. For from dawn until dark while "on shell" all is work on a pearling lugger.

Francis Paddy, to a spray of bubbles, sank down into the gloom. He was anxious to win all the shell he could, he had lost much time through over indulgence in the poppy and through the Liebglid murder case.

Once on the sea floor he signalled "Bottom", adjusted his air-valve to the water-pressure, then walked slowly forward over an uneven bottom of plant life luxuriating in mounds like well-tended rockeries. Here grew sea bushes and grasses whose silk-like tendrils moved dreamily to the tide. Presently the bottom changed to a broken coral patch where "coral cups" taller than a man stood up, to which clung huge vegetable shapes like bloated black rubber.

Francis moved through the gloom looking as monstrously weird as any of the queer life around, his air-pipe and life-line disappearing hazily above like tentacles of some deep-sea monster. There arose in front of him a ghostly gravel patch with a large shellfish lumbering across it, now stalked by a marauding crab. The lithe, grey shape of a shark glided by. Francis gave the tiger of the sea hardly a glance. A shoal of tiny fish fled frenziedly past. Behind his face-glass, Francis scowled. These sardine-like fish seemed harmless as flies, but Francis was wise in the underwater life. A silver streak shot past followed by another—then another. Francis scowled again: kingfish were chasing the herrings!

A shoal of herrings like a cloud emerged from the gloom. They massed around the diver enclosing him in atoms of frenzied life that rapidly darkened vision. Despite his waving arms and shaking life-line, despite a liberated burst of bubbles, he was engulfed in a moving darkness of countless tiny, frantic bodies. As if at a signal they turned straight in on him and glued themselves to his helmet, swarming to his neck, his chest, his back, swarming like bees especially under his arms and massing between his legs, gluing themselves to him, a compact mass of living fish. He heard the swish! swish! swish! of the pursuing fish; felt the thud! thud! thud! of impact.

He could barely move now. But still he fought like a man standing within a swaying coffin. He was in a rage lest he should have to be hauled up. As another shoal in dumb horror seeking protection swarmed upon him he felt their vibration in the writhing mass encasing him. Within inky darkness he tugged feebly at the life-line, screwed close his air-escape valve. As the dress inflated it refused to rise under the weight; considerably more air than usual must be accumulated. Again came the dull thud! thud! thud! only faster this time as more large fish arrived and charged again and again.

Slowly the dress began to ascend as the tender above shouted to the crew to lend a hand to this unusually heavy haul. Very slowly up towards the surface came the mass of the diver surrounded by the dense cloud of tiny fish with voracious big ones darting amongst them, snapping left and right. As the mass broke surface the fish dissolved and the domed helmet came into view. As they hauled him to the side herrings splashed back from his neck, his shoulders. Weakly he grasped the ladder, swearing like a fury inside the dress. The fish slipped down from his legs, they glued themselves to the keel and sides of the lugger, a living mass blindly seeking protection.

On such occasions there is wisdom in their blindness. For, when they charge, the protruding snouts of the big fish may strike the vessel's sides and not get as clear a snap at the prey as when the victim is fleeing through clear water.

In a rage, Francis sat on the hatch. He might have to wait an hour or more; certainly the tiny fish would not flee their sanctuary until the large ones went. Now the ocean around the lugger was streaked with foam as swarms of kingfish arrived and gulls in shrieking thousands swooped among them to gobble up the frenzied little things that leapt from the charges of the voracious big ones.

The tender shrugged.

"Up mains'l! Up fores'l!" he ordered.

So can a herring upset the well-laid plans of a diver, and force a lugger to sail away.

Broome: Sheba Lane.

CHAPTER IX
Time and Life and Death

Lay-up season had come again; the fleets were all home. Broome was sweltering under the wet-season heat; a mutter of thunder came and went over sea and land. Red dust was thick on the roads; in the brilliant sunlight the feathery fronds of the poinsettias were drooping. On shaded verandas of the pearlers' pretty bungalows easy chairs and hammocks were overworked by men in whites discussing the price of shell, of pearls and buyers, or news brought by the very irregular papers. Cool drinks and charming company made the hours there pass pleasantly. Boisterous shell-openers crowded the foreshore camps determined to make their three months ashore particularly lively. In the packing-sheds busy experts stacked unbelievable quantities of shell into cases for export to the markets overseas. Shell was keeping at a good price; business was thriving; the few hotels, whether in the white quarter or up town, did as usual a roaring trade: the gambling-dens were reaping a clinking harvest. Legitimate pearl-buyers bargained with the pearlers over the season's pearls, while snide-buyers, white and brown and yellow, were even busier under cloaked activities.

This small isolated town was alive with restless progress, with schemes of coastal commercial exploration, with the development of its fleets, the formation of bases and development of known shell deposits, the struggle for oversea markets for shell and pearl, the increasing problems both local and foreign of coloured indentured labour. Pearlers were busy prospecting for new shell-beds farther north along the dangerous and uninhabited coast.

Syndicates were formed to follow the patrols of the mounted police into the desert country inland in the hope of finding pastoral country or mineral. Enterprises were set on foot towards the well-watered but far more rugged country north of the desert belt. Apart from pearling, the life of Broome lacked nothing in fullness, adventure, and enterprise. Entrancing material awaits the future writer who delves into this particular forty years of Broome development

Toledo lost his new white girl. In the overwhelming shock of losing the pearl and his desperate attempts at its recovery he had hardly thought of her. She had outgrown her momentary infatuation and was now weaving a romance of dreams around the figure of a particularly handsome bank clerk.

Toledo haunted the telegraph office, and the afternoon that word came through that Charles Hagen, Simeon Espada, and Pablo Marquez paid the full penalty for their crime in Fremantle jail, he acted. He hurried to the Rio de Janeiro, slipped in around the back and into old Sulu's garret while that slave was washing up in the kitchen adjoining. Toledo pulled the garret to pieces, he examined the roof, the walls, he even tore up the floor. He found nothing. He cut the old man's pallet to shreds—unavailingly. He stood there breathing miserably, gazing around in despair. A large black-and-yellow hornet came buzzing in, an inquisitive fowl poked its head in the doorway.

Toledo was bitterly disappointed. With humped shoulders he sat on the remains of Sulu's pallet, waiting till he came for his afternoon siesta. And he did not know that through a nail-hole in the wall his activity and despair had been watched from the wash-house. When Sulu entered the garret Toledo was on him like a tiger, throttling him.

"The pearl!" he hissed in Malay. "The pearl!"

Sulu's eyes bulged; his tongue protruded. Toledo loosened his grip. "The pearl! My pearl! The pearl Pablo gave you. Pablo stole it from me. Give it me."

Sulu gasped while stubbornly shaking his head.

"I have no pearl," he mumbled. Toledo struck him across the mouth.

"Sulu! Pablo is dead. Hagen is dead. Simeon is dead. They swung! The news has just come through on the telegraph. You cannot get away from me any more than you could from Pablo. Now where is my pearl?"

"I have no pearl," mumbled the old man.

Toledo bumped his head on the floor but into the withered old face stole the fatalism that defies even death.

"Very well then," hissed Toledo. "Join Pablo in hell!" and his grip tightened as he pressed his knee into Sulu's stomach.

"Why are you murdering the old man?" inquired a suave voice in Malay.

Toledo glanced over his shoulder. Gomez stood there. Toledo had almost placed Pablo's noose around his own neck. He crouched there with convulsive face.

"You too!"

"Three men have just swung for murder," said Gomez softly. "You had better put away that knife!"

"You would never have spoken while there was a chance he might show me the pearl. Yellow dog! You seek it for yourself."

"I know of no pearl. I only know I just came in time to save my old friend's life."

"Lying dog! You would poison him if only you knew where he has hidden the pearl!"

He glared at Sulu stretched out beneath him.

"Sulu! I give you warning. The pearl is mine. Pablo stole it from me. Return it to me. I will sell it and give you enough money to take you back to Manila. But"—he pressed cold steel upon the old man's throat—"if you sell my pearl to Gomez I will follow you to Manila and slit your throat on your doorstep!"

Mad with rage he sprang through the doorway, knocking Gomez violently aside.

Sebaro was happy, sitting in his little cottage yarning to Bin Mahomet the quiet Malay. Sebaro was a good diver always sure of employment; above all he was an honest man. He would never rob his employer. But he saw no harm in selling a pearl for another man on commission. Fairly often a coloured crew-man would sidle up to him in the dark or come sneaking into his little cottage. The man would hand him a pearl whispering, "Get me twenty pounds gold money for this!" Sebaro might get a hundred pounds. He would hand the man his twenty sovereigns and keep the rest as commission. But, please let me repeat that Sebaro was an honest man who would never rob his employer; never betray a trust.

There was never any difficulty in selling a pearl. Besides the legitimate buyers there were the "coloured heads" of the town. Some Chinese storekeepers also bought pearls. These shrewd, silent buyers invariably drove too hard a bargain. But the shrewdest man will occasionally make a mistake. And whenever a Chinese snide-buyer was thus caught, the delight of Asiatic town was hilarious.

Sebaro was chuckling now, chuckling over a disappointment that would have driven some white men almost to suicide. He was examining a blister almost the size of the bowl of his pipe. Had that blister been the pearl it appeared to be, a king's ransom would hardly have bought it.

A Malay had brought him the shell in which was the gigantic blister. Sebaro's eyes had almost popped from his head when he opened the shell. He grunted "Wah!" Words were superfluous. The Malay had watched in trembling silence. Bin Mahomet just sat quietly there; the business was none of his.

The apparent pearl was still glued to the shell. Carefully Sebaro examined both. The Malay's heart thumped as Sebaro began cleaning the back of the shell. But, carefully as he cleaned there was always left, right behind the pearl, a tiny round, blackish-grey spot. No word was spoken. The Malay was almost crying when Sebaro picked up a fine needle and placed its point fair on that almost invisible spot. He began to bore.

Slowly the needle bored right through the shell, right on for half an inch fair into the heart of the apparent pearl. The Malay sobbed.

Sebaro laughed at the Malay. Bin Mahomet looked quietly on.

"By gum! we catch some damn Chinaman thief with this blister," chuckled Sebaro.

The Malay sighed; the tension relaxed from his face. "Kismet!" he muttered. With cloudy eyes he stared dully at the floor.

The pearl was a blister, a bubble of nacre filled with caked mud. A shellfish had bored into the oyster which had formed a coating of nacre over the wound. This gradually grew into a blister after it had formed as a bubble of nacre. And mud of the sea had gradually filled up the bubble through the tiny entrance hole.

With a chisel Sebaro detached the blister leaving plenty of the back of the shell upon it. Easily and completely he disguised the presence of the tiny bore-hole. That evening, with the Malay and Francis Paddy he strolled into town and visited a Chinese storekeeper. Casually he asked to buy a handkerchief.

The three worthies pored over the handkerchief. The storekeeper leaned over the counter.

"You got something?" he whispered.

"Suppose I got? You can buy for hundred pound gold money?" inquired Sebaro.

"Lemme look see! I mus' look first time!"

Sebaro rolled the phenomenal blister on the counter the Chinaman's eyes looked comical.

"How muchee you wantee?" he asked excitedly.

"Hundred pound gold money."

"Too muchee! Too muchee! No can do!"

Sebaro reached for the blister but the Chinaman clung to it. "No can do! No can do! Let me look first time! More look! Suppose he got hole inside, me beggar up! Me losee money!"

"He no got hole," spat Sebaro. "S'pose he good one pearl inside, you make plenty money. You no give me fellow none. You only give me little bit. Damn you!"

But the huge size of the thing moved the Chinaman to a corresponding degree of caution.

"More better you take two pounds first time," he suggested

ingratiatingly. "Suppose he all li, me give you more by em by."

Sebaro snatched the blister. But the Malay seized his arm and drew him aside.

"More better you take two pound," he whispered. "He only got mud inside."

Sebaro frowned, then slung the blister back on the counter. "All right, you take him," he agreed. They accepted the money and walked away chuckling over how they had sold the Chinaman "two pounds' worth of mud".

"He proper fool that one; 'e only mud inside; ha ha ha!" chuckled Sebaro.

"He no more get back money to-morrow!" roared Francis Paddy.

"We make him proper sure," laughed Sebaro. "We drink him money."

So they went and drank the two pounds. The joke grew hilarious.

Several days later, when Sebaro was passing the store, the Chinaman was waiting for him. "Hi! Come here. You lookee see. Me losem two pounds nothing."

"Ah, go to hell!" sneered Sebaro—which is the Manilaman's favourite expression of contempt. "Me know nothing bout him. Suppose he got someting inside, you no give me nothing. Supposing mud, alla same. Go to hell!"

But if Sebaro had only known it, that blister, even though filled with mud, would have been bought by almost any legitimate white buyer as a gamble for a hundred pounds or more.

And now for a little incident that goes to prove that even a hardened old nor'-wester can develop a few "white ants", as well as the veriest new-chum. Little Captain Owen did not think so. Clad in spruce whites with moustache trimmed in that "damn 'em all!" Celtic style he marched away down along the tram-line that leads to Broome wharf, and the monthly steamer.

She had commercials aboard, eager to entertain and be entertained. Pearlers, business men, and Government officials were drifting along like night cameos in white; cigars glowed like fire-flies along the dark wharf; ghostly dresses swished; snatches of hearty laughter broke on the clear air. The steamer at the long wharf end was a fairyland of lights. As Owen came under the gangway a voice bellowed from above:

"Ahoy there! Captain Kettle!"

"Hullo, Dick! How many unfortunates have you robbed today?"

"I was too busy watching the pearlers!" came the instant reply.

"How's the snide market?" yelled another to an immediate laugh from the jetty.

"Hullo, Tom! How are the forty thieves?" called up a pearler. Then a bull voice roared, "How's the liquor?" as all hands trooped aboard. Some had brought their wives. Some wives brought themselves. Other wives stayed at home.

Captain Owen joined in a game of "Go as you please poker". No limit. Drinks after every round. Owen was a fast player. He did not get merry of course; you haven't met a Welshman yet to admit that indiscretion. They would have loved to make him merry, but he smiled kindly while resolutely refusing to be over tempted. He knew his carrying capacity and it lasted until an hour before daylight.

"Can't stay here all night like you grass widows," he declared eventually in cool, precise voice. He stood up, very erect, sternly pleasant, very efficient; a master pearler who sailed his schooner and managed his own fleet; made a success of the game.

They saw him to the gangway, each earnestly pressing him a last "Doch-an-dorris" with an embracing insistence on the "dorris." But with a majestic wave of the hand he marched down the gangway without a tremor.

The tram-line meanders for nearly a mile along dark roads then skirts Chinatown and ends at Streeter's Jetty. The captain stuck to the rails along the streets, smiling at his bushmanship. He hugged them too through Chinatown. Though now in darkness, he just saw several shadows turning into a lane. There were always shadows in or around Asiatic town. At Streeter's Jetty the captain paused. The schooner, a dark outline just visible, lay some two hundred yards out from the end of the jetty. The sleepers of the jetty on which he now stood were two feet six inches apart. Up through the awkward vacancies between each sleeper came the smell of black mud and water.

This was Streeter's private tram-line for loading, running on trestles out through the mangroves. Past its farthest end was visible the dim light of his schooner *Anthon*, pride of his eye.

There was no moon. The captain was alone with the night and the sky and the universe. Presently he came to earth; became immersed in proud memories. The *Anthon* was the largest schooner in all the fleets, a depot ship, under the command of Captain Owen. The captain stepped on to the narrow jetty and glanced cautiously around. Streeter's big shed was a blur in the darkness. Everything slept. Just as well. For if any one saw him crawling on hands and knees along the jetty, how the town would laugh!

This jetty was just a narrow truck line. It was like an embankment except that there was no embankment. You had to step on the sleepers; if you didn't you fell through into the water. The captain could step it like a bird in daylight but instinct warned him not now, loaded as he was above the Plimsoll.

"Dash it, if they see me tackling it on hands and knees I'll be the laughing stock of the town," he whispered. "Anyway, that would be better than breaking my neck—and there is no one to see whether or no."

With a last furtive glance around, he started to crawl. It was a long, careful crawl with frequent pauses for breath and equilibrium and a swear word to pull out splinters. Nervousness gave way to a confident smile, he grew immensely proud of himself, he had not once fallen into the water, he would arrive at the schooner without one splash of mud on his spotless whites. What better test of a man's sobriety? At long last he arrived at the very end of the little jetty. "By George you're lucky!" he smiled to himself, "getting here safely and not a soul the wiser!"

Seating himself cautiously upon a crosspiece he doubled his legs over the beam, collected his voice, then strongly and confidently shouted, "*Anthon*, ahoy!"

An answering hail came from the schooner. "Dinghy!" shouted the captain.

He waited comfortably until the dinghy should come. Waited some time, though he did not notice it. He was humming a ditty, expecting the creak of oars when a voice spoke softly below him. Malay hands were helping him on with a pair of diver's leggings.

"Ruffo," thought the captain, "a leaky dinghy! Assan my boy, now you are in for a tongue-wagging!"

Malay hands helped him down to the water's edge. He stood solidly. A Malay shadow stepped out, here came the gentle tugging of a hand at his sleeve. The captain stepped out, following the piloting shadow.

Suddenly he realized it! Heard his footsteps crunching on sand. The tide was out of course, the schooner high and dry! He could have walked to it!

He did not say a word. If only he could have done so he would have turned around and kicked himself. With bated breath he watched the outline of the schooner growing more clearly ahead. A light showed up there by the gangway. He heard the calm voice of Mrs Owen directing the bosun to lower the ladder from the top of the gangway.

"Hullo, so you've come!" she challenged.

"Yes, I've come. What about it?"

"Well, I advise you to get a pair of wheels and fit them on the dinghy. Or else arrange for more water."

Captain Owen mounted the ladder wishing he could muster the courage to demand whether the water was meant for the whisky or the creek.

The fleets put to sea again. And Toledo sailed with Mark Rubin's fleet. He must earn his living now and meanwhile play a waiting game, a game of life and death. Old Sulu dared not sell the pearl. There was no escape, for he could go no farther than his own home village.

Time was on Toledo's side. The old man was very old. If he did not die soon in Manila he would die in Broome. Fairly confidently, Toledo worked while he waited for the old man to capitulate, to hand over the pearl and accept what largess Toledo should give him.

For old Sulu, lying on his pallet away back in Broome, the nights were longer. Hate was concentrated in the last energy of his fading life.

Night after night as he lay, staring up at the hornet's nest, he was wishing that his hate might be a dagger in Toledo's heart so that Sulu might escape.

Among Sulu's race is a belief that should an enemy deeply and maliciously wound you, then, if you are able to deeply enough and constantly enough wish him injury, that injury will surely overtake him should certain spirit forces not be capable of guarding him.

And so, day by day, night after night, old Sulu willed that Toledo should die.

Another lay-up season came and went.

In creek for the lay-up season.

CHAPTER X
Down Where the Dead Ships Lie

April 1908 brought its first willy-willy in a tornado of destruction and death. In dead of night the *Anthon* stood into the gale, forced to ride it out, the wind shrieking against a racing tide that smashed the colliding seas into whizzing sheets of water. Against a thunderous wave the anchor chain snapped with screech of rending steel, all seemed lost as the *Anthon* plunged back into darkness. In that pitching inferno they struggled to get another chain up from below, while Mrs Owen clung lashed to the mast holding aloft a hurricane lamp.

Suddenly they were in a vortex of terrifying silence, a ship deep within a black funnel above which twinkled stars. With a frightful thunder-clap the cyclone revolved upon them, the wind howling from the opposite direction while the stars vanished as a hissing sea swirled across the deck. When it was gone the woman still held high the lamp, water surging around her waist.

Farther north, Pat Percy's schooner *Gwendoline* was similarly battling it out, Mrs Percy lashed to the poop. Somewhere out in the blackness Bernard Bardwell's *Phyllis* was going down as, near by, the *Lilian* plunged to her doom with a fatalistic diver locked in her cabin, resigned to sink with his belly full of rice. As the white owner of the *Lilian* was drowning Bardwell remembered his oft-heard old nurse's prophecy that he could never drown—he had been born with a caul. For nineteen hours he battled with a furious sea and was thrown ashore, still alive. Toledo was clinging to a grating, all alone on the maddened sea, never knowing that far away in Broome an old man lay upon his pallet staring up at a hornet's nest praying that Toledo might drown.

All along the tortured coast were tiny vessels and tiny men and half a dozen women battling for their lives. When the willy-willy fury was past, lonely beaches were strewn with wreckage; wavelets were crooning around the bodies of fifty dead men. The price they pay for pearls.

Sulu was heart-broken. Toledo had returned. He had clung to a hatch for twenty-four hours and had been washed ashore near Beagle Bay.

But, grim as Fate, old Sulu lay on his pallet at night staring up at the hornet's nest.

Toledo went to sea again, and again signed on in the fleet of Mark Rubin. That once footsore wanderer was now, not only a "pearl king" owning his own fleet, but one of the greatest pearl-buyers Australia has ever known.

Mark Rubin's pearling fleet cruised prettily in line, a lively flotilla upon an emerald sea. But they were searching for dead things, ships and men gone to Davey Jones's locker in the willy-willy of six weeks ago. As the line of little vessels came slowly sailing towards shore keen eyes from the mastheads sought any trace of a ship in the shallow water below. It was Captain Gregory, on the poop, who saw the broken tip of a spar tonguing up through the waves.

"Looks like one of them, Young," he nodded as he handed the glass to the mate.

The mother ship this, the *Kelander Bux*. A graceful schooner with her rigging lined with men in waist-cloths and red caps, brown men all staring towards the cruising luggers alert for the signal that should tell a sunken ship had been located. Six were down here somewhere, close by on the bottom of the sea. As the *Kelander Bux* bore down upon the spar the mate said:

"I believe you are right, sir. That spar is not drifting any!"

It could not. For a strand of rigging held it as a buoy. And the anchor of that buoy was the *Gracie*. Up forrard, as the crew pointed out the forlorn tell-tale, low talk broke out in rapid Japanese, in Malay, in "pidgin".

Was there a lugger below? Which would it prove to be? Would there be men aboard?

They glanced at one another, the Japanese rather quietly, the Malays and Manilamen whispering uneasily. But the chocolate-brown, deeply-creased faces of the kanaka bosun and sailmaker simply stared ahead. It was all in the day's work to them.

At a signal, the luggers closed in towards the schooner as she neared the spar. Bringing the schooner up into the wind Gregory ordered the two divers overboard from the nearest lugger. They were Manilamen, unusually slow in donning their dresses. Gregory watched with narrowed eyes. A tall, powerfully built man was Captain Gregory, well-cut features, direct voiced, somewhat stern of face, active on his feet; not a man to be trifled with. The mate, elbows on the rail, stared down at the lugger. The schooner crew stared down, silently sympathizing with the apprehension of the divers. Those men down there donning their heavy woollens so hesitantly were not afraid of the bottom of the sea but they *were* afraid of sea ghosts. And so was every coloured seaman in all the fleet.

Down on the lugger's deck the crew manned the air-pumps, each tender stood by his life-line with his assistant at the air-pipe, and the divers at last waddled to the short ladder overside.

"Click-clack! Click-clack!" came rhythmically as the crews bent to the air-pump handles. Gregory from the schooner poop above watched suspiciously as each diver slung himself backward from the ladder and each helmet sank to a spray of bubbles.

"Bottom!" called the tenders to a tug on the life-lines. Up to the surface came little air-bubbles that marked the divers' progress below. Gregory watched those bubbles, knowing the superstitious horror of Manilamen where dead men are concerned.

"They'll be looking for their sea ghosts," whispered the mate. "They won't be able to hear a thing except the air-pumps, and they won't be able to turn around and see what's behind them."

The skipper grunted. The groups of air-bubbles were slowly moving out in two wide circles.

"They are not going near her," growled Gregory. "They are simply crawling around her. I wish I had two Japanese divers here."

"Are the Manilamen too scared of the sea ghosts?" inquired the launch engineer as he came and learned over the side.

"There are none below. But I'll not be able to trust the divers' report. Whatever lugger it is down below she's worth five hundred pounds if we can raise her."

"Ah!" exclaimed the mate. "They've signalled the tenders to haul up. They've hardly had time to wet their feet! Here they come, up on their own air. Quick work!"

Sitting on the lugger deck with their helmets unscrewed, the divers called up a shamefaced report to Gregory. The lugger was the *Gracie*; she was smashed beyond hope of repair.

"Get out of those dresses!" shouted Gregory and turned to his own crew. "Who will come down with me?" he asked. And there was scorn in his eyes.

Now Gregory was a man whom the crew would have followed anywhere in the material world. But down to the *Gracie*—with her dead men aboard!

She had dived straight down with hatches and cabin scuttle closed. All on deck had been washed off and lost except one man. He told how Tomumuki the diver and five men were in the cabin—were there now!

Old John Magron the sailmaker stepped forward and quietly began to undress. Good old South Sea John! Superstitious as the Malays, but braver.

They went down together with the air hissing into the helmets in a riot of sound, the wreck coming up to them as a weirdly magnified *Gracie*. They reached bottom almost side by side and stood gazing at the wreck while adjusting their air-escape valves. She was lying on her side towards them, her mainmast broken off, shadowy ropes leading up to the floating spar above. Five fish glided across the vessel and vanished in the gloom. The even click-clack, click-clack of the air-pump above came sharply down into Gregory's helmet, all else was silence in yellowish-green gloom. Looking up through the shallow water Gregory could plainly see the bottom of the schooner, and the attendant lugger. He stepped towards the wreck, peering through his face-glass.

The *Gracie* appeared all shipshape from this side, no strained planking, no gaping hole. Carefully he climbed up on to the sloping deck, old John was already groping towards the hold. In slow movement they unfastened the hatch and peered down. A ghost would have got a fright had it looked up at those two domed heads peering there. It was quite dark down below, no gleam of lighter water betrayed a hole. They worked back aft, noting that the deck was sound. They came to the cabin. Crab fashion, Gregory squatted on the deck on a level with the cabin scuttle. His hands, weirdly white and magnified in the water slowly groped upon the scuttle. After some trouble he managed to slide it back and as he did so a bare foot thrust out and touched his face-glass, the toes waggled. Gregory's hair rose on end.

"Good God!" he thought, "is he alive? He can't be. He's been here six weeks." With nerves still tingling he tried to peer in under the body, it was right up under the cabin roof. So far as he could see there was no hole either in the cabin bottom or walls aft.

Satisfied that the *Gracie* was sound Gregory signalled the tender, and salvaging operations commenced. Up above, big whales came gliding that were the bottoms of oncoming luggers. Gigantic, bloated spiders came gliding down that were divers descending to help. Ropes and chains came noiselessly down until the dead ship was enmeshed with air-pipes and lifelines, ropes and chains. Grotesque figures crawled over the sunken vessel like water-spiders upon a body.

Lest when raising the wreck her mast should poke a hole through the bottom of the schooner, they pulled out the broken stumps by leverage of a tackle worked from the schooner. The *Gracie* had sunk at her anchors, so they had the awkward job underwater of unshackling the anchors and chain. It proved too difficult to unship the rudder so they sawed the rudder-post off and the saw made not the slightest sound. Chains were secured in a bight in the *Bux*, two ends of a chain were worked in under the forefront of the wreck then aft over the deck and the ends brought up through the rudder-trunk. Long spars were run out from the schooner above in the wake of each mast, with tackles on the ends which were connected to the chains under the wreck, the tackles leading from the schooner's mast-heads to the windlass. To the bellow of John Hokobotong the bosun, the crew manned the windlass and it slowly turned to a South Sea chanty. The leverage thus exerted on the pulleys was gradually trebled as the wreck began to lift. As slowly she began to rise, the schooner gradually developed a list to counteract which the mate lashed all the whale-boats to the opposite side and filled them with water. While this work above was going cheerily on queer indeed were the antics of the workers below in their slow, clumsy movement amidst the great silence to signals of a white hand. And the hand also tugged signals to a tender above who shouted those signals to the mate officering the schooner.

As the wreck in shadow form appeared rising up through the water the schooner crew stared gaping as they toiled, the crews on the luggers stared silently. Slowly she came almost to the surface and stopped, at Gregory's command.

Her underwater weight was considerably less than her weight would be in the air. With her decks thus just awash that foot was still poking out of the cabin scuttle. Japanese seamen leapt overboard and swam to her. They helped the owner of the foot out of the cabin. As he floated triumphantly on the surface a cry arose from schooner and luggers.

"Tomumuki!" Breathlessly they stared for others, but no others came. They lifted Tomumuki into a dinghy.

"Take him ashore and bury him according to your custom," ordered Gregory, "and the others too, when you get them out." But the others were in pieces. And no man was game to go in and get them out. Then they lashed the wreck to the side of the *Bux* as a mother swan might protect its cygnet with its wing.

With launches towing the *Bux* they made slowly towards the beach and at high tide dropped the wreck in the shallows of Geoffroy Bay. At low water next day she was just visible. The crew were superstitiously afraid; the handful of whites aboard the fleet had to lead the working parties and force their toil by command and example. Except that the giant bosun with his cheery, bellowing laugh needed neither command nor example, nor did old John Magron the sailmaker. They made a coffer-dam around the hatch, building it up with canvas and planking above the surface of the water, then pumped the hold out. And as the water was slowly emptied so the *Gracie* began to rise. As no other would volunteer, it fell to the lot of old John Magron to get the five bodies out of the cabin. Philosophically he carried out his grisly work, remarking:

"Some day you may have to do the same for me. Who knows? Perhaps soon!"

But none would follow him down into the dank cabin.

Presently his voice came hollowly, as if from a tomb:

"Look! See! I have found ten hands. The skin comes off like gloves!" They heard him slushing about, but they all stood back. Presently the giant bosun came along with a bag.

With temporary repairs effected, the luggers gladly sailed away out to the shelling-beds while the mother ship towed the derelict back to Broome. Leaving her burden on the beach she spread her wings and sailed back to her chicks.

In the following months the *Gracie* was refitted. With new masts, new rudder, new gear, freshly painted, with all aboard spick and span she was again launched for her reincarnated life upon the ocean wave.

As was expected, it required all the psychological knowledge, all the "Number 1" manner of the captain of the fleet to sign on a new crew, all the half-laughing, half-bravado chaffing of the big bosun of the *Bux*. Fearing shame before their comrades a crew at last signed on. Shiosiki was the new diver. True, he would not descend in Tomumuki's diving-dress but he was the new diver of the *Gracie*. And the *Gracie* sailed for the open sea.

By this time but little more remained of the season. The *Gracie* immediately did wonderfully well. Her captain invariably selected his drift with uncanny judgment; Shiosiki invariably found good shell. And then, almost at the very last of the season, he found a pearl!

That night the *Gracie* anchored off Geoffroy Bay, the whole crew in excited delight. They went to sleep quite happily.

In the dead of night, Tomumuki woke Shiosiki. Shiosiki lay there with his heart painfully contracting. The drowned diver stood before him, the water-drops fading from his ghostly form. Gradually he developed shape quite as if human again. Reassuringly he smiled. Slowly Shiosiki's heart pulsed again, his terror faded as the water-drops had faded from the spirit standing there.

Then softly Tomumuki whispered not to be frightened, that it was he who guided Shiosiki to good shell, that he was grateful to Captain Gregory for allowing his countrymen to bury him ashore and according to the custom of his race. He and those with him were in measure in debt to the captain. He would become the spirit of the *Gracie*, he would continue to show Shiosiki shell. When Shiosiki was down below he would ever be at his elbow urging him towards the good shell. For as he was a man drowned at sea he was a water ghost as well as a land one, and he could do these things. And the *Gracie* would now always be a lucky ship.

Tomumuki smiled, made the Japanese salutation, and faded through the side of the ship.

And the spirit of the *Gracie* has kept his word.

CHAPTER XI
The Wreck of the "Kelander Bux"

It was now 8 December 1908. Beautiful weather except for the momentary rain-squalls that came in blasts from the cock-eye bobs. All the fleets and all the sailormen were looking forward to the return to Broome and Christmas and the lay-up season. Captain Gregory's command was again off the Eighty Mile Beach intent on a final search for other of the vessels sunk in the April blow.

A pretty sight, those twenty-six vessels in line, drifting across the sea. All under mizen and jib, all with their divers down; the schooner's launches speeding from lugger to lugger. Below them, on the bottom of the sea, twenty-six divers groped forward not seeking shell but a wreck. Like a swan sheltering her cygnets glided the mother ship, pride of the fleet. A beautiful schooner of a hundred and fifty tons, she fed them and watered them and relieved them of shell, so enabling them to remain at sea throughout the busy shelling-season. Nothing short of the dreaded willy-willy could break the guardianship of the *Kelander Bux*.

Far away to shoreward appeared bluff Cape Frezier with the sun gleaming on the white sands of the Eighty Mile Beach, grave of many a pearling ship. Ghosts in hundreds walk that beach at night—so the coloured seamen say.

"Ensign at the mast-head of the *Postboy*, sir," called Young the mate. "She must have found something!"

Towards the schooner raced a launch at top speed. Very proud of its launches was this fleet, for "engine boats" at this period represented the last word in modernity.

"Kondo the diver reports he has found the *Zoe*, sir!" called up the launch engineer.

"Splendid, Mr Tillen! See that a buoy is secured to the wreck by a length of cable. I'll be aboard at once."

While the launches and diver were busy attaching buoys to the sunken lugger the schooner crew were hoisting wire ropes from the hold, heavy blocks, and other salvage gear ready for work at daylight. Sunset saw them furling awnings, cleaning decks for the night.

"The aneroid is not working well to-day," observed the skipper thoughtfully.

"It's been fairly steady," replied the purser. Miller was the ship's weather-prophet.

"Yes," emphasized the skipper, "it has done its afternoon drop but is now seven and does not show any inclination to rise. With this south-easterly wind and drizzly rain, if it were a month later we would stand a good chance of a willy-willy."

"Machan Siap, tuan!" reported the Malay steward, and the four Europeans turned into the comfortable saloon. Breakfast and tiffin might be often a hurried affair, but dinner aboard the *Bux* was quite a state occasion. Any pearler in the fleets gladly availed himself of an invitation to spread his legs beneath the *Bux's* hospitable table. Snow-white tablecloth, polished silver, the steward in spotless ducks, the Chinese cook at his best. But on this somewhat oppressive evening Captain Gregory, Young the mate, Tillen the engineer, and Miller the purser dined by themselves.

On the main hatch on deck the petty officers dined, John Hokobotong the bosun, old John Magron the sailmaker, sworn pal of Hokobotong, the three Japanese carpenters, and the two launch engine-drivers.

A Solomon Islander, a gigantic man this bosun. of the *Bux*, famed as the strongest man of all the pearling fleets. He could lift up three hundredweight and carry it away with a laugh, he could lift a man across each shoulder, pick up one under each arm and dance under the load. His great voice and unfailing good temper were as famous as his strength. His one idol was Captain Gregory: the skipper could do no wrong; he was the greatest captain that ever sailed the seas.

A quiet chap was old John Magron, the sailmaker. A Solomon Islander, too, his smiling, patient ways had years ago made him a favourite on land and sea.

Up forrard, the rank and file of the *Bux* ate their curry and rice. A picked Malay crew these twenty odd forecastle hands, the envy of all seamen of the pearling fleet. Fine sailors, great whale-boat men, all with that wonderful gift that God has given their race, "the laughing heart". Gregory swore by his red-capped *Bux* seamen; sternly disciplined, extra paid men. Any Malay entitled to wear the red cap of the *Kelander Bux* considered it a *hari besar*—a great honour. Squatting around their curry bowls they were discussing the morrow's salvage operations, making laughing bets as to who would be the first to catch hell from the old man in the morning. As each was a picked man and proud of it, it looked bright for no mistakes in the salvage operations to come.

Sitting smoking on the hatch, the bosun's rumbling voice was discussing the lashing of the gear, the placing of booms and spars and pulley blocks; the carpenters were discussing the caulking preparatory to and after pumping out the sunken *Zoe*; old John Magron was explaining the making of a coffer-dam like the one he built for the raising of the *Gracie*.

The Japanese, discussing diving, glanced up at the mention of the *Gracie* for the visit of Tomumuki was known now to all the fleet.

Down aft in the cabin the whites were discussing the probable lifting-weight of the *Zoe*, the slinging and rigging of tackles, the strength required of the spars and booms. By eight bells the softly laughing voices over all the fleet grew quiet, stars gleamed down on a silent sea. Not even the lap of water, not even the flop of a fish. All hands were turning in, all except the watch and the restless skipper of the *Bux*. He felt a queer urge to listen out into the silence, a vague feeling that all was not well with the night. Thoughtfully he studied the glass:

"Even the mercurial is convex," he thought. "I don't like it, it seems impossible at this time of the year. Probably we will only get a northerly swell in the morning, even if anything does come out of it."

He took a turn on deck. It was a night of ghostly blue, the sky blue, the sea blue, and transparent blue in between. He could just distinguish shore along the Eighty Mile Beach, like a faintly smudged line. For a mile around the schooner were velvety black dots upon each of which a solitary star dimly shone. Like jewels set in the cup of eternity were those luggers.

"Mr Young!" called the skipper sharply.

"Aye aye, sir!" came the sleepy voice of the mate from below.

"Call the bosun pipe all hands. Stand by till ten o'clock."

"Aye, aye, sir!" And the mate was on deck and wide-awake.

An hour later and a sudden awe silenced the crew. It was as if the air had been chilled by some icy breath.

"Mr Young!" ordered the skipper sharply. "Strike all spare gear below. Double lash the launches and boats."

"Aye aye, sir!"

Instantly the atmosphere aboard ship seemed changed. Gone was the breathlessness, the brooding quiet. All hands sensed something coming— quickly! Before the gear was lashed a gust came out of the night to whistle through the shrouds and moan away.

"Stand by the windlass!" shouted Gregory as old John Magron stepped to the wheel.

"Heave up!"

A hiss came in a spurt of icy wind. To the creak of the windlass with the grind of the anchor chains came the bellow of the bosun, the pattering of feet, the deep breaths of men throwing their weight into the ropes, the rumbling growls of the unfurling sails all in the tense atmosphere of a something coming. The quiet, dull sea had reacted in slow movement even as the *Bux* bore down upon the sleeping fleet. Forrard in the bows with cupped hands the bull roar of the bosun spread over the waters:

"Luggers ahoy! Heave up! Sail for Bossut Creek or stand for the open sea. Heave up! Heave up!"

Shouts of haste, patter of feet on tiny decks, clank of windlass powls, rattling of blocks heralded white specks of sails fluttering up into the night. Musical commands, flecks of bow-clipped foam below the little mast-head lights now bobbing, and the scattering fleet was under sail. The mother ship had warned her chicks.

"Both tops'ls and flying jib, Mr Young!" came the clear command from the monkey poop.

"Aye aye, sir!" and swinging up to the mast-head went the big gaff topsails of the *Bux* as she raced for the open sea. A wind gust tore through the shrouds, the stays vibrated with that shrill, icy whistling fearful of awful things to come. A sea whipped up and spray hissed flying. The gust passed. Topsails and kites were furled; the night turned inky black. Old John Magron at the wheel, the mate beside the captain forrard. The schooner's bows rose dizzily to dip, then plunge. Another gust came and the rigging boomed like organ-pipes to a shrieking from the stays. The gigantic figure of the bosun loomed forrard as the ship trembled up, his great voice boomed out some joke in pidgin-English as a howling wind bore down. The vessel trembled, lurched over, she came to again as a sea crashed aboard in sobbing water that swirled to the knees of the crew. "Hell!" glowered Gregory, "she makes heavy weather of it."

"It's a willy-willy!" replied the mate. "We're in for it now."

Stronger and fiercer came the squalls, sail after sail was furled. She slid on into darkness that engulfed her in a whirling inferno of sound. The great swell fast growing carried her up high to suck her far down and then come rolling in over the bows, smashing against her sides. In two hours she was making very heavy weather and yet was still only in the outer fringe of the willy-willy. Gregory, constantly conning the ship, strove to drive her out to sea against the cyclone now driving her back to land.

Came a shock, a grinding crash, vicious water in pounding bulk smashed in stinging sheets that slapped and blinded, the starboard launch was stove in. Before she could recover, a following wave had smashed the after whale-boat as a boot crushes a match-box.

The heart of the sailorman feels desperate when his boats go one by one.

"Cut away both launches!" shouted Gregory. The carpenters sprang to the tackles and cut away the motor-launches that were the pride of the fleet.

By 3 a.m. it was blowing full hurricane force, the schooner battling for life. Under close-reefed foresail and fore staysail she was head reaching. Gregory kept her lying close to the wind; fighting to keep up to it, to hold the weather lest it blow him right back to the shallows of the Eighty Mile Beach where the great rollers pound and grind. Every yard ahead now was a yard gained, the land was not forty miles astern, while this cyclonic wind at a hundred miles an hour was howling to blow them back to it.

Dawn broke wild and furious; sky and sea had met and mixed. Seas rolled down on the *Bux* and out of the mist came other seas rolling, rolling, rolling. To ease their breaking, the engineer and launch boys sweated to make an oil tuk, struggling across rolling decks awash with water to get it over the sides. Constantly they fed it with oil-bags pierced with small holes which dripped a film of oil causing big waves to surge sullenly by without breaking on the vessel. Then stronger blew the wind, and the *Bux* trembled in the grip of an overwhelming hand.

"Unbend fore and main tops'ls. Send down both topmasts!" shouted the skipper and all hands laboured in the pitching inferno where only expert seamanship born of strict discipline told against unbridled fury of wind and sea. With the topmasts down and lashed the skipper shouted: "All hands to coffee!"

But the cook was washed out of his galley. To the bosun's roar and pointing hand they stared to sea where through the foam-sprayed mists a tiny vessel rode like a gull. They were nearly upon her, this sea-sprite appearing and vanishing in a cauldron of flying foam. The sea howled and flung her up beside the schooner. They saw a man aboard with arms upraised. But the little thing fell away into the mists.

"The *Vera,* one of Clarke's fleet," shouted Gregory to the mate. "I would rather be aboard her than here!"

"Me too!" howled the mate with a grim glance at the labouring schooner.

Then the wind whipped around to the north and the mate looked at Gregory and shrugged. This placed the vessel on a lee shore, the land now directly astern, the wind beating down on her directly ahead.

Despite all those battling hours the *Kelander Bux* was driven steadily backwards, her bows pounded by mighty seas, her drenched crew panting for their lives across Hooded decks. Her masts swayed bare to the driven mists, her mascot was drowned.

"All hands rig sea-anchor!" shouted Gregory.

To the bosun's bellow the scared crew came leaping, sliding, clutching towards their posts.

Across the heaving deck they manhandled the big topmasts of the *Bux,* then sawed them in halves and lashed the spars together in the form of a triangle, hanging on like spiders when the bosun's roar warned of a wave tumbling aboard. They spread a sail to the deck and lifted the huge triangle upon it, folded the canvas over it, and lashed it with practised knots. With great difficulty they carried up a small anchor from below and waiting their chance carried it across the water-sluiced deck. They weighted the triangle with it, lashed it to the end of a six-inch coir rope, then, waiting their chance, launched all overboard. It fell with a great splash, sogging over the bows there ahead. Presently they saw that its sagging weight was checking the drift.

Young, breathless from exertion, made his way aft to the skipper.

"Checked her somewhat, sir?"

"Yes," growled Gregory, "but she's still making leeway. Considerably less though."

Then the wind note changed into a moaning shriek that eerily twisted away and they were surrounded by a rumbling that swirled far out around them.

"We're in the centre," shouted Gregory.

"My God!" replied the mate. "If these black walls close in!"

"They won't. The cyclone revolves around its centre; but when it travels again ..."

"Good-bye!" finished the mate.

"We're not gone yet," answered Gregory grimly. "I wonder how much is left of Broome! This willy-willy came from the north. It will wreck Port Hedland if it doesn't swerve inland or blow out to sea!"

For another twenty-four hours they fought it out, making steady leeway despite their sailing cunning and the checking drag of the sea-anchor. Then the ominous call from the leadsman:

"Twenty-four fathoms, sir!" (Dua pulo ambat, tuan!) Their hearts fluttered. Several hours later:

"Eighteen fathoms, sir!" The strain showed plainly in their drawn faces, the muscles in arms and bodies no longer bulged taut and strong. Their salt-stung eyes showed thoughts of death as they listened to some ceaseless, confused thunder that was not the howl of the cyclone.

"Wonder it does not pound the very earth to death!" mumbled the mate.

"God!" whispered the engineer. "Fancy being pounded to pulp in that surf!"

"Our only chance is to anchor and hang on and hope for a shift of wind!" shouted Gregory. "Stand by the anchors!"

"Aye aye, sir!" came the bosun's voice as if at a parade ashore.

"Let go anchors!"

"Let go!"

Down rattled the anchors; they let the chains run out to the bitter end, then toiled near exhausted to fit great springs to the cable ends so that the frantic plunging of the bows would not snap the chains. Then each man sent his silent prayer to his God, to Mohammed, to Buddha, that the anchors and cables would hold. Now really they had done almost the very last thing to do. Gregory cupped his hands to his mouth.

"Stand by to cut away the mainmast."

"Aye aye, sir!" and bosun and crew ran to cut the lanyards while the carpenters hissed as they sank their axes into the solid oregon. Chips flew to be howled away by the wind.

"All clear, sir," shouted the bosun. Then his roar: "Stand clear!" and over came the towering spar to plunge clear into the sea: Gregory breathed in relief. Not a man hurt; no damage done and those two anchors gripped, the tautened cables held the weight of the plunging cripple against the tearing sea.

At eight bells that night the battered schooner tossed invisible in an inferno of terrors, the seas now breaking clean over her. At two in the morning came a cannon-shot with a frightful crash of wood. Both cables had parted; the starboard one catapulting back on deck smashing the forrard deckhouse like a pack of cards. In the pandemonium of winds and waters they rushed the windlass, and to the bosun's stentorian chanty heaved the cable ends aboard, and shackling them together fastened them to this their last anchor. They toiled with the strength begotten of the madness of fear. They let go this anchor and when she tugged to the limit of the cables they crouched there, gripping what they could, staring at one another, staring towards the captain.

One hour later the cable parted, the doomed ship lurched back into the darkness.

"Stand by! Stand by!" shouted Gregory.

To the bosun's cheery roar they came huddling aft in wild hope of perhaps yet another forlorn chance.

"Hoist close-reefed fore stays'l and close-reefed fores'l!" shouted Gregory. "We are going to run for the beach!"

As they leapt to the task two Malays screamed in relief that at last the long vigil was over. The *Bux* was going to die fighting.

As the schooner was paying off there came a rending, a flapping, and a shriek of tatters as the foresail blew out of the ropes. They leapt instinctively for safety as a sea came rolling aboard making a clear breach over her, but they got her before the wind and their hearts beat again. Pursuing seas came thundering over the stern.

"All hands aft!" roared the bosun.

They came in tatters, bloodshot eyes gleaming under salt wet hair.

Gregory gazed a moment, hurt by the hope in their eyes.

"We are running for the beach, men; it is our only chance," he shouted clearly in Malay. "There is nothing left to do but beach her now. The beach cannot be far away. If we can run her into shallow water past the outer breakers some of you might have a chance to battle your way ashore. But it means every man for himself. That is all. Now stand by."

As he closed his mouth the vessel sheered straight down and struck bottom with a jar that threw every man to the deck. The remaining mast trembled like a shaken stick. With a slow shivering she began to pick herself up between the water walls again, rose tremblingly, then plunged far down. As she struck again her timbers shrieked like the cries of drowning men. Then the sea rolled her on her side and walls of water crashed down upon her.

Broome: Along the foreshore.

CHAPTER XII
The Swim of Captain Gregory

Only those who came to the surface heard the sea thunder through the ship, heard the water-drowned roars of her bursting, heard splintered timbers flying before the cyclone's fury. Gregory shook his head in wounded alarm as a flying beam whizzed by. He was in more danger of having his head knocked off than of drowning. He snatched at a spinning petrol drum and was lifted straight up. He clung a while, though whirled around and flung up and down in the lashing of the waves. A brown hand reached up out of the sea, clawing fingers gripped the drum and there arose the gasping face of John Magron.

"I come too, skipper," puffed old John.

"It is not much good, John," said Gregory soberly. "It floats too lightly, it will tear your arms out. I am going to let go."

"Well, shake hands, captain; and good luck."

They shook hands, smiled, then Gregory let go. The drum spun away into darkness. He swam and floated, keeping low to dodge blows from floating wood while seeking something more solid than a lively drum to cling to. Something spun along and he snatched at it but winced from the piercing cut of a nail. It was the cabin door. As it spun around again he ducked in time to save his skull, then rose and grasped it cautiously. He clung to it for two hours until a boat boom came floating by. He grasped its greater security: ropes and boom were easier to cling to than wood and nails.

Day came in grey light making clear neither sea nor sky, it was all mixed up with sheets of driving spray, squalls of violent rain, warm rain luckily. He clung all that day in a torrent of movement; by late afternoon he felt that centuries had dragged by. A nerve-racking strain were the pyramidal seas, rolling monsters piling one on top of another as they roared down to wrench the boom from his arms. On these occasions, only, he had to swim; to take a deep breath and sink just before the break of the plunging waters, then leap up and stare and swim desperately for the bobbing boom. As afternoon merged into evening that boom had grown very precious, it was all he had in the world, and these jealous waves surged to tear it away. As evening howled down he clung with a strength grown cunning in competition with the pyramid waves.

It was a grim struggle; though he did not feel it much, for mind and body were concentrated on beating those waves. Only occasionally he realized that he was Captain Gregory, late of the *Kelander Bux*, fighting for life. Generally at such a time a pyramid had almost beaten him, and he had had a frantic struggle to find and once again clasp the cherished boom. He would straighten up and stare around and raise his gasping face to the unseeable skies and realize there was a God. In a quite impersonal way he realized this, he, Captain Gregory, adventurous wanderer, careless unbeliever, doer of deeds judged harshly by men, knew there was a God. Not that he was greatly interested. He had lived hard, fought hard, but there came quick memories of little kindnesses he had done, and these now brought a strange strength. And he awaited the next pyramid with a wonderful glow that he could fight to the last and die, if die he must, like a man.

All through the next day he clung and swam, and clung again. But he only had to swim when the pyramids came, he did not have to see them now, he knew their gathering roar above the surging of the other waves, he felt the quiverings and swirlings as the oncomers gained mass and height and nearness, and he clung until the final second when with a great breath he vanished as the breaking furies collapsed above him. Then up through the raging whirlpools he would shoot and stare wildly about for the bobbing boom.

In late afternoon a man with a horse and cart came trotting along, and pulled up.

"Jump aboard," he invited. "I'll give you a lift."

"All right. Take my boat boom too!"

"No. It's too heavy. Leave it behind."

"I think I'll hang on to it," answered Gregory doubtfully; "It might save me."

The man whipped up his horse. Gregory watched him drive away. He stared then into the mists, with fear at his heart. He struck the boom with sodden hand, for he wished to feel something tangible; something solid. He struck his head. "Thick enough," he growled, "I must be going batty."

He struck up a sailor's chanty but it would not come. In bewilderment he felt that his tongue was swelling, his lips cracked.

In the mists of evening he suddenly looked interested. The man who had driven the horse and cart was coming to him in an outrigger canoe.

"Give me your boom!" the man called.

"What do you want it for?" inquired Gregory.

"To make the outrigger bigger and stronger. We can both get in then and might reach the shore!"

Gregory clung to the boom.

"Come on," called the man. "The sun is going down; another night is coming!"

Gregory clung to the boom. The man scowled, and paddled away.

The breakers were heavier, more continuous, surging more furiously. His storm-deadened ears registered the pounding thunder on that mighty beach; wildly he hoped he was on the edge of the ground swell that rolls irresistibly in from the sea. As night wore on he was certain he was in the outer line of breakers and a great fear came-fear that a change of tide might sweep him back to sea!

That fear was the father of strength. With a madman's cunning he swam with each breaker, then, nursing his strength on the spar, swam again as the following breaker rushed upon him. Though he could see nothing but seething foam he felt he was travelling—drawing near land—every nerve was singing. He felt the breakers losing their mountain height. His toe—his foot touched bottom. Land! The mad thrill plunged him fighting ahead with maniacal strength.

In the small hours he was wading ashore, still fighting, hanging to his boom against the backwash, pushing it before him when the backwash passed, never knowing he was done. With the water swishing at his knees he picked up the boom, steadied himself and staggered ashore carrying it up to the base of the sandhills. He fell to his knees and the boom rolled from him. It was raining in sheets. He rolled on his back, thrust out his under lip and pawed his hair down over his forehead, the rain trickled down the hair and into his throat. He enjoyed a wonderful drink.

Weakly he scratched a hole in the lee side of a sandhill, crawled into it, and clawed the sand over him. He slept. Just at dawn he was washed out of his lair. He flung out frantic arms ... he could not find it ... he plunged seaward and touched and gripped it—the boom, his boom, just being washed away by the tide. He held it for some time before realizing he wanted it no longer. He was on land ... on land! Day broke with a hurricane wind from the north-north-west; he started to walk the beach, instinctively heading north. In the greying light he almost trod upon a dead man lying there with arms outflung, his rain-sodden chest bare to the sky

"Wassa!" he exclaimed. "Poor devil," he muttered hoarsely. He gazed down on the quiet brown face. "You've built your last ship, Wassa." He stooped and dragged his second carpenter up above tide-level. "You're heavy, Wassa," he gasped. "I thought I could lift a little Jap like you with one hand!"

He walked on along that beach of dead men. It was not the only time that its white sands had mothered the quiet sleepers. Dead fish were strewn far and wide, dead sharks in plenty, dead birds; bits of boats, broken spars; what the sea had taken it was returning. He dragged four of those sleepers up out of tide reach; after that he let them lie, he was too weak. But later in the day he did drag John Magron the sailmaker away from the lapping sea. He could not let Old John lie there with the sand in his hair and a dead shark beside him. Castilla Toledo lay there too, very still and silent. "Poor devil!" muttered the captain. "He was once a handsome man."

He walked throughout the day, towards Broome. He wanted to walk inland, for two stations lay there—somewhere. But he remembered that running in there somewhere parallel with him was the Madman's Track! He staggered on, knowing he must keep the sea to his left if ever he was to go anywhere. But his mind would persist in running away to the bush. There were wells in there somewhere—water! In this arid country every man's thoughts are of water! He could survive if only he could find permanent water. Grimly he trudged on, keeping the sea to his left.

In late afternoon he battled against the wind with phantom company. Old shipmates strolled along and talked to him, walking beside him, keeping him company. He blinked his eyes and they faded away. But presently some other well-known form would come strolling towards him; they would meet and talk gravely, trudging along side by side, tramping towards Broome

Suddenly he stopped, staring as if he saw a ghost. And the thing stared too, sideways, sneaking away as if from something it knew full well was no ghost. He gave chase and it ran, this hoppy-legged, broken-winded thing, this storm-battered gannet. The only live things on all the great beach. Both wanted life, had fought the sea and the tides and the wind to keep it, and would run now to the last gasp to hold it. The gannet stretched out and raced, not feeling the pain of its broken wing. Gasping to the thundering man behind, it heard his pantings too and spurted as the giant flung himself flat towards it, was showered with sand from those snatching fingers. With this heaven-sent respite the gannet slowed down, but soon heard the thunder of gaining feet behind and it stretched out again. It had nowhere to go but straight ahead, the raging sea to its left and sandhills to its right. In its path were gigantic things it had to spurt around or leap: pieces of wreckage, dead sharks that were mountains of flesh to it. Once almost a dead man killed it; it leapt on his chest but the spring off carried it just out of reach of the live man's hand. But he fell flat on it at last and wrung its neck and staggered up and walked, feeling his thumping heart might burst. Plucking the feathers from the gannet, he made to sink his teeth in its breast. The gannet expanded to the size of a turkey!

Amazed, he slowly realized his lips were so swollen he could not bite; his tongue so swollen he had no feeling of taste or size or grip. He walked on, trying now and then to gnaw the gannet in bits; but he could not work up enough saliva to oil his tongue and teeth and jaws.

He was staggering at evening, the gannet clenched by the neck. But his own neck was hanging low, his shoulders bowed, his chin on his chest; he was talking to a whole host of sea mates who plodded beside him, all walking up along the coast, all trudging along to Broome.

But he was past talking, it was only the mind of him that was carrying the body along. When the body fell, the mind went to sleep.

In the morning it took him a long time to stand up; the weak blood slowly coursing through those tired limbs had the faltering strength of a lamp that is burning very low. His mind insinuated that he was done, but he defied the thought by striding forward; he thought his sagging jaw was firm and set. The sun shone brightly; the rain had gone and much of the wind. He did not hear the ceaseless roar of the surf and was unaware of the growing odour from the beach.

Towards midday he became certain of a large black thing before him; blink his eyes as he would it stayed.

He stood gazing up at a lugger, one of his own fleet, flung like driftwood far up on the beach. "The *Langdon!*" he muttered. He had christened it himself; it carried his mother's maiden name. A host of memories of the men who had manned this ship revived him to the present. He climbed aboard, then among broken timbers down into the wrecked cabin. There wasn't a thing to eat but a tin of beans. He smashed it open and thrust a handful into his mouth. He could not swallow. Through sand and muck and wreckage he crawled to the water-tank. It was a long while before he could swallow, but he had plenty of time; time meant nothing. Because he could not swallow, gradually he washed the beans down his throat. He did not want to eat, he wanted strength, but he must eat to live. He rested a long time while the water was bringing back life to the muscles of his throat and tongue. Presently he crawled about again and in a cracked looking-glass stared at a nightmare. Mad, bloodshot eyes, swollen, cracked lips, hair matted around a long, deep cut. The wrecked cabin smelt companionably, like the water-wet presence of men. He rolled into bunk with a long, tired sigh.

Far north along the Eighty Mile Beach the schooner *Alto* was high and dry far up on the sands. Every man aboard was saved. Grig Wilson the engineer and Billy Deering had armed the crew with shovels. They were working back south along the beach with Zumpfeldt, manager of Anna Plains station, burying the cyclone's harvest.

Word was spreading far and wide. Broome was a wreck; the few scattered stations a wreck; townships farther south were wrecked;

telegraph lines down everywhere for hundreds of miles. Zumpfeldt with all his station-hands had ridden to the coast, knowing well the Eighty Mile Beach, hoping he might give help to some few survivors of the pearling fleets. Wilson's gangs came on a well-known, unmistakable figure stretched out on the sands.

"Hokobotong, by God!" They grouped around him, staring down at the gigantic figure of the bosun.

"The sea can beat even giants," said Deering at last.

"My God!" replied Wilson, "what a fight he must have put up. Look at him. Cut to pieces!"

They dug a big grave above high tide, then carried the bosun to it. The hole wasn't big enough. They enlarged it, then bent to lift him in again.

"Eye belong him he move!" exclaimed a Malay superstitiously. Wilson bent down and lifted the eyelid:

"Give me the brandy bottle!" He forced the spirit down the throat of the living corpse. The bosun gurgled, choked, coughed, drank. "Ah-h," he rumbled, "— —good!" Presently he sat up, his face in slow contortion. He began rubbing his eyes, his rugged forehead a maze of frowns. "Give me 'nother drink!" he growled. They did so and he glared vacantly around. "By gum; that good!" he grumbled. They helped him rise so that he stood with his back to the grave.

"Where's da skipper?" he inquired dazedly.

"Oh, he's drowned with the rest of the crew," answered Deering.

"He not drown," frowned the bosun. "S'pose everybody drown *he* no drown."

Deering shook his head.

"Yes he is, bosun. It is three days now since the bodies began to come ashore."

"He not drown. He *any* place can swim."

They led him away and gave him food, then took him the five miles back along the beach to where the *Alto* lay. And with every step he obstinately swore that the captain would *never* drown. They put him to sleep on the *Alto*.

The bosun's faith was great. He awoke at daylight and immediately roused the *Alto* crew to search the beach south for Gregory. But they would not be convinced. His big eyes flashed, he swung his arms. "I go myself!" he roared.

They made him wait for breakfast. "Then I go with you," promised a Malay.

"And me too!" answered his mate.

"It is hopeless, you old fool," said Deering sadly. "But eat first. You will need it, and we will prepare you food and water to carry."

The three set out carrying bottled brandy and milk. They plodded for twenty miles down the beach; then they saw far away, a black dot erratically moving. They hurried; soon they could tell it *was* a man. He was staggering along, swaying from side to side. Again and again he fell to his knees. Very slowly he crawled up, the sea-gulls swooping above him. Each time he fell he rose again, and came staggering along.

The bosun ran with all his lumbering gait. He flung his great arms around Gregory, hugged him, and burst into tears. Gregory stared at him, holding tightly by the neck a dead gannet.

The diver's life is in their hands.

CHAPTER XIII
Con Makes Love

An unhappy Christmas this for Broome. The town in ruins, citizens in mourning, many financially broken. But they immediately proceeded to rebuild the residential quarter and the town.

The foreshore camps were re-erected by men who seemed working in a nightmare, for shed after shed was quickly filled by quietened, often cowed seamen, survivors of wrecked luggers. Vessel after vessel, some being towed totally dismasted, others crawling along under jury-rigged jib and foresail, came creeping back to port. Search vessels were still combing the uninhabited coast north of Derby for vessels that had gone ashore and for survivors who, there, were at the mercy of wild aborigines.

But in a mourning Broome one heart beat with delight. Old Sulu now knew that Toledo was dead. Dead and buried with many others along the Eighty Mile Beach. His ghost would walk at night when the crews of dead ships rose up to walk the beach.

Old Sulu sold the pearl to Gomez, sold for hundreds what was worth thousands. But those few hundreds were a fortune to him; he would return to Manila a very rich man.

When at long last the steamer came, quite deferentially Gomez saw him off. Sulu watched Broome slowly fading in a blur of tears. He was going home at last. He passed the voyage in dreamland, staring out over the bows, the foam below whispering songs of Manila, Pearl of the Orient. At night he stood with starlight on his face while the voice of Toledo crooned up from the bows.

When the steamer arrived, old Sulu could hardly walk down the gangway, his knees were trembling so, his heart was beating painfully—he could barely see. With a set smile on his lined old face he walked gropingly along the wharf. He stretched out his foot to step upon his native land and fell—dead.

Con the bosun was tired of sea-life. He had sailed the Seven Seas and received nothing but blows and hard fare. He decided to retire; to build a cosy nest ashore and make money in comfort. He was sure he could, for now he had overcome his worst enemy, the drink. Besides, Con's chief pleasure was the study of his fellow men. After each lay-up season he had enjoyed studying the new crew of a schooner. But when, in a few months at sea, he knew each man "inside out" from the master to the meanest Koepanger, the remainder of the season held for him only the longing for the next lay-up season when he could go ashore and study men and make love to every nice young coloured thing he could cast his wiles upon.

Con bought a secluded little cottage on the outskirts of the white residential quarter about midway between the town and the pearlers' bungalows. Here were numbers of tree-shadowed little cottages occupied mostly by coloured families whose breadwinners were generally bosuns, divers, tenders, or shore aristocrats. Unlike the widely spaced bungalows of the white quarter, these cottages were built fairly close together. Con's cottage adjoined that of his bitterest enemy, "Puppa" Lorenzo, a shore man. Con's idea was that by having his enemy living under his eye he would have the less chance to do him harm. Lorenzo saw him with consternation. Con smiled benignly across the veranda. Lorenzo literally staggered inside, his eyes fearful. The most dreaded hoodoo man on all the coast had come to live beside him.

Con enclosed his veranda with a dark green lattice. From behind this, seeing but unseen, he could spy upon his enemy's house. They would never be sure whether he was there or not. He could leave the cottage, ostentatiously by the white picket gate, or at night come and go unseen by a loosened sheet of iron in the back fence. True, by the back way, he had to manoeuvre through other people's yards. But among those trees and shrubbery he was like a shadow in the night. And he made it his business to become friendly with every dog in Broome.

In impish delight Con settled down to know, unknown to them, every soul he could in Broome. To learn the business of the town. To hold any coloured enemy under the spell of his black magic. To earn his living, and enjoy his lovemaking. Henceforth Con's life was to be occupied indeed.

Comfortably settled in his little cottage, he gave considerable thought to his next move, which was to be a steady, "independent" job. A job in which he would not be bothered by the boss once he had proved trustworthy.

Sitting thinking there in the dark behind the lattice, he could hear soft conversation from the veranda opposite across the fence, see the glow of his enemy's cigarettes, see the very eyelashes on a swarthy face as the owner lit a match.

He finally decided that, as hotels had kept him poor all his life (according to his reasoning) it was up to an hotel to keep him. So he got a job at the Continental in Broome. There, he is now part of the stock in trade.

Settled in a home and a job Con engaged on a series of amorous adventures the course of which rarely runs smoothly on sea or land.

"If I catch you hanging around my place I'll sool my dogs on to you and tear you to pieces!" growled old Tommy Raymond. Con's eyes blazed as he whipped out a razor:

"If one bites me I'll cut him into ham sandwiches!"

It was only by chance Con had that razor; he was taking it to the sharpener. Tommy Raymond was a retired pearler for whose wife Con's present sweetheart worked as maid. She was a young quarter-cast with soft brown eyes and skin of olive which coloured warmly under Con's honeyed soothings. Her soft, dreamy voice, her languorous smile had for the time being captured Con's butterfly fancy. The memory of her slim, clinging figure had haunted him at sea, but he desired more than memories now.

"Your eyes is like stars," he smiled in a lingering drawl. "Your lips is pomegranate! Men have died for beautiful things like you."

"G'wan!" she chuckled. "You make love like the white men!"

"Better!" whispered Con, "like this!" And the lesson proceeded in blissful delight.

But Raymond the old pearler was the ogre in this romance.

"Only just let me catch you! Only let me catch you in my yard once!" he roared.

"You'll have to wake up early!"

"I'll never sleep for the pleasure of catching you! And when I do I'll smear your insides around the yard!"

"Then you'll wake up!" sneered Con and walked away along the footpath.

"Why you persist in a vendetta against that coloured man beats me," protested Mrs Raymond. "If he wants the girl fair and square and she wants him, why not let them alone!"

"He doesn't want her fair and square," growled Tommy. "Besides she was made for better than the likes of him. She's a nice girl and I'm not going to see her life spoilt."

"Get out with you!" protested his partner in life. "That's not your real reason. Why not let Con alone; he'll harm no one if he is let alone."

"We're enemies," answered Tommy stubbornly. "Sworn enemies. I've threatened to shoot him if I catch him prowling around my house. He's threatened to cut my throat. What can be fairer than that?"

"But why interfere?"

"I tell you she's made for better than him. Besides, this little feud gives me an interest in life."

"Ah! I thought there was something in it! You hate sitting here on the veranda all day like an old derelict with nothing to think about."

"That's it. Con Gill thinks all day about how he will meet the girl at night, and I think all day about how I'll prevent him."

"H'm. Pity you hadn't something else to think about. Con Gill is dangerous."

"That's why I'd like to spike his guns," declared old Tommy grimly.

The girl's little sleep-out was snugly placed in a latticed-in portion of the veranda, and she was forbidden to leave the bungalow after dark. It had the usual large grounds with trees and shrubbery and garden, all flower scented and shadowy at night. Sometimes old Tommy would sleep all day the better to catch Con at night. But on such days, as Con walked home in the late afternoon along the footpath fronting the bungalow, he would see a large, green watering-can under a certain tree. This warned him that Tommy had slept that day. And Con would pass on smiling and retire early to a virtuous bed.

A savage dog that Tommy especially trained to prowl the grounds suddenly died. Tommy secured a ferocious mastiff from a French pearl-buyer, but it, too, departed this life. In a cold fury Tommy bought two savage dogs and spent grim months training them to prowl in company. But Con hoodooed these dogs; made friends with them and induced them to love the touch of his hot, caressing hand, his soothing voice. At night they would become aware he was in the grounds and come to him instantly, making not a sound.

Con on his nocturnal visits was invincible. His skin ·was the almost black of the British West India man, his hair of the tiniest black ringlets. He wore a black flannel, black trousers, no boots, no hat. He cut the buttons off his trousers for a button "pings" upon a wire fence. He marked a tall poinsettia near the fence: If interrupted in his love-making he would run straight for this with hand outstretched, and as his hand lightly touched the tree he would leap straight over the fence and be away noiselessly and invisibly within seconds.

And the girl loved the excitement; it added delicious tingles to an already thrilling love-making. Her work by day was made pleasant by dreams of night. She would creep to the veranda and meet Romeo within hearing of the deep breathing of Tommy inside the bungalow. Let his chair or bed creak once, followed by the soft thump of his feet on the floor, and she would be gliding back along the veranda while Con would be flying for the fence.

On some nights the old man would sleep softly; then Con was particularly wary. He used to watch the shadowy shed down the yard. When he saw the faintest reflection of light upon the shed door he knew that danger was tiptoeing down the house passage.

When Tommy crept out the front door to essay a rear surprise, Con had to rely on an uncanny intuition. He possessed a sixth sense of approaching trouble—particularly if he happened to be alert, and if that trouble happened to be an active, creeping human. Besides which, his eyesight at night was almost supernatural; I have seen his eyes actually glowing in the night. His hearing too for the softest footfall was uncanny. But let him once lose caution and these acutely developed senses seemed almost to desert him. It was a worrying strain to enjoy ardent love-making and at the same time keep alert for a creeping foe.

When Con became aware that Raymond was creeping close around the garden he would step on to the veranda and with the girl tiptoe along it behind the lattice. As Raymond would creep to the back of the veranda, Con would be kissing his sweetheart farewell at the front steps, the two big dogs affectionately sniffing his feet.

So, amid varying alarms Con carried on. And he had ample evidence that Tommy would make good his threats if possible. Raymond was a man still noted for his great strength. If he could lay hands on Con he would slowly crush him to death. If he could shoot him, he would.

A fine type of young white man came to town, saw the girl and was smitten. They arranged that he should come one evening. The girl encouraged the white lad in the hope of a thrill should he for a while succeed in luring suspicion away from her lover.

She got her thrill. The appointment was made for an evening when Raymond had slept all day. Now. he was quietly seated amongst the shrubbery in the garden. Con was away in the shadows outside the fence, awaiting what should happen. The dark form of the would-be wooer came uncertainly along the footpath, clinging to the shadows by the fence. The girl had not warned him about the dogs. He stood there a while, listening. All was silent; the stars shone dreamily upon a night of pale light and shadows, a night that lovers love.

Cautiously the young fellow got through the fence but—he made a noise! Flame spat from the garden followed by a sharp report, then another and another; a bullet struck a wire and screeched horribly away; two great dogs came rushing. The lad bounded back over the fence and fell heavily on the footpath. He was up on the instant, running for his life. Con laughed silently as the lad sped up the street frantically kicking back at the dogs.

A hoarse chuckle rumbled from the garden, it growled on to fresh outburst. Then old Tommy stood up and, still chuckling, stamped heavily up the garden path and inside, heartily pleased with himself.

"My heavens!" exclaimed the wife. "Did you hit him?"

"I did! He fell over that fence like a ton of bricks."

"Well, you've done it now, you'll have the police down here in ten minutes."

"Let 'em all come!" growled Raymond. "Any man can shoot a burglar in his own home. And this burglar won't come again, believe me!"

He didn't. But Con at that moment had his arms around the girl, both giggling to the chuckles of Raymond as he stretched out on his bed inside.

The rebuilt fleets put to see again, brilliant sunlight bathed the mounds and the sand-dunes of Broome and the pindan scrub that led inland to the spinifex fringing the desert. A little man dressed in white with panama hat and white shoes came hurrying down the dusty Broome road to Otto Blackman's. His big blue eyes were open wide; his rather long nose suggested business:

"Otto, I hear you've got some proper barrack [baroque]. How much?"

From the cool veranda Blackman waved to an easy chair.

"No time," snapped Rubin. "A pearl-buyer has to make a living, he's got no time to loaf in creeper-covered verandas with a decanter by his side."

"I notice the hard-working pearl-buyers don't go to sea and fish the pearls," growled Blackman.

"No jolly fear; they stay in the towns and travel the seas on liners."

"Where's this barrack?"

"Take a blooming chair and I'll get it," grumbled Blackman as he rose and went inside.

He returned with a canister full of baroque. Rubin tipped it out on the floor; spread it out with a touch, and had appraised it at a glance.

"How much?"

"Threepence a carat."

"Otto, you are thieving me!"

"Take it or leave it."

"I'll take it; I've got to. What weight?"

"Ten thousand carats."

"All right."

"If it's a fair question: what do you want it for?"

"Ah! I have that Elles working for me and I'm going to make him earn his money."

"I reckon you'd make any employee earn his money and a bit over—a good bit."

"Same as you do your crews," answered Rubin placidly.

Blackman frowned.

"It's not as easy as that," he grumbled. "There are a few rogues among them; they take watching. They're clever, too."

"I'd rather have a clever rogue working for me than an honest fool," snapped Rubin. "You can watch a clever rogue but no matter how you watch an honest fool he won't make any money for you."

"If you could watch the entire crew of a pearling fleet," replied Blackman energetically, "you'd have more eyes than an octopus has tentacles."

"You don't watch them with your eyes," said Rubin witheringly. "You watch them with your brains. Good morning. I must be going."

"So long. And look out you reach your office before sundown," called Blackman sarcastically. "You might miss a pearl."

Rubin laughed from the gate, and waved his hand.

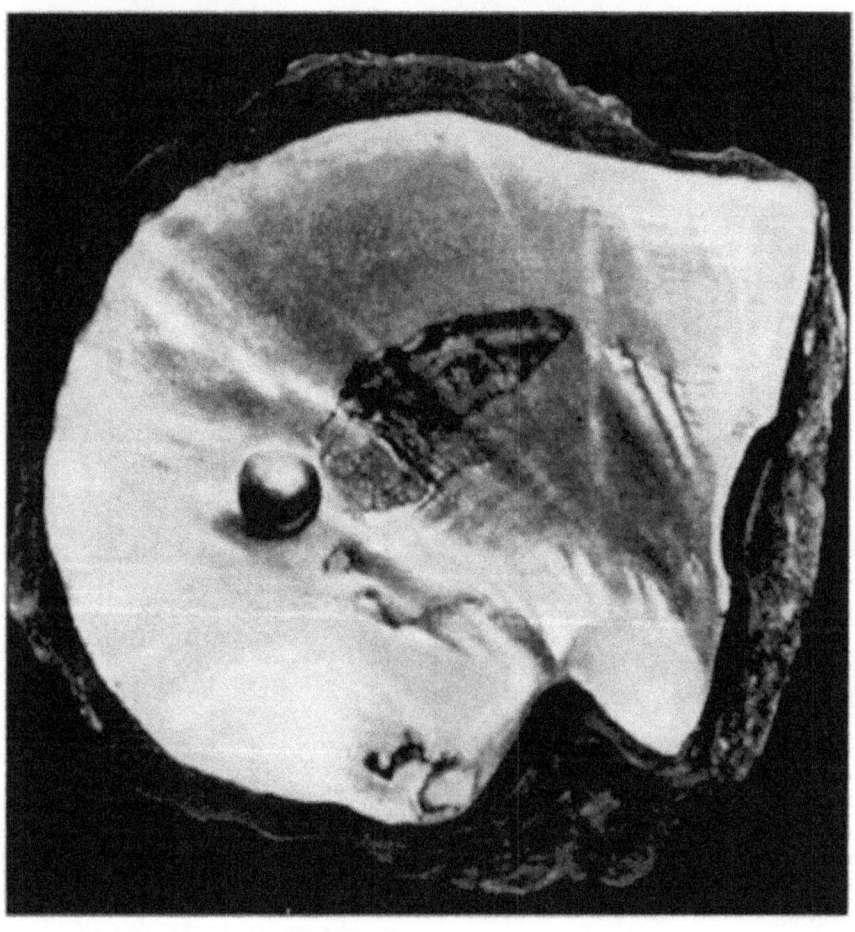

Blister pearl worth £1500: Fished by Mr S. J. Pryor

CHAPTER XIV
A Sleeper in the Night

Coming jogging down the quiet residential street to the town was an old creamy pony, pulling a sulky. The pony was taking its time; it always did. Sitting straight up in the sulky was an exceptionally tall, grave, handsome man with somewhat melancholy eyes. His moustache and closely clipped beard were golden brown; he was neatly dressed. Looking straight ahead, he saw everything to right and left. Occasionally he would wave courteous greeting to a wave from a bungalow, or a salutation from the footpath; as courteous to a passing coloured man as to a pearler.

This was Davis the pearl-buyer, brother-in-law of Mark Rubin and his manager in his absences. Davis ran his business on a strict code and believed his duty to a client to be exactly as is a doctor's. Silent as the Sphinx on business matters he was trusted in consequence. He was a thinker, quick and witty when he chose, a brilliant Jew. Versed in history especially, he could carry a debating hall with him. A highly strung man, depository of many a secret, strict in his religious observances. He arrived at the office on the heels of Rubin.

"Hi, Elles! Here!" called Rubin as he banged the tin of baroque on the office table.

Noiselessly and unhurriedly a man stepped in from an adjoining work-room. He stood there with the shadow of a smile on his smooth, dark face. An excellent "poker" face had Elles the Cingalee, probably the most wonderful pearl-cleaner the world has ever known. His sensitive finger-tips seemed both to impart to and feel "life" in a pearl, his eyes seemed capable of seeing into the very heart of a gem. His fingers were worth thousands of pounds per year to Rubin, who paid him a handsome retainer.

"Here's something to keep you occupied," said Rubin. Elles smiled, softly running his fingers over the baroque. He knew perfectly well that he had to sort and class and clean anything worth cleaning off this baroque because Rubin feared that otherwise his fingers might clean a pearl for someone "privately".

"Very well, Mr Rubin," he said suavely, and took the baroque away.

Like many others, the Cingalee had come to Broome a wanderer. In his struggling days he had got in debt to the extent of eight hundred pounds.

"Go bankrupt," advised a friend.

"No. While a man has two hands he should never go bankrupt."

He went to sea in a lugger and at the end of the year paid all his debts.

Now he was on the path to fortune with romance in every pound he earned, for it all came out of bringing to the light of day the wondrous glow hidden in pearls.

"That man has got a king's ransom buried in his finger-tips if he only knew it," remarked Rubin.

"He does know it," replied Davis quietly.

"H'm," growled Rubin to a knock at the door. "Come in!"

Bernard Bardwell entered, smiling pleasantly, a parcel in his pocket. Intuitively Rubin knew that Bardwell was forced to sell. Davis retired to his own office.

"Sit down, Mr Bardwell," invited Rubin busily. "I know you haven't come to sell me pearls, because all Broome knows I am full up."

Bardwell took the parcel from his pocket and spread the contents on the table, a parcel of exceptionally nice baroque.

"Pouff!" exclaimed Rubin with deprecatory gesture. "Full up I tell you. I show you."

From the safe he brought out a parcel sorted, classed, and cleaned all ready for London. The baroque in biscuit tins at so much per carat, the pearls in clusters of rounds, drops, and buttons at so much per grain. Bardwell's heart fairly thumped at sight of the beautiful things. Fifty-five thousand pounds' worth.

He sat back with a sigh, knowing that Rubin was deliberately devaluing his own little parcel.

"One of these days I'll bring you in some beautiful pearls like those, Mr Rubin," he said, "and you will be eager to make a deal. Meanwhile, how much for my baroque?"

"Ah!" waved Rubin deprecatingly. "How much you want? I tell you I am full up."

Rubin laughed Bardwell's price to scorn. He flung open the safe drawer and brought out another tin of excellent baroque.

"I don't give one-third for this what you ask for that rubbish!" he pointed scornfully.

Bardwell thought rapidly in an attempt to gain time. "Why don't you clean that blister?" he parried. "You gave two hundred pounds for it and you've had it in your safe for donkey's years."

Rubin frowned at the large blister that Bardwell had pointed out.

"What you know about it?" he demanded. "How you know I give two hundred pounds for this?"

"I know a lot about it!" smiled Bardwell. "I was outside when it was found. I examined it myself at sea, and I know that Mr Davis gave two hundred ponds for it."

"Abe!" yelled Rubin. "Come here at once."

Bardwell smiled; he had not expected his ruse to prove so successful.

The blister was still attached to portion of the shell. A magnificent blister. If there was a corresponding pearl inside, it might be worth thousands.

Davis came in, big and polite. "Yes, Mr Rubin."

"Send for Elles and make him open this blister. What for you keep my money tied up for years!"

Elles came in softly. As he picked up the shell and examined the blister, a cynical smile spread over his well-fed countenance. He carried a tiny tool in his hand. Without a word he tapped the blister in one exact spot, then laid the shell back on the table with all the feline satisfaction of a cat.

"Oh, hell!" cried Rubin and leapt up. "Look what he's done with my two hundred pounds! Look! Look what my beautiful manager has done with my two hundred pounds! Look what I pay for! Hell!"

The blister was full of mud. Rubin stormed while Elles stood complacently by, Davis standing silently, his eyes perturbed.

Rubin had made the same mistake more than once. But never would he admit such mistakes. Davis had to stand by while fierce wrath descended upon his head. Meanwhile, Bardwell was sizing up *his* opportunity. That blister, with the mud cleaned out by acid and with a hatpin stuck in the hole made by Elles, would make the most magnificent hatpin in the world.

"Two hundred pounds!" shouted Rubin in hoarse exhaustion, "and not worth twopence!" He Hung the shell violently on the Hoar.

"I'll give you one pound for the blister!" offered Bardwell.

"You will not!" cried Rubin. "And I will not buy this stuff!" He pushed the baroque contemptuously aside.

"The sooner you start buying the sooner you will make up that loss of two hundred pounds," insinuated Bardwell craftily.

Rubin was about to fly into a fury again. Instead he snorted and eventually bought the baroque, taking full advantage of his intuition that Bardwell must sell at a sacrifice. Elles was the only one who enjoyed the joke.

Routine had hardly quietened to a stormy normal when Long Jimmy James breezed in. Rubin greeted him darkly.

"Why the storm clouds?" demanded James as he stretched his long frame in the most comfortable chair. "Any one would think there was a war on!"

"There soon will be a war," answered Rubin darkly; "a bigger war than you ever dreamed of."

"What on earth are you talking about?"

"War. War-war-war—war!" shouted Rubin.

"Rats!" replied James.

Rubin glowered, then shrugged. "All right, you'll see."

"How's the pearls?" inquired James.

"I've got half a million tied up in pearls. The world does not want pearls!"

"What does it want?"

"Wool! There is going to be a war—mark my word, James—a war in two or three, perhaps four years."

"Well, what are you going to do about it?"

"I'm going to buy sheep."

"What?"

"I'm going to buy a sheep station. Perhaps more than one."

"What do *you* know about sheep stations?"

"I'm surprised at you, James, asking me what I know about anything!" said Rubin scathingly. "You know as well as I do you can always buy brains!"

He could. And he bought his sheep stations. He had known what it was to be without a shilling in the world. Now he was buying stations to grow wool that would help clothe troops in a great war the possibility of which was denied by almost all the world.

That evening, Jimmy James was strolling down the road towards the wharf, wondering if there really was anything in this warning of a great world war coming. Rubin was a clever man and a world-travelled one, but his latest belief did really seem fantastic. It was a lovely evening, one of the quietly peaceful evenings of Broome. Behind him, the occasional lights from the bungalows; laughter from a party at the Residency. Around him, the mangroves of the foreshore and the bushes lining the road. As he walked, James's shoes made no sound. He was near the long wharf when he noticed movement among the bushes near by. In three strides he was there and had seized a Malay by the shoulder.

"Oh, Master James," gasped the man, "I been think you policeman comin'! I been swallow one pearl!"

"Oh, did you! How far has it gone?"

"He been go right down!"

"You fool! You'll get snide poisoning now!" To the Malay's and his squatting comrade's obvious discomfiture he added: "Serves you right! Who did you steal it from?"

The abashed man glanced down at his mate: "I no tellem you," he mumbled.

"So long as it wasn't from me, I don't care whether it kills you or not.

Cough!" James shouted. The startled man coughed violently.

"He go right down—he no more come up!" he spluttered.

"How big was it?"

"Like one pea," replied the man, and made a representation of a nice sized pearl.

"H'm. You go straight back to camp and take half a bottle of castor oil and three packets of Epsom-salt. Hurry now or that snide will poison you."

"By and by suppose that one pearl come up, by and by me wash him I sellem you. You buy?" inquired the Malay.

"No, you won't!" roared James. "You give him back longa owner or I tell policeman—send you jail, you scoundrel!"

But the Malay never recovered the pearl. The acids in the stomach may have dissolved it. Anyhow, it did not kill him, though the quantity of oil and salts almost did. Now, James was never a buyer of snides; but this particular snide intrigued him.

"Pearls before swine!" he murmured as he walked away. "Now if I had that pearl I would call it Jonah. And if the boys asked me why, I'd bet them they would never guess ... By Jove they might though; it's an old trick."

Gomez had cleaned his pearl. In the heart of his ramshackle boarding-house, within four iron walls he had stood and gazed while a coloured expert skinned the gem. Taking only three skins from it, it had unfolded as a perfect round with a soft rosae glow; a magnificent thing, warm and beautiful; a pearl of perfect loveliness putting to utter shame the corrugated walls of the dingy room.

Gomez paid the cleaner his rich commission and with a glance warned him what would happen should be speak. For past misdeeds, Gomez could have put him in jail with a word. The man nodded, and slunk away. But the pearl had entered into his soul. A pearl of great price was and always would be a gem. But this was a glory. No man, once he had seen it, could resist telling others of it, even if he did not actually long to possess the glorious thing.

Gomez locked the pearl in his safe along with others but not for long; it worried him night and day; ate into his thoughts. He took the pearl from the safe and sewed it into a tiny bag and hung it around his middle. It was always with him then, night and day. He intended to ask ten thousand pounds for it. He would sell it with other pearls when the fleets sailed in during the next lay-up season. He already had a rich little parcel in his safe. This glorious gem would sell the parcel at a great price. Gomez would retire to Manila an exceedingly rich man years before he had anticipated.

One night Gomez slept soundly. Very soundly. He had blocked his keyhole; had put a mat hard against the bottom of the door. His iron-walled room was suffocatingly hot, but this was immaterial to Gomez the cunning. In the small hours of the morning, a long, straight piece of wire was gently pushed under the carpet that sealed the tiny space under the door. And through the aperture thus made a long, thin tube was stealthily poked. And through this was blown, in noiseless puffs; a powder. In the almost hermetically sealed room, Gomez presently began to inhale that powder. That was why he slept so very soundly. Half an hour later and an ordinary iron cutter, well oiled, was cutting a round hole through the wall next the door. Through the hole came a sinewy brown hand feeling about. The bolt was drawn, the hand groped about, pulled the plug from the keyhole, inserted an oiled key.

The door opened noiselessly, admitting a naked, oiled body. The building was so quiet that the snores of sleepers sounded droningly from distant rooms; a cockroach scuttling over paper made a loud sound.

The visitor took no chances, his eyes gleamed as he held a tube to his mouth and blew a puff of powder right below the sleeping man's nostrils.

Truly, Gomez would sleep very soundly.

The visitor stepped out into the passage, closing the door. He waited a few minutes, then filling his lungs with air threw open the door and stepped again into the room. Swiftly he ran his fingers over the body of Gomez, he felt the little bag. A knife gleamed and the bag was in the man's hand. He was out in the passage again, closing the door. Not a soul had seen him; not a soul heard.

Very late next morning, Gomez awoke. Dazedly. He lay for a time staring up at the roof, his senses gradually returning. Automatically, his hands felt for the tiny bag.

With a cry he leapt from the bed. Trembling in every limb he stared down at his middle, his eyes glaring, his mouth opening pathetically.

Slowly he turned towards the door. Then throwing his arms above his head, he ran screaming through the house. He ran amuck. Ten minutes later he committed suicide.

Through one stolen pearl four men had already died violent deaths. And Toledo had been drowned; and old Sulu had died of heart-failure when he still might have been alive. Six men dead so soon through one stolen pearl.

Streeters, selling pearls from their Broome verandahs.

French D'Antoine and members of the local Badi-Jawi tribe help with his beachcombing business, small pearling and shelling, Broome 1920.

CHAPTER XV
Men and Fate and Destiny

However, a stolen pearl was of but passing account in the destiny of Broome. Very few white men knew that this particular pearl existed. They still believed that Hagen, Pablo Marquez, and Simeon Espada had been hanged for killing Liebglid in the attempt to sell him a lemonade stopper wrapped in a handkerchief as a pearl. Life in Broome went busily on, seeking other pearls and, above all, shell.

The pearlers had plenty to think about; the marketing of shell, the commercial and sea-going management of their vessels, the indenturing of labour and the management of the crews. Trouble sometimes brewed. The Japanese were beginning to preponderate; securing an ever larger share of the diving, the tender and crew work. The Malays, Koepangers, Amboinese and others resented this; resented particularly the increasingly masterful manner of the efficient Japanese. Deep racial antipathies occasionally led to violence on sea and land. The owners sent the vessels to sea under mixed crews with each man allotted the job he could do best. Under this system the different groups watched one another, there was less possibility of loafing, less chance of pearl-stealing, less chance of running away with the vessel. Though one group might scheme against the master another group would definitely say "No!" if only through racial antipathy.

That the few white men controlled these simmering racial troubles with only an occasional serious flare-up in a vessel here and there, is remarkable. Many a lugger had only one white man aboard, living lonely and aloof among a mixed crew. On his management of this sailing hot-bed of jealousies and sometimes hate depended the success of the season's cruise. Now and again, through the years, there was mutiny and murder, perhaps followed by the total disappearance of a vessel. But that happened rarely.

The Japanese, once established, quickly consolidated. Then the good divers began to sell their services to the highest bidder apart from the usual agreed-on terms, quietly pitting one pearler against another, comparing results meanwhile, and so causing new problems to enter into the signing on of the crews.

In the bargaining that followed, the pearlers found themselves compelled to offer an advance considerably above the usual terms. When Gibson gave a crack diver seventy pounds advance the pearlers were staggered. Outside, a boom swung over, struck the diver on the head, and knocked him overboard. He was drowned, and the pearler lost his money as well as the diver. Mark Rubin, bidding for the services of crack men, gave some divers a hundred pounds advance; even went considerably above that. Fatality and loss also followed here, for one of his luggers was never heard of again. Whether the natives massacred the crew, or she cleared for Java or Malaya, no one ever knew.

In numerous ways the Japanese began to prove their shrewdness. When Hunter secured the services of diver Ramatzu on consideration of a hundred pounds advance, Ramatzu came to him next morning and offered him the loan of a hundred pounds at ten per cent. By these and other means the Japanese insidiously and constantly strengthened their position, not only against the coloured crews but against the whites. Immediately they gained one point they quietly consolidated, and proceeded to gain another until they became a force to be reckoned with. The old happy-go-lucky pearling days were gone for ever.

One anxiety of the pearlers began to be somewhat allayed, the dread that they would work out the known pearl-shell beds. The beds proved harder to work out than imagined, while again and yet again venturesome craft would locate a new bed. They prospected the coastal waters as prospectors pushed out into the continent seeking goldfields. But, whereas the land prospectors could see the surface of the ground, the pearl-shell prospectors could not see the bottom of the ocean. Prospecting for shell was thus immeasurably slower, more hazardous and costly, than prospecting for gold. And always dangerous. The coastline north was mainly uncharted. There was only one naval survey vessel to cover an enormous area. The magnificent work of the naval surveys is only now being realized.

Through the years the little luggers on the western coast were ever creeping north, then east; while those from the Coral Sea came west until the tiny sails had fluttered along six thousand miles of practically unknown coastline. The eastern coastline fleets prospected our Great Barrier Reef for its length of twelve hundred miles, then cruised the thousands of square miles of coral reefs in between. Thus the fleets of east and west worked the entire Coral Sea, the north-western coast, the Arafura and Timor seas, and the south-western New Guinea coastline. A mighty work that held within it an ocean of adventure and romance which alas will never be written.

It was nearly midday in September 1911, off Wallal in ten fathoms. The weather blowing a bit, the *Mars* with her nose to the wind dipping to a choppy sea. Diver Takahaise was working on the sea bottom, the tender standing by the rail with the life-line in his hands. That rope was of new coir, one and a half inches thick, sixty-six fathoms long. Syd Pryor always liked his gear to be in apple-pie order, for one never knew what was going to happen at sea, especially aboard a pearling lugger. He glanced towards the dinghy which, while lashed against the seas on deck, was roped in such a position as to be ready for an emergency.

A tomahawk, razor sharp, was handy to the dinghy. Everything aboard shipshape, ready to be handled in a moment should need arise. Pryor felt satisfied. He smiled a joke towards the Malay crew who smiled reply with flash of perfect teeth. Each man at his job, each man cheery. Abdurakin Haji Dollar was busy by the pump preparing the midday meal. A smart hand, Abdurakin.

Pryor stepped below; he had work there to attend to. He was hardly in the cabin when a startled cry rang out above. He leapt to the deck to see the tender braced there with the life-line hissing through his hands. Pryor jumped to a bight of the coil and took a turn around the halyard rack. The tender gasped his relief and leapt back beside Pryor. With hands soon burning they clung to the hissing rope, steadied as it was around the rack. With bated breath the crew waited as the life-line hissed out—gave a jerk as the lugger trembled and plunged forward—then broke and slapped back upon the waves. Helpless, they watched the air-pipe hissing out as a line hisses when taken by a fish. Then the air-pipe changed course; the tender leapt to the tiller to sail the lugger with it, but the pipe sped out to its limit, stretched and—snapped.

Diver Takahaise was gone, life-line and air-pipe broken by some leviathan of the sea.

The surface heaved in broken waves as sunlight gleamed upon a huge black body. The crew screamed with pointing hands, for there, sprawled helplessly across a whale's back, was diver Takahaise. The leviathan snorted and rolled with a shaking that slapped against the waves. They sighed as the diver rolled helplessly off.

Pryor sprang for the tomahawk and with three blows cut the lastings of the dinghy while Abdurakin beside him helped throw it overboard. They leapt straight over into her. As she fell away Abdurakin seized the oars with Pryor standing up straining for a sign of the diver. Takahaise was slowly sinking, his air-inflated suit buoying him up. The frightened whale was surging around and around in wallowing circles, Pryor dared not look at it lest he see the maddened thing coming to swamp them. Shouts from the lugger advised him when the dinghy was above where the diver was last seen. Peering overside he saw Takahaise about twelve feet down, slowly sinking. He leapt overboard and swam down. There was just one chance. If he could only grasp the broken life-line and it should prove long enough!

He swept past the face-glass of the sinking diver and saw the horror upon the convulsive face inside. Seizing the broken rope he swam up, dreading to feel the weight that would prove the rope too short.

He broke surface with a gasp and seized the dinghy as Abdurakin snatched the rope end and made it fast around a thwart. Guarding against capsize Pryor climbed in, then laboriously they hauled on the diver, a ticklish job in that choppy sea with the whale snorting and circling around them, around the lugger too as she came manoeuvring towards them trying to dodge the whale while careful not to run down the dinghy. The two panting men hauled the diver up to the stern of the dinghy, then Abdurakin hung back on the rope by the bow while Pryor leaned over and managed to lift helmet and corselet to the stern—a herculean task. There he lashed the diver with what remained of the life-line; feverishly unscrewed the face-glass, and looked into the swollen, blackened face of Takahaise. Skilfully the tender brought the *Mars* down to the dinghy so as to give the tiny craft a lee, the crew rigging a block and tackle while keeping an eye on the whale.

They hauled the diver aboard. And Pryor laughed his relief as he followed side by side with Abdurakin. Strong brown hands reached over and with the rising of a wave the dinghy was lifted aboard.

Chattering, willing helpers quickly undressed Takahaise. They propped him up so that he could see the whale now encircling the lugger in more dignified gait. Grimly the recovering diver stared at the huge thing whose bovine clumsiness had entangled his lines and almost sent him to a terrible death.

The inflated dress had saved Takahaise—that and the quickness of Pryor. The diver had just inflated his dress ready to ascend when the whale became entangled in the lines and in its mad rush carried the diver to the surface. When the lines broke the inflated suit kept Takahaise from sinking quickly while at the same time allowing him to breathe the imprisoned air in the suit. But it had been a very close go.

Takahaise went back to work on the bottom that same afternoon, after the whale had swum away. Fatalism, in the life of divers, shrugs at death.

CHAPTER XVI
Hazards of the Sea

A dark night, with stars like fire-flies blinking through spectral clouds. A heavy sea with a racing tide that hissed and sighed with the wind. A will-o'-the-wisp, bobbing away in the darkness, was the riding light of the lugger *Phil*, anchored off Guerdon Bay. It was ten o'clock and all hands forrard asleep. All except the diver Ishi Moto, nicknamed "Gin-bottle" by the Japanese of the pearling fleet. He had one now clasped in his arms, a grin of alcoholic cunning on his weather-lined face. Clad in snow-white pyjamas fitting tightly around the neck with rubber bands at wrists and ankles, diver fashion, he crouched like a hazy ghost there by the mainmast, his only company the wind, the sea, the sky and—the bottle.

Ishi Moto well deserved his nickname, he would drink a pannikin of square-face at a time. A potent brand reinforced with chillies, hot enough to heat a boiler without fire. Ishi grinned as the bottle gurgled at his lips. He grinned at thought of how he had bamboozled the lone white skipper asleep in the cabin aft! True, they were only a day's sail out of Broome and there was no telling what another search of the vessel might bring forth. Still, this night at least, Ishi was safe with his smuggled firewater.

Lying down aft in his bunk, Harry Macnee was listening uneasily. Usually the diver slept in the cabin too but this evening he had smiled an excuse and had gone forrard with the crew. Which was natural, for they were only a day out and all hands had memories to talk over. The hurricane lamp burned dimly. The little vessel was all a-tremble; he could feel the anchor chain quivering as she faced the tide; hear a sighing rumble as she came back a bit with it.

The wind was on her beam, the fresh breeze whistling through the rigging. Through the open scuttle Macnee could just catch a glimpse of black sky and a solitary star as she rolled. His eyes closed sleepily.

A splash, and Macnee had leapt up the scuttle and peering overside saw a ballooned ghost drifting by from which grinned up the silly face of Ishi Moto the diver.

"Man overboard! Launch the dinghy," shouted Macnee and leapt straight over. Two strokes took him to the floating man whose fists clawed out in drunken protest. Macnee thumped him on the jaw into semi-consciousness; grabbed him under the armpits and, leaning back, kicked out. He drew in a breath and shouted again.

As a wave carried him up he shouted with all his might, awed by the distance already between him and the masthead light. My God! how that tide was racing him back away from the lugger. Then he glimpsed a swinging ray that was a hurricane lamp and he breathed thankfully. What a fool he had been! Leaping straight overboard and the crew asleep. If someone had not heard him shout ...

He settled down to the task of keeping himself and the diver afloat. It was comparatively easy for he used the strength of the tide. The roll of the waves gave both men buoyancy which Macnee helped by keeping stretched out and kicking under and down with his legs. The diver lay limply, the wind making a balloon of his battened down pyjamas. Very thankful Macnee felt for the style in diver's pyjamas that favoured belt and wrist and ankle cuffs tight fitting.

When surging up with the rise of the wave-crests Macnee shouted, holding his head back while trying to throw his voice up and out towards the lugger, trying to beat the wind with his lungs. He heard no answering hail, no sound save the whispering of the water, the soughing of salt-tinged air as he glided back down into the troughs. Presently he saw no more the lugger's riding light; he felt a terrible loneliness there with an unconscious man rocked on the bosom of the sea.

He shouted regularly, straining his ears for a reply, his eyes staring up to the star-sprinkled sky. His main fight was to keep kicking and keep his own and the diver's head up; the man being in a state of coma helped considerably. He settled down to steady work, his fingers gripping firmly yet loosely the armpits of the diver. He felt like punching the soggy fool until he woke up yelling. Racing away with the tide on a pitch dark night with a speck of a dinghy trying to find them—all for the sake of a drunken Japanese! He checked his anger and clung the tighter, for Japanese have similarly saved white men. As they rose on a wave he shouted with a long, strong call.

Quite soon they were a mile astern of the lugger, racing away on the crest of a terrible loneliness. An hour later Macnee realized he was growing tired, yet fought on with a grim conservation of strength. Half an hour later he caught the click of rowlocks. He almost leapt from the water, shouting in a mad exultation. A faint answer floated back on the wind, creak of rowlocks hard driven. Macnee laughed to the skies.

A hurricane lamp appeared bobbing above the waves, then came the sweet yell of Yabbi the Japanese. Macnee never felt so fresh in his life, he felt the strength of ten men ... Suddenly he thought of sharks ... Which would come first? Shark or boat?

Plainly now came shouts of "Master! Master!"

Like a black bolt the dinghy came sweeping down upon them. They lifted Ishi by the shoulders and dragged him in over the side like a big fish. Macnee, in gasping delight, climbed in over the stern. Smilingly he slid down into the stern panting his thankfulness.

The two Manilamen at the oars were dog tired. They had followed a line with the tide directly from the stern of the lugger, rowing to race the tide too. Wearily they turned the dinghy's nose back into the darkness. Manilamen and Japanese chattered in strong language towards the unconscious form of Ishi.

"Master, s'pose you no catch him, he proper die!" growled Yabbi.

"Yes, he die all right!"

"He drunken fool—proper drunk!" growled Donarto contemptuously.

They tried hard to row back but the winded men could only just hold the dinghy.

"If Araki will only think to lift anchor and drift back with the tide!" thought Macnee anxiously.

Araki had already done so. A smart tender Araki, sharp brown eyes gleaming above the little black moustache. With hand on the tiller and eyes on a star he kept her drifting back in a direct line with the tide, a crew-boy on the masthead seeking a momentary gleam that would be a hurricane lamp.

In the dinghy Yabbi shouted, standing erect as he waved the lamp. Excitedly they called as the gleam of the riding light appeared in the darkness. With rejuvenated energy the rowers bent to the oars. As lugger and dinghy came drifting towards one another Araki slackened the chain so that the anchor would check the lugger. Strong hands clutched the dinghy.

Araki had a lot to say in rapid Japanese to the unconscious Ishi. They pummelled him into sensibility, punched and rubbed and rolled the excess gin and water out of him. After which Araki said a lot more. But old Gin-bottle merely squatted like a limp sack on the deck and wanly smiled. "Why wastem gin!" he protested. Macnee in disgust went below to bunk.

Ishi Moto, anxious to condone his dire disgrace, worked well and long on the morrow, despite his awful head. For this was the time of the favourable tides and clear water. Tides regulate—really control—both the work of the pearler and diver. Spring tides often stir up the sea bottom and the diver cannot then see to work below. On the other hand, during certain months the sea will make "springs" quite clear and the diver may be able to work right through. Neap tides with their lesser movement mean clear water and the diver reaps his harvest. It is a quaint fact that the sun and the moon, a fiery and a "dead" world millions of miles away, should actually decide when an insect called Man may work on the bottom of the sea. Nay more. Forces regulated by this same sun and moon sometimes kill man, even though he be right on the bottom of the earth's sea. Truly, the laws of the infinite universe chain us more closely than we dream.

During the monsoon (called the willy-willy, the cyclone, or the northwest) season, with its storms and squalls and swells, visibility is invariably poor down below; hence the fleets seize the opportunity to make this the lay-up season. When under great pressure the diver can barely move down below unless there is at least slight movement in the water such as occurs just before and just after slack water. Should there be no movement in the water, the diver feels as if he is pushing his way through almost a solid body, though at shallow depths he is not quite so oppressed.

Because of tides, seasons, winds, and human and mechanical sickness and engine trouble the diver only works the bottom during approximately two hundred and thirty-five days each year. So both master and diver go their hardest while opportunity allows. Divers are tempted to take risks, and the more fatalistic the man the more liable he is to chance it.

"I cannot die," he says with a smile, "unless it is my day to die."

In King Sound where the tide rushes in and out the great inlet at eight and ten knots an hour, divers have been caught by the water forces and paid the penalty. There is sometimes a thirty-foot rise of water here. Imagine it! The vast inlet is, then, really a walled sea packed with an excess depth of thirty feet of water. When the tide turns, that mighty volume packed thirty feet high for forty miles inland comes out through the narrow channels to swirl around the islands, first sighing and whispering, then hissing, then roaring as it creates a foam-tossed maze of cross currents and whirlpools. The narrow channel where the *Karrakatta* was wrecked, Pearl Pass, Meda Pass, Escape Pass, Whirlpool Pass and other death-traps have all their tragedies. The water in spring tides comes rumbling through these passes in masses of foam with a strength that causes a sighing through the air. Luggers trapped there come shooting out like logs caught in a flood-race. The temptation with divers has been to stay under too long, refusing to come up from dangerous places before the turning of the tide. Since the finding of new shell-beds in recent years the Sound is seldom fished.

But not only in the Sound is there danger. The Roebuck Deeps just out from Entrance Point lie in the open sea practically within sight of Broome. The dangers here are the deep holes in the sea floor. The bottom is lined with "dead" shell (shell in which the fish once inside have been killed or died), one foot thick in places. This low-value shell may be quickly obtained, and in this hope ·divers returning disappointed to Broome have risked the forty fathoms depth. A diver might win almost a ton of shell in a day, and though of low value it would help enrich his disappointing take for the season. But the Deeps are the extreme of diving depths, and paralysis lurks there. Here Fuji, the No. 2 diver on one of J. T. C. Mackenzie and Lyons's luggers was caught by the tide entangling his life-lines. The alertness of the tender saved his life with only seconds to spare. The tender with the life-line in his hands felt the ominous drawing taut of the line that quickly drew into a strong pull. He tugged, and felt the definite fixity that is not the flexible feeling when the line is attached to a free-moving man.

"Overboard lines! Overboard dinghy! Anchors astern!" he shouted as the tide dragged the vessel away. Men feverishly threw overboard coils and coils of life-line and air-pipe while other men raced astern and dropped two anchors. They stared then as the vessel swayed away while the life-line and air-pipe rapidly tautened to their limit, the anchor ropes tautened astern. Would the anchors grip in time and hold?

They gripped—and held. With life-line and air-pipe stretched taut forrard the ropes astern were quivering from the weight of the lugger pushed by that terrific tide. Should the ropes break then the weight of the lugger would wrench both life-line and air-pipe from the diver's suit.

For five terrible hours Fuji crouched there below expecting the wrenching pull on his life-line that would tear him in halves. Though people watched from the shore they were powerless; it would have required a steam tug to pull the lugger against the tide back over the entangled diver. When the tide turned and Fuji felt the life-line easing he cried from relief. The lugger sailed back over the diver with the tide; the lines slowly drooped; were easily untwisted, and Fuji rose to the surface to see another day.

One of Harry Macnee's divers was less fortunate: his "day to die" had come. Both life-line and air-pipe became fouled around a coral cup. A stiff wind had lashed up a heavy sea and the tender lost his head. The vessel in the grip of the tide wrenched out the fastenings of the diver's lines; the sea rushed into the suit and drowned him. Had the tender instantly slackened the lines and manoeuvred the lugger forward over the diver it would at least have given him a quick chance of freeing himself.

"The day" had come too for Yoitz, one of Piggott's and Long Jimmy James's divers. Yoitz was doubly unlucky for the tender was not only skilful but a seaman, and gave the doomed man every chance. Yoitz's lines became fouled below in the Lacepedes. With skilful manoeuvring and expert seamanship the lugger was held above him for hours—all through a raging tide. They kept the lines free; kept the weight of the lugger from wrenching the lines away. When the waters slackened, another diver went down and freed the lines. But Yoitz was dead; the weight of the vessel had flattened the air-pipe where it was entangled round a rock and Yoitz had slowly smothered to death.

For one of Captain Talboys's divers, too, "the day" had come. When he was down below, the air-pipe burst. Frantically he screwed shut the air-escape valve. Alas, the retaining valve had broken—the air rushed out in ballooning bubbles, the victorious walls of the sea crushed in upon him. When he was hauled up, his head was so swollen by the pressure that they had to cut it out of the helmet.

Extraordinarily lucky was Yatam, the Malay diver working for Kennedy. The air-pipe became entangled around a coral cup; Yatam cried to Mohammed while struggling madly to free himself. He saw the air-pipe stretching out ... out ... he whirled shut his air-escape valve as the pipe broke at the helmet valve causing only one little leak. But the breaking of the pipe freed Yatam; by the life-line they hauled him up to deck in the nick of time; his suit half full of water, his lungs gasping for air.

Mishaps such as these are all in the diver's life. He treats them as we do accidents on land, meanwhile growling at simpler things. He frequently complains of the seasons under the sea, as the farmer complains on land. But the diver's plaint is the reverse. "Too much grass!" he mutters. "Want a big storm down below."

A prolific season down below results in a luxuriant harvest of seaweeds, grasses, sponges, and a bewildering variety of sea vegetation so thick as at times to cover the pearl-shell beds. A violent storm down below is then needed to clear them: a cyclone which tears up and sweeps away the weeds as a bushfire clears rank growth on land. During a recent year on the north-western coast, in many places the reefs carrying shell were completely covered by a thick carpet of green, moss-like growth. These lawns of the sea are anathema to the pearl-shell diver. They cover the shell as bush covers mushrooms on land. And sea-snakes, turtles, spiders, centipedes, beetles, and innumerable other wogs, also have their seasons down below. Occasionally these things cover areas of the sea bottom in "plagues," as rabbits and rats and grasshoppers do the land.

Where life is normally abundant on the sea bottom the pearl-shell oyster is more active and larger; fish are more plentiful; the locality more interesting. All marine life is particularly abundant in rock- and reef-strewn waters. At the same time, not all reefs either of rock or coral, nor all grassy patches or gravels give welcome harbourage to the shell-oyster. The diver has to serve a long apprenticeship in learning where to look for the shell, just as a prospector has to learn the likeliest places to seek for gold.

The diver can rarely complain of no variety in the scenery down below. He may be working among sea-gardens, weird places of fantastic vegetable growth wherein crimson bulbs blink, then vanish at his approach. Or he may find himself beside a shadowy cliff from which the tide trails long tendrils of sea maid's hair. Perhaps he lumbers through clusters of sponges, or over plains dense with sea-grass, or among the fantastic beauties of coral grottoes where brilliant fish glide with shimmering scales and opalescent eyes. He may grope in almost darkness wherein the nearest thing looks only a confused shadow that seems to take form as he stares, or he may walk over far-reaching gravel patches, or sand. Always the scene is changing.

While the diver is groping along obliquely to the tide, the tender in charge on the lugger above under short sail keeps the vessel head reaching, that is, keeps her close up to the wind. This prevents the tide drifting her away too fast, for the lugger must move only at the speed of the man drifting, walking, or working below.

The diver's work is from sunrise to sunset, for just after sunrise light suddenly appears on the ocean bottom and blots out suddenly just before sunset. Thus again we learn that the sun, though millions of miles away, throws out rays which pierce even to the shallows of the ocean's floor.

But stygian darkness dwells in the depths, relieved only by the uncanny glow of trillions of specks of phosphorus in ghostly pulses of blue and green. Helped too by the shimmering glow and dimming of phosphorescent fish and snakes, the dripping reds of dull beads of light in underwater ferneries, the sickly sheen of "black light" trickling in diluted green among flabby monsters that seem to be partly plant and fish and animal.

In tropic seas, especially in the Coral Sea three thousand miles east of Broome, on warm, quiet nights certain fish, under certain atmospheric conditions, leave a trail of light when they charge like that left by a falling star. In proportion of course. But as you are so very close the whirling phosphorescent pearls are more lovely than the dying star. This beautiful phenomenon does not come from the body of the fish. The sea is so heavily charged with living, microscopic beads of phosphorus, that the charge of a swift body through them flames its pathway into a blaze of light.

Other lights come floating by down there; but these are self-contained and of fairy-like loveliness. They pass like tiny parachutes of illuminated silk glowing with the sheen of mother of pearl. From these hang clusters of red and green beads, and luminous tendrils drooping down all tasselled with glowing fire. Beautiful tassels, yet tipped with a deadly sting. Far below these fairy lamps of the sea are ugly fish that stealthily cruise with a tiny bell of light hanging out over shadowy snouts. There are, too, big glowing seaworms, and countless other fantastic forms of life in this weird world at the bottom of the sea.

The tide, the power of which will shift banks on the ocean floor, also carries food to the myriad things of the sea. This tide is really the pulse of the ocean heart that keeps the sea alive. If the tides ceased, the sea would become stagnant, dead. And the stench of its billions of tons of dead things would poison the air for human beings. So that the sun and moon and movement of the earth in causing the tides are really helping us to live.

Because the tide carries vast quantities of food, the diver always looks in a tide-way for the pearl-shell oyster. Generally, the stronger the tide-way, the more baroque in the oyster, for the enclosed tide being in concentrated volume carries more foreign matter such as grains of sand, as well as more food for fishes and vegetable things.

Baroque is really misshapen pearl. The oyster breathes and eats, hence its gaping "lips" in the tide-way below. It, apparently, allows the tide-drift to enter through a fleshy curtain that hangs round its body. Its food is absorbed through this spongy curtain as it were, the oyster closing its shell to squirt out any sand grains or other matter offensive to its appetite. An unlucky oyster sometimes cannot eject a grain of sand. To stop the irritation it coats the grain with succeeding layers of nacre and thus gradually forms a pearl, or baroque. The nacre is a sort of saliva which, when ejected, quickly solidifies. These layers of nacre are the coats or skins of the pearl. Some skins may be slightly discoloured, dinted, or spotted. One skin may be perfect and beautiful. To find this perfect skin is the job of the "pearl doctor", the man like Elles.

Sometimes a shell-oyster, being unfortunate or foolish in its choice of a sea-bed, finds its growth continually interrupted by a necessary but incessant closing of its shell, and so is unable to get rid of its surplus saliva. This may solidify, cause irritation, and in time be covered by succeeding layers of nacre until it too becomes a pearl. Coarse particles of sand flowing in a strong tide current will compel the oyster to close its shell, as will the passing of enemy fish, the raids of starfish, crabs, and certain boring shellfish. For an oyster's life is not all beer and skittles. Sometimes a shellfish will come along armed with a natural drill; will bore right through the shell of the oyster and enjoy a meal. If the enemy is not one that can suck up the oyster by degrees through the drill-hole, then when it ambles away the oyster protects itself by covering the tiny wound with a layer of nacre which sometimes forms into a bubble under pressure of the water. This bubble soon solidifies and appears to be a pearl; it is really a "blister", which is gradually filled with sediment of mud forced into it by water-pressure.

These boring shellfish are dreaded enemies of the pearl-shell oyster. To guard against them it camouflages its shell with sea-growths. When discovered, desperate "slow moving" fights take place between the boring shellfish and the oyster.

Some boring shellfish have a marvellous foot of varying shape according to the use it is put to. Some use it as a spade to dig into the sand in search of soft prey; others as an augur to bore into the hard shell of other shellfish. Some species possess a hard tongue armed with hooks. This is their augur. With it they bore through the shell; then, twisting the long tongue deep into the fish inside, withdraw it with the hooks clogged with flesh.

Naturally, a big and vigorous pearl-shell oyster puts up a fight against thus being eaten alive. If it cannot shake off the "old man of the sea" that clings like a limpet to its "back", it fights hard to prevent it boring into a vital part. When that happens, paralysis kills the oyster if the enemy does not.

Perhaps the hardness and thickness of the shell defies the hard working enemy; perhaps some other enemy engages it in turn; perhaps it bores into the oyster and kills it; perhaps it merely starts the work which will result in a wonderful blister pearl for man.

But the diver does not bother about these trials and tribulations of the oyster. All he wants is its shell, and a pearl if it has one. Like the oyster, the diver has his good days and his bad days; days when everything goes well; when he finds abundant shell; when he feels like whistling all day long. There are other days when everything goes wrong, when he finds little shell; when everything seems against him; when the work feels hard and lonesome; when he tires quickly and is depressed with that "what's the good!" feeling.

I remember a day on the Coral Sea when all aboard the lugger felt that way. All alone on a great big sea, the tucker bad, the water smelly, no one to love us. While toiling at the air-pump, one man thought his mate was loafing on him so he started an argument that flared into a sudden fight, they dropped the pump-handles and got well and truly into it. Shouts from the tender; screams from the air-pipe attendant, while the shell-opener dropped his knife and sprang to the pump-handles. We had to kick the two struggling men apart. They would have torn each other to pieces without the slightest thought of the diver below whose air-supply had been so unceremoniously cut off.

The diver signalled immediately to be hauled up, and the things he said when on deck cleared the air.

CHAPTER XVII
The "Koombana"

I never learnt who actually stole the pearl from Gomez. Rumour spread, particularly after the drowning of Toledo, that there was a curse upon the pearl; that he who possessed it died; and that it would return to the sea. Maybe three coloured men living could connect the particulars; but they keep the secret, superstitiously awed by the fact that the curse worked out so truly. Perhaps it is as well that the history should simply fade away. There was a lugger under close-reefed sail during a wild night in the Bonaparte Archipelago. The steersman was knifed and flung overboard, his cry but a wail in the wind. He too had sewn the pearl into a tiny bag concealed around his middle. But they guessed it was there. He was "lost at sea", and the pearl entered another chapter in its tragic story. I could only find traces here and there of succeeding chapters. Dark hints and whispers. Hence, I will pass by these shadowy episodes until we come to the last chapter.

South of Port Hedland a lugger was anchored. An early bird; for the main fleets were still in port because March is a dangerous month in the willy-willy season.

A black night, quiet and still. All aboard the lugger asleep: the white master soundly so in the tiny cabin aft. Gradually, he became aware of an increasing pressure on his shoulder. Sleepily he awoke and saw eyes staring into his, a finger raised to warning lips. The visitor beckoned as he noiselessly stepped back towards the scuttle and climbed out; then his head appeared vaguely as he beckoned again.

The master glanced at the opposite bunk where the diver lay sound asleep, then quietly drawing his blanket aside, he stepped on bare feet to the scuttle and climbed on deck. A Malay crew-boy stood before him, holding out his hand. The white man stared. A lovely pearl glowed within that brown palm. The glory of the thing held him speechless for seconds.

"Where you get him?" he whispered slowly. "No, never mind, I know you won't tell!"

With gentle fingers he took the pearl, and saw at a glance that the Malay could not have stolen it from his own vessel. The gem was perfectly cleaned.

"Any other man longa crew know 'bout this one?" he whispered.

"No."

"How much you want?"

"Two hundred pounds—gold money!"

"All right, I give. To-morrow morning-time then we sail for Broome—I sell pearl there to big buyer—I give you two hundred pounds gold money."

The Malay nodded assent. "You no tell no man," he whispered urgently. "Tell no countryman belong me, no Manilaman—*no* man!"

"I tell no man," whispered the master. "Only you—me know."

The Malay nodded, then tiptoed away forrard.

It was the wonder pearl, the glory of the seas. And the diver at that very moment was crouching by the scuttle. He had not been asleep. He watched the white man sitting there on deck oblivious to everything but the beautiful thing in his hand. In the hurricane that was even then developing far to the north-east the diver was the only man saved in the wreck of this lugger. Otherwise this last chapter in the story of the wonder pearl would never have been written.

Next morning the lugger sailed for Broome but on the way the master called at Port Hedland. It apparently occurred to him that a visiting buyer might well be there. At this small north-western port, home of a small local fleet, such was often the case. If so, he could sell the pearl with considerably less risk of any one being the wiser.

And the S.S. *Koombana* called too. Davis the pearl-buyer was aboard, on a business trip. Convinced that Mark Rubin's prophecy would prove correct, he had bought de Vahl sheep station, inland from Port Hedland. Swan the manager met him, and they concluded business.

"Swan, bring along your port," suggested Davis. "A little holiday will do you good, you've been working too hard. I'll pay your expenses. Come with me to Broome for a few weeks." The manager shook his head regretfully.

"I can't, Mr Davis, there is too much work."

"Nonsense! there are plenty of men on the station, and you have a capable overseer. Bring your port from the hotel."

"No, Mr Davis, I must get those rams to work."

"Never mind the rams, get your port."

"You don't understand, Mr Davis. You are a pearl man, I am a sheep man. Those rams must be put to work within this coming fortnight."

"Oh, very well, but I believe you could do with a holiday. All work and no play ... you know the old saying."

Swan smiled.

"True, Mr Davis. But I'll accept your hospitality when the station is running smoothly."

Then a man wished to see Mr Davis privately. He was a pearler, had just come in from outside and had a magnificent pearl. He had fished it himself south down the coast.

Davis bought the pearl in all good faith; everything apparently was all clear and above board. This was a recognized pearler selling a pearl he had fished from the sea himself. But of all the gems that had passed through Davis's hands this alone was priceless. He congratulated himself that he had arrived at Port Hedland just when the pearler sailed in.

The lugger put to sea straightaway. She only just managed to sail outside, for nasty weather was already blowing up.

The *Koombana* was a doomed ship; a great tragedy. Yet Fate that links the lives of men deliberately prevented individuals from sailing in her. Swan had been sorely tempted to accept Davis's invitation. Sense of duty saved him. Before this, when the vessel had sailed from distant Fremantle a traveller had rushed on to the wharf just as she steamed out. He cried "I'm ruined! I'm ruined!" He should have sailed in her to take up an important appointment in the East. At more than one port up along the coast similar incidents had occurred. And now from the station country inland from Port Hedland Mick Meehan, the shearer, came riding into town.

"Why don't you sell your horses and go up the coast in the *Koombana* to Derby," a friend advised. "All blade shearers there. You would knock up a big cheque."

"That's a bright idea. If I can sell my horses I will."

"Knock off a tenner and I'll take them," offered a prospective buyer.

"Not on your life! I'll ride the Madman's Track first." And he did. Faced the waterless track back of the Eighty Mile Beach, and was saved from a watery grave.

Tullerman the contractor came in from the bush looking for Roberts, and was told he had better hurry to the wharf for Roberts was sailing aboard the *Koombana* for Derby. Tullerman found him aboard as the *Koombana* was making ready to cast off.

"Been looking for you all over the place," said Tullerman. "I want you to put up a cattle-yard for Jack Stanley."

"Blow the cattle-yard! I'm going to Derby."

"You're not!" declared Tullerman. And he seized Roberts's swag and threw it down on the wharf. Then took the man's arm and still arguing urged him to the gangway. They had to jump to reach the wharf. The *Koombana* (on 20 March 1912) steamed out into the teeth of a willy-willy. She was never seen again, nor any soul on board.

But the life of Broome flowed on despite such incidents as stolen pearls and racial fights of coloured crews on land or sea; despite success or tragedy among the lonely vessels prospecting along the wild coast north.

Despite disaster in the occasional mining ventures of her citizens too. Life went on just the same. And fortune favoured one man, frowned on another-just as usual.

On one bright day of that same year Syd Pryor was whistling like a schoolboy around his foreshore camp. He was going to Brisbane, a little trip half-way around the continent, to visit his parents. He hadn't been home for years.

"Why not cut out the blisters from these dud shells, Syd," remarked Jimmy Taylor his partner, "They make acceptable ornaments, hatpins and 'pretties' like that. You're sure to meet a girl or two in Brisbane. A blister made into a brooch is an acceptable present, you know."

Pryor looked at the shells lying around the camp. Some had quite large blisters—of no value of course.

"It would take several days to chip those blisters from the shells," he said doubtfully.

"Get to work then. Your female relations and their friends will expect you to arrive home loaded with pearls. If you arrive with a pocketful of blisters you won't disappoint them so much."

Syd laughed.

"I'll do it. You never know your luck. I might meet something fascinating in Brisbane."

"Nothing fascinates like a pearl," said Jimmy. "And if you haven't got a pearl give her a blister."

Pryor spent several days chipping the blisters from the shells. Result: a tinful, some of which when cut and polished and set in silver and gold would make fine presents. His back ached: it was tiresome work. He gazed speculatively at a large shell that had been used as a door-jamb these last two years. A big, hard blister had grown right into that shell; it would need patient chipping to prize it out.

"You look tough," murmured Pryor, "but I may as well. You're the last."

He reached for the shell as Donald Macdonald strolled along for a yarn. Donald sat down and glanced at the blisters.

"How about giving me one, Syd," he suggested, "the one on that big shell for preference. Taylor tells me you're chipping them off to give them away."

Pryor started work on the shell.

"I won't give it away. I'll sell it to you for a pound."

"Give you five shillings."

"Why. man, the shell is worth two shillings and the blister may be worth ten or fifteen! Still, you may have it for ten shillings as you fancy it."

"No, five bob is my price."

"Nothing doing," said Pryor, and proceeded to cut out the blister from the shell. After careful labour he completed the job, then took a chisel and flaked away the shell still adhering to the back of the blister. And stared curiously.

For this shell showed the usual bore-hole from some shellfish, but the bore-hole, instead of penetrating the blister, apparently had gone to one side of it. With a tingling of excitement Pryor flaked away at the blister. Macdonald leaned closer. A wonderful smile spread over Pryor's face—the bore-hole travelled right away from the blister!

"Surely not!" murmured Macdonald. But it did. Soon, all trace of the bore-hole was flaked away. The blister was solid. And in the heart of it was a fine round pearl twenty-five grains in weight.

"Oh, what a holiday!" yelled Pryor as he leapt up. "What a pearl some girl has missed!" laughed Taylor.

"And I could have had it for ten bob!" exclaimed Macdonald ruefully.

Next day they sold the pearl for five hundred pounds.

With the help of southern meteorological stations the towns and fleets were learning to foretell a coming willy-willy during the hurricane season and take precautions accordingly. Improved methods of working, too, were being introduced. An air-compressor was appearing on a lugger here and there. McLaughlin had been the first man to introduce an air-compressor but he had gone down in the 1908 blow. Very soon, engines would increasingly replace the hand-pump; and engines would, before long, appear in the luggers as auxiliary to sail. This would mean the beginning of the end of the mother ships (the schooners) for, with power, the luggers would be independent.

The technique of diving was being steadily bettered. Soon it would be universally carried out at the "drift", the diver being suspended just over the bottom as the vessel slowly moved over the surface. Many a diver to-day is voyaging down below over the ocean floor. When he comes to a reef on which grow sponges and sea-plants he signals; the tender brings the vessel into the wind and the diver settles on the bottom to walk about and seek his shell. So much time is saved; more shell is won.

If the diver decides he is examining a valueless patch of bottom, he simply inflates his dress, rises a little, makes a loop in his life-line, sits in it, then signals the tender who sails slowly on with the diver suspended as before. Thus far greater areas of the sea bottom are "covered" than in the old style of fishing with the vessel at anchor.

And the Japanese were bringing about another great change. These men had almost displaced the Manilamen and Koepanger divers; were displacing the Malays even. In the near future nearly all divers and tenders would be Japanese. Fatalistically brave; quietly efficient; experts at learning; keen not to lose a moment; determined to make every shilling possible to take back to Japan after their term had expired; they have built up the most efficient diving service the industry has yet known.

And they are responsible for a more dangerous problem. They have come to almost man the fleets of all the pearling centres from Broome to Thursday Island — three thousand miles of coastal waters. Broome, when the events here recorded happened, was midway through forty years of prosperity. Only a very small place, it probably was (per head) one of the richest townships in Australia. Pearl-shell, with occasional lapses, kept at a profitably high price, and there was a keen demand for Australian pearls from the world's markets.

The shell won was and always has been the basis of the industry; the pearls were the occasional plums. The Golden Lip (our mother-of-pearl shell) is the best in the world. The Black Lip comes second. Most of the pearl-shell won in other seas is Yellow Lip, with species of lesser value. A cyclone every five of six years may wreck portion of the fleets and damage the scattered coastal townships, but both will build up again stronger than ever.

"It's the luck of the game!" said Syd Pryor with a laugh. He had returned from his wonderful holiday, and in the *Patience* was fishing off Wallal on this beautiful twentieth day of March 1913.

Taylor was back in Broome looking after the shore end of the enterprise. Pryor felt one of the happiest men in the world. "The luck of the game!" he laughed as he held aloft a shell to the sympathetic grins of the crew. Stuck to the shell was a big blister pearl which proved a hundred and twenty grains in weight.

Schaumer, of Bauer and Schaumer, bought the blister on the shell just as it was for fifteen hundred pounds, probably the highest price ever paid for a blister pearl in Broome.

Just the luck of the game. The ups and downs are often strange as they are true. J. T. C. Mackenzie, when managing director of James Clarke's fleet, forwarded a parcel of pearls to the Pearl King who was then directing his far-flung activities from headquarters in Brisbane. Clarke, and George Southern his secretary, hurriedly checked the pearls and placing them in the safe turned their attention to more pressing business on hand. A few days later they were staggered to find that a fine round pearl, thirty-five grains' weight of perfect lustre, was missing from Mackenzie's parcel. The office was thoroughly searched; the carpet was pulled up. Not a trace of the pearl was found. Southern was very worried but Clarke took the loss philosophically.

Three weeks later Mrs Southern was pressing her husband's trousers. The iron came in contact with something hard in the turned-up trouser cuff. She turned down the cuff, and a lovely pearl winked out at her.

Southern had been walking about Brisbane for three weeks with a pearl worth over twelve hundred pounds in his trouser cuff!

Elles, the Cingalee pearl-cleaner, was prospering, with a shop and office of his own; the craft of his finger-tips was bringing to light the liquid glow on many a "tear of the sea".

Davis's lovely bungalow came into possession of a pearler and one night he awoke to an unearthly visitant. Nothing would convince the man that a well-known figure had not stood by his bed. Word flew round town that the pearl-buyer had visited his earthly home and that pearls were buried in the garden—a belief that has persisted throughout the years and been the cause of much surreptitious treasure-hunting in the garden. Even some cement garden ornaments were broken up in the hope that the alleged pearls might be inside.

It is hard to understand why a visitor from the other world should be interested in the pearls of this one. To the pearler who owned the bungalow real pearls would have been a godsend for his fleet had gone down in the great willy-willy. He never recovered from the blow. The bungalow was eventually acquired by the Anglican Church and was henceforth known as the "Bishop's Palace," which it is to-day. The Right Reverend Dr Gerard Trower, Bishop of the North-West, took up residence there.

CHAPTER XVIII
A Quiet Night At Sea

The schooner, under foresail, mainsail, staysail, inner and outer jib and main topsail was bowling along with a steady roll that rose evenly to the oncoming waves.

Marab, his brown body a picture, his muscular legs firmly apart under his scarlet sarong, stood gripping the wheel with the sea-love in his eyes. Pedro, the bosun, stood beside him chewing a quid, his little eyes missing nothing in the crew forrard. A wicked little man Pedro, the original yellow of his skin had been tanned brown under the sun and wind of many seas. He was a Chilean fire-eater who had lorded it in Chilean and American sailers until fate took him to the Australian pearling-seas. Appearance was against Pedro. He had been compared to a "villainous little scorpion." His thin body was all whipcord, his bandy legs ridiculous in contrast with the sturdy legs of the Malay steersman. His whisky-stained moustache framed two yellow teeth, his eyes nursed the baleful glare of a waiting shark. But he was an excellent sailorman. And as for his physical handicaps—well, the crew respected the nasty knife at his belt.

The *Eva* was bound from Broome with fortnightly supplies for Hunter and Blackman's fleet fishing off the Eighty Mile Beach. The lookout was even now seeking the first sails of the fleet. Welcome always was the supply schooner with her news of Broome, with her longed-for mail from the great world outside, with her good things in that slop-chest.

A big chest this, a great storeroom built in the hold forrard of the cabin; and it was stacked with cases and crates and bags of food-stuffs and tobacco; with calicoes, knives, sarongs, looking-glasses, and a thousand and one things that sailormen love.

Skipper Claude Hawkes, in immaculate khaki, stretched his tall form with a quizzical glance at the sky.

"A high glass!" he remarked to the mate. "Likely to have a strong sou'-east blow in the morning. Must be careful how we anchor. Don't get too close to the luggers when we near the fleet."

"Aye, aye, sir. The sky does have a sou'-east look about it. We'll have to water the fleet and get the shell aboard immediately the sea goes down."

Calm good humour, a somewhat prominent nose, a slow smile, marked the face of the captain; it was his first cruise in this particular schooner. It was difficult to fluster skipper Claude Hawkes. Fortunately, for a schooner's life in the pearling-seas goes through many alarms. A pearl-buyer now, the skipper takes the *Eva* to sea no more.

Harry Macnee was a ball of energy down below. Now manager of this schooner and the fleet, he had the certain and the uncertain requirements of seventy men to attend to, not to mention the interests of Hunter and Blackman. The net profit for this year was to prove ten thousand pounds, and the gathering thereof was keeping Macnee a busy man. Short and powerfully built, his wideawake face expressed a restless store of Scotch-Australian energy.

In late afternoon a hail from the look out announced the sails of the fleet. An hour later a Red Ensign fluttered at the *Eva's* mast-head, signal to her chicks to gather around her. In the glory of a beautiful sunset they came gliding to anchorage a few miles off the Eighty Mile Beach. Shell-openers on many decks dropped their knives; crews chattered excitedly; tenders signalled to the bottom of the sea "Supply ship!" And up came monstrous shapes from the sea floor.

A quaint scene. The setting sun gleaming on thirty domed helmets coming crawling up the luggers' sides; the white sands of the Eighty Mile Beach stretching away to north and south—the most wonderful, but most treacherous beach in Australia.

"Lower fores'l!" echoed the bosun to the skipper's orders; the crew jumped to the peak and throat halyards.

"Lower away!" Down came the gaff rumbling to the boom as the crew swarmed it, furling sail.

"Make fast! See that the anchor chain is a couple of shackles clear of the windlass."

As the crew made fast to the gaskets, the bosun saw to the anchor as Macnee came forrard.

"Down stays'l—go stays'l halyards!" And down they came to the Malays' echoing "Harrier" (let go).

"Down jibs!"

"Harrier jibs!"

"Haul the mainsheet!" As she came right up into the wind she lost way; then: "Let go forrard!"

"Harrier anchor!" chanted the Malays, and down went the mudhook with a splash.

"All gone, sir!" called Macnee.

"Down mains'll" chanted the Malays, and down came the big sheet.

"Make fast!"

To the patter of feet orders were smartly obeyed. The bosun set the lamp-trimmer to attend to the lights. From the crowded decks of the scattered luggers came shouts of greeting and more distant hallooing, for they had come among three fleets; Streeter's and Gregory's were there too. From luggers near by, dinghies were slung overboard and quickly manned by coloured oarsmen boisterously fighting their mates for a seat. The quietening waters echoed musically to racing rowlocks, to laughing shouts in English, Japanese, Malay and "pidgin", to the creak of windlasses as distant luggers heaved up to come gliding closer to the mother ship. Careful were these captains not to anchor astern; for a schooner has a playful habit of dragging her anchor, and woe betide the little vessel she bumps in the dead of night.

These dinghies coming racing were those of the captains and white shell-openers eager for gossip and mail. The real raid upon the schooner would start to-morrow when from daylight until midday the slop-chest would be opened.

Twenty white men sat at the schooner's table for dinner—all like happy, noisy boys wild for mail and news of the war.

For the prophecy of Mark Rubin had come true. The world was at war; and the world *did* want wool.

A boisterous crowd; revelling in company and a change of food; indulging in horseplay as a heaven-sent relief from the cramped quarters of their own tiny luggers. After gossip came the hush. Instinctively they crowded around the table for the lustre of a pearl was there, glowing under the hurricane lamp, like a tear from the eye of the moon. One by one they examined it, balancing its weight, judging its shape, its lustre, its depth, estimating its value per grain; questioning whether the removal of another skin would enhance or dim its sheen.

Then another gem was produced, carefully wrapped in cotton-wool. It was a nice pearl, a "round", glowing with depth and lustre. Macnee spread a piece of black velvet on the table and slowly rolled the pearl over it while they all feasted their eyes. The "roll" of the pearl seemed "invisible"; that is, it rolled so evenly as to prove its shape perfect. Any slightest unevenness would have been instantly apparent. On the smooth black velvet the life in the glow of the pearl was also brought out with perfect depth and evenness. Daylight, of course, would be the best light. Their talk was hushed as they lovingly handled these treasures from the sea, their faces lit with the glow of possession or the longing of desire. For all pearls won the shell-openers would, in due course, receive commission. As each man handed over his pearls and baroque (if any) Macnee carefully entered details, received the pearls, and locked them in the schooner's safe.

With noisy cheer they sat round the two tables in the cabin while Guno, clad in a smile, shiny brown skin, and clean lava lava brought in huge plates of corned beef, spuds, and carrots, crowning all with a beaming smile and a pudding. After which there was song to the accompaniment of the accordion, later challenged by the gramophone, opposed by bridge and poker. So passed a happy, clear south-eastern night.

Hawkes and Macnee were thankful to get two hours sleep that night. Before daylight they were awakened by the clamour from approaching dinghies, the patter of many feet on deck, the voluble chatter in half a dozen tongues. The crews of the three fleets had swarmed aboard for the opening of the slop-chest.

When they crowded down below, Macnee blocked them off into crews, sweating as he worked, and swearing occasionally to add to the confusion of this babel in divers tongues. South Sea Jimmy did hectic duty as schooner policeman, a hard-bitten old South Sea Islander this, with curly hair and a chest like a baboon.

Starlight and peace. The last of the whites, except Dick Gregory, had pulled singing away towards their shadowy luggers. Stretching miles away, little mast-head lights shone dimly on invisible vessels. Song came floating across the starlit water. The sea was so quiet you would never dream it could brew such a squall even as a cock-eye bob.

"Going to be a quiet night," ventured Dick Gregory. "H'm!" murmured Hawkes. He was always suspicious of the sea.

Macnee was too dog tired to say anything. They were stretched out on deck-chairs, enjoying a final pipe. Without remark they watched a dinghy that had come from the direction of the *Ida Lloyd*. It seemed to be going nowhere while going in all directions at once. When it wasn't jerking forward it was lugging astern only to change course and violently attempt to go two ways at once. A shadow stood up in her and, waving an oar at the sky, howled loud and long.

"Looks like a coon in that crazy dinghy," said Hawkes. "He's boozed."

"Jimmy," called Macnee sharply, "you go and catch that feller over there. He drunk too much!"

South Sea Jimmy grinned, his hairy paw stroked a muscular chest. He leaned back from the rail and walked cat-like to the stern. Soon his dinghy shot out, propelled by powerful strokes. When he reached the shadow dinghy he became a shadow too. Both clashed, while out of the mix-up came maniacal screams with the shadowy clubbing of an oar. They separated violently, Jimmy pulling back to the schooner, the wild oarsman back into the night.

"Surely he hasn't thrashed Jimmy?" drawled Hawkes.

"It looks like it!" said Dick Gregory incredulously. "He must be a man-eater."

"Mad, more likely," growled Macnee. South Sea Jimmy tied the dinghy astern and came sheepishly aft.

"What was the trouble, Jimmy?" inquired Hawkes.

"Oh, he proper drunk that feller; he big buck nigger man. He got 'em bottle gin. I chuck it overside. Good gin too!" added Jimmy regretfully. "I hit him longa head—he go back longa boat."

Sudden screams, yells, and howls rang through the night. They leaned from their chairs, staring towards the shadowy mast-head of the *Ida Lloyd*.

"Sounds like murder on an ambitious scale," drawled Hawkes, as blood-curling yells howled again into the night.

A dinghy came racing for the schooner, the rowlocks sharp and clear as she took shape from the gloom.

"A nigger's gone mad!" called up "White Jack" Macdonald. "He has cleared my decks with a tomahawk—the crew leapt off the boom like monkeys. They're food for the sharks now. He's hacking at every man who attempts to climb aboard."

"We'd better organize a capture," drawled Hawkes.

"That tomahawk might be sharp!" suggested Gregory. "Advise the crew to stand clear until we arrive to rush him."

"Let's go and see," Hawkes stood up. "Man the dinghy," he ordered.

"Any particular fancy in coffins?" called Macnee from the schooner as the dinghy pushed off.

The crew rowed in unusual silence; their eyes gleaming, white teeth flashing in excited grins. Soon the black shape of the *Ida Lloyd* loomed up. Then tiny shapes came, bobbing heads and gleaming shoulders as swimmers closed around them with terrifying whispers of the bloodthirsty maniac aboard.

The dinghy crept on. It was turning bitterly cold with gusts of a south-easterly whipping the waters into snappy wavelets. They quietly shipped the oars when under the lugger's stern. Loud commands, oaths of fearful menace, came howling down to them from above. The big buck coon was enjoying his first command, and it was going to be under the skull and crossbones. "Hoist da Jolly Roger!" he roared. "Get out de guns an' knives! Fetch me a bucket a blood to drink youse——s' death!"

"When I give the word," Hawkes whispered, "all hands leap on deck and rush him from rear and front."

They did so with a will. In five seconds he was sprawled on the deck shouting his command to the mainmast with the ship's knives and axes lying around his great, outflung arms. They jumped atop of him and he grunted like a grampus, they had him handcuffed and thrown into the dinghy while he was groaning for breath. He was still wheezing when near the schooner, but the cold revived him and he attempted a fight. He tried to kick his foot through the dinghy but they grabbed his legs and arms; snatched his hair and the hair of his chest and helped him aboard, where he roared like a bull as the crew manhandled him forrard. Anchoring him to the anchor bollards, they stood back panting while he glared like a wild beast.

"A good fighting brand," breathed Hawkes as the whites resumed their chairs. "I shouldn't care for his head in the morning."

"This breeze will cool it before then," Gregory said with a shiver. "That last blast was icy. I think I'll go aboard and turn in now the excitement is over."

It may have been the voice acting on a muddled brain but the coon forrard shouted a tirade against Gregory, a string of beastly curses that almost made their hair stand on end. He kept it up, a bull voice roaring appalling threats, unthinkable insults. Hawkes stood up:

"Let's go below," he said. "Evening tea is ready."

They were hardly comfortably seated when a South Sea man came bouncing down in a great state.

"Hey boss! I lendem my pipe belonga that nigger there! He break him!"

"More fool you!" exclaimed Macnee savagely. "Go without a pipe now! Get to hell out of this!"

Wind-blown down into the cabin came another roar of abuse.

"I can't stand much more of this," exclaimed Gregory, and jumped up as Tommy Tocus, a South Sea man, poked his woolly head into the cabin. "Boss! that nigger there more better you put rope round his waist." He grinned amiably. "When he swear, drop him under sea. When he stop, pull him up. Alla same South Sea fashion."

But Macnee refused to keel haul him. "No! You stand up there with bucket of water," he continued. "Suppose he open mouth, you bang him bucket water. When he stop you stop."

A pleasant smile enveloped the face of Tocus. He vanished. Leisurely he walked along the deck seeking the largest bucket on the schooner. The cynosure of the entire crew he came forrard humming a ditty, then ostentatiously tying a rope to the bucket heaved it over and drew it brimming full to the deck. The pirate king, shivering at the bollards, paused with a throaty rattle, wondering at the bucket before him, the South Sea man waiting by. Gathering a great breath as Jimmy picked up the bucket he opened his mouth for a roar and the next instant had swallowed the mighty sea. Choked, blinded, half paralysed, he thumped back against the bollard, his body convulsing for breath. Calmly, Jimmy filled the bucket again. The unsympathetic crew roared delight; they crowded round, their glowing eyes daring the prisoner to open his mouth. Uncontrollable fury convulsed his face as he did so, he tore at his chains as the water dashed him back to the bollard again. Only once again did he open his mouth.

When things quietened forrard, Gregory took his departure. His dinghy had hardly vanished in a now tumbling sea when another dinghy appeared out of the dark.

"Who's this coming aboard this time of the night?" exclaimed Hawkes.

"Going to be a quiet night," prophesied Macnee. "We've had enough for one night. We'll get all the trouble we want when this westerly blows up."

The dinghy pulled alongside with a bump and a monkey-like figure crazed with importance leapt aboard. He sprang to the open hatch and, though not very big, expanded his chest with a magnificent gesture. He threw his arms about shouting:

"You're barby tana" (sons of pigs).

Thus Pedro the bosun took command. In a shrill voice blown away by the wind he abused all and sundry. He flung his arms to the skies, he invited every one to fight him. Magnanimously he allowed them choice of weapons; they could have knives or guns or tomahawks. He was willing to fight the world with claws and teeth alone. He shrieked a special invitation to the two white men.

Macnee picked up a pair of ship's irons. "Be careful!" warned Macnee. "He is holding a knife behind him."

Macnee whipped the irons behind his back and walked straight up to the Chilean, glaring at the man, staring him in the eye.

"What you mean by this?" he demanded, then sprang forward swinging the irons as the Chilean whipped out a gun. The irons caught Pedro under the jaw and he groaned back—straight down the hold.

"So hath the mighty fallen," murmured Hawkes. "We might get some sleep now, all's quiet."

"A quiet night. I wonder if Pedro is dead—or if he merely sleepeth!"

"He'll wake in the morning," growled Macnee, "or else we'll hold his funeral."

They retired below, donned pyjamas, and stretched luxuriously out on bunk.

A patter of bare feet and the pugnacious face of Cah Wee glared in at the cabin door.

"Me wantem bottle port wine," he demanded.

"No. You ask skipper," growled Macnee.

Cah Wee turned his port-wine blear on Hawkes.

"I wantem port wine," he squeaked.

"No. Can't have."

"Me wantem bottle port wine," he insisted in crescendo.

"No!" stormed Macnee. "That's the end of it—Finish—You've had enough—Get out!"

But Cah Wee had been indulging in the poppy: it gave him temporary courage and cunning. He produced a packet of greasy testimonials.

"I gottem letter—I velly good cook," he insisted. "I you cook ... long time ... I pleasee master. You leadem letter, give me port wine."

"Take them away. I'll read them in the morning," growled Macnee.

Following a string of Chinese oaths Cah Wee came stepping down into the scuttle. "Get to hell forrard out of this!" yelled Macnee and leapt for the scuttle. Cah Wee bobbed back on deck. They listened to his pattering feet accompanying his excited oaths. Macnee went on deck and called for Marab. The muscular Malay came noiselessly.

"You look out cook!" ordered Macnee. "He drunk. See he no come aft—he too much humbug. Get Guno watch too!"

A grin spread across the keen brown face. "Me look!" he answered softly.

Macnee went below, satisfied that Marab and Guno would watch Cah Wee with a cat-like patience. So they would. But they were not to be proof against the guile of the wily Chinese. A tot each of vile overproof rum, in which was mixed thumbed charcoal of the poppy, would effectually dull the watchfulness of both Marab and Guno when Cah Wee's moment arrived.

"This peaceful pearling fleet," murmured Hawkes, "is turning into a nest of pirates."

"I try to have eyes at the back of my head while we are at Broome," growled Macnee. "But Satan himself would not have cunning enough to stop a coloured crew from smuggling firewater and poppy aboard a supply schooner."

"They must make a tidy bit retailing it to their thirsty mates on the high seas."

"They do—so long as I don't catch them!"

A long-drawn howl came from somewhere out in the misty night.

"Is it like this every trip?" drawled Hawkes. "If it is I'm resigning."

"Oh, this is a bit fresher than usual," answered Macnee. "What about turning in?"

"Finished with the light?"

"Just a second. I'll just make sure." Macnee climbed up the scuttle and looked forrard. A chink of light streamed from the galley, the dim forms of Marab and Guno were standing by the fo'c'sle head. Macnee walked noiselessly forrard and peered into the galley.

In there under a dim hurricane lamp, amidst his pots and pans, Cah Wee was industriously sharpening a butcher's knife, murmuring to the trilling steel, caressing its edge with his thumb.

"What are you doing here?" demanded Macnee. "Get to hell out of it and go to bed!"

Cah Wee curled his upper lip, then lowered his glance and sullenly put the knife away.

"Get to bed," advised Macnee gruffly, "and sleep it off." He turned and walked back aft.

"Only Cah Wee sharpening the carving-knife," he explained to Hawkes.

"Whose throat?"

"His own I hope, if I was only sure I'd sleep sounder."

"Where do you keep your revolver?"

"Under the pillow."

"You need a machine-gun by the look of things."

They doused the light. Barely half an hour later both heard the expected patter of feet on the deck above. The taut, drawn face of Cah Wee came poking down the scuttle. Pale skylight was framed behind his crouching shoulder. Held up behind his back Macnee caught the gleam of steel. Cah Wee must have seen the stealthy movement under the pillow for he yelled piercingly:

"Me wantem port wine."

"I'll settle you!" yelled Macnee, and leapt for the scuttle.

Cah Wee reached the forrard deck first and slammed the galley door. The bolts grated home.

Macnee bolted the door from the outside. Cab Wee was alone with his favourite carving-knife.

Dawn of a beautiful morning showed numerous divers of the far-flung pearling fleet going down for their first morning dip. On the schooner was sorrow and repentance—and business. Pearl-shell was already being stored for the return trip to Broome. They took the big coon off the chain; Pedro the bosun climbed up out of the hold and got to work; Cab Wee was busy in the galley cooking breakfast.

Hawkes yawned brightly in the cabin. "Nice morning," he called. "Any corpses?"

"No," shouted Macnee busily from the deck, "nothing doing ... Quiet night."

CHAPTER XIX
Lost on the Bottom of the Sea

In cheerful mood Hamaguchi the diver dressed himself as if for a trip to the North Pole. Really, he was going to the bottom of the sea. He stood on deck while the tender supervised the crew at their jobs. Hamaguchi pulled on two suits of pyjamas of the finest flannel, each suit fitting tightly around neck and ankles; then drew on two pairs of thick woollen socks that reached to his knees; then he took a strip of flannel eighteen inches wide and four yards long, and wound it round and round his abdomen. For, though brilliant sunlight bathed the lugger and a bead of sweat already glistened on Hamaguchi's forehead, it would be cold on the sea floor. And cramp and rheumatism await the diver particularly should his stomach become cold.

Then Hamaguchi drew on a pair of heavy woollen drawers reaching from just above the ankles to well above his waist. This was followed by a heavy woollen sweater reaching from neck and wrists well down to the thighs. Three sweat beads gleamed on his forehead. But he added two pairs of heavy woollen stockings that came right up to his thighs. After that he was helped on with the tough canvas diving-dress enclosing the feet. The greased sleeve-cuffs, of finest rubber, through which he thrust his hands, were very tight, as was the rubber collar around his neck. He sat on the hatch then while the attendant pulled on the great boots, each with a leaden sole weighing fourteen pounds.

Then Nishi Shigetaro the tender screwed down a copper corslet around the rubber collar, taking great care with each butterfly nut. For Nishi Shigetaro was a good tender, a trusted tender, he took no chances with his cruel mistress, the sea. His little brown face crinkled as his deft fingers tested once again the screws and helmet valves the least displacement of which might mean the life of a man, a life that from now until Hamaguchi rose from the deep would be in his hands.

The *Leighton* was drifting on a strong tide. Half a mile away the *Bintang* and the *Douglas* were lazily drifting under jib and mainsail. Sea-gulls wheeled overhead, cheekily swooping almost to the deck. A beautiful day, this twenty-sixth of August 1915.

Idly Hamaguchi wondered at the life in the air and on the earth so different to the creeping, gliding, darting life in the dim world within the great silence below. This sweet sunlight made one feel it was good to be alive. And the cruise so far had been profitable. Pleased were the crew and pleased would be Miss Withers, the girl pearler of Broome who owned the *Leighton*.

The tender inquired, "O.K.?" Hamaguchi nodded, stood erect, and cumbersomely walked to the side looking tremendously broad for his short height, his brown face and little head with jet-black, bristly hair doll-like above the corslet. He turned, stepped carefully overside on to the short ladder, and climbed down three rungs until he could lean forward with his corslet supported on the rail.

Those ladders, of four-inch thick coir rope, are fitted with rungs that suit the individual legs of each diver.

Shigetaro the tender leaned over then and fitted on the heavy leads which fit down the back and over the chest, fastened so that the weights won't wobble and thus capsize the diver should he bend incautiously while picking up a shell. Made sure that the air-pipe which fits into the helmet was all clear; saw that the life-line was securely fastened around the diver's chest and under his left arm so that it came up the back and could not interfere with his vision and movements.

Then Shigetaro lifted over the big domed helmet of copper and screwed it into the corslet until he had the small brown face of Hamaguchi squarely framed in the face opening. Then into the helmet he screwed the face-glass recently cleaned by a dip into vinegar and water so that it would not "smudge". As he screwed it on he signalled to the men at the air-pump. These coloured hearties, standing with their heads on a level with the hatch immediately bent to the pump-wheel and its rhythmic click-clack, click-clack, hissed the air into Hamaguchi's helmet where various little gadgets spread it evenly.

The Koepanger attendant stood with the air-pipe in his hands, its coils beside him, while Shigetaro now stood with the life-line firmly held in his hands, ready to pay out. Guarding against the roll of the vessel, Hamaguchi threw himself backwards into the water. Partly submerged, he wallowed there while with his right hand he adjusted the large screw on the side of his helmet which regulated his air-supply valve, waved his hand to the tender, then slowly sank to a stream of bubbles, through light green water that gradually darkened to a deepening green through which he could see clearly for sixty feet around.

The bottom came up to Hamaguchi like a hazy blanket of plant growth. Blocks of weed-draped coral loomed up like stumps vaguely seen in a misty field. When he felt his own weight on his feet he tugged the life-line once as signal of landing. He stood there adjusting his air-escape valve, regulating it to just withstand the now increased pressure of water against his diving-dress, whilst ensuring a constant supply of pure air. He was at eighteen fathoms depth (one hundred and eight feet) under a pressure of fifty and a half pounds to the square inch. At this pressure the efficient diver works carefully. Double that pressure is almost extreme diving depth.

Up above, the tender kept a sharp eye on the Koepanger paying out the air-pipe, while attending to the life-line himself and the management of the lugger. At such times the vessel is drifting while head reaching; that is, the tender keeps her close up to the wind. This prevents the tide from drifting her too fast. Otherwise Hamaguchi would be dragged along like a dog tied to the tail of a car. So Shigetaro kept the *Leighton* almost bow on to the wind, thus neutralizing the speed of the tide. The tiller was left alone, the vessel being regulated by the main sheet, according to Hamaguchi's signals from below. For, although at the bottom of the sea, he was really sailing the vessel on the smiling surface above.

On Hamaguchi signalling "Bottom!" Shigetaro hauled in the slack of the life-line and called the Koepanger to haul the air-pipe until there was just sufficient slack for the diver to work comfortably and safely.

Hamaguchi slowly walked along the ocean floor, his head within the suit constantly turning to peer this side and that through the side-glasses, keen not to miss a shell. If he did, he would not be able to walk back for the tide was a moving wall pressing him forward.

To him came reassuringly the murmuring cluk-clok, cluk-clok (at this depth) of the air pump on the vessel above. Now and again he breathed a whiff of engine oil sucked down the air-pipe. All else was a clammy silence.

While peering for the gleam of mother of pearl among that riotous vegetable life a living silken bowl pulsing with the sheen of the moon came drifting towards Hamaguchi. Twinkling eyes of green and yellow gleamed amidst the moonlight. And from the bowl drooped tendrils glinting like threads of glass. Altogether lovely this wraith of the sea. But the ends of its tendrils held a paralysing poison. Yet. between those tendrils swam six small fish protected thus from enemies not immune.

Hamaguchi gave not a glance to the jelly-fish drifting by. Before him loomed a coral cup, a huge post of coral overgrown with a colony of plant-animal things strange beyond the imaginings of man. Among it all Hamaguchi could spy no pearl-shell; so he passed slowly on, a grotesque thing as weird looking as the weird life around.

The diver has to be keenly observant, for the big, dull grey shell of the pearl-oyster is often almost indistinguishable. Against its many enemies it camouflages itself; encourages smaller shellfish, sponges, weeds and various plant life to grow upon it, and thus disguise it still further from fish and crab and cuttlefish, and from those enemies that would drill a hole through its shell and suck its very vitals. Keen must the diver's eye be to catch the "puff" of water that betrays the closing, or the glint of mother of pearl that reveals the open lips of a shell.

Presently Hamaguchi saw his first shell, or rather he saw. the starfish. There ahead of him, crossing a clear gravelly patch, was a large, bright blue starfish, grim purpose in its bunched-up legs as it humped its way across the gravel. This starfish in a hurry knew that the pearl-oyster was there; had spied on it previously. But the oyster had seen or felt the starfish before the starfish saw it; Now, the starfish knew that the shell-oyster would have its mouth open drawing in food from the tide. With concentrated malignity it came sneaking up behind the oyster upon whose shell was growing a russet spray of sea-fern.

Upon that spray the starfish seemed to spring and instantly its five arm-ends were in the mouth of the shell which closed upon them, struggling to cut the tough limbs, while against this squeeze the body of the starfish struggled with the fierce contortions of a wrestler. Rocked by this fight to the death the fronds of the tiny sea-fern were gently trembling. With two arm-tips pressing down upon the lip of the under shell the starfish strained with its other three arms to pull the upper shell apart as an ape man might fight to wrench apart the jaws of a crocodile. As Hamaguchi came up level he signalled the *Leighton* "Stop!" and stood looking down. Not that the fight interested him; he saw similar fights almost daily. But where this small pearl-oyster was there might well be others.

For a time the bivalve held its pressure against the wrenching arms whose grip it sought to ease by smothering them with slime. But when its muscle began to feel the strain the contortions of the starfish redoubled; it snatched a better grip and levered to straighten out its stubby legs now vivid blue and swollen. This would be a short struggle for it was an old-man starfish and its prey only a baby pearl-shell oyster. Otherwise the man would have wrenched the starfish away and taken the pearl-shell.

Presently the oyster gaped a little and immediately the starfish's knotted arms thrust farther in and up as it pushed to force its body deep between the shell edges, thus securing leverage to force wide its arms. Hamaguchi felt the tide pressing him; he obeyed with slow steps forward. The shellfish slowly opened, the sea-fern tilted back, the starfish squeezed farther in while opening its stomach upon the fish, seeking to suck it up from its shell. It squirted acid things to shrink the oyster and help it digest it as its levering arms prized open the shell. Then its sucking stomach widened and lowered to engulf the convulsive thing.

Hamaguchi stepped forward, pushed by the tide. Suddenly he felt the master's hand. Ice touched his heart as he felt himself being drawn strongly backward instead of being urged forward. He signalled instantly for more line and the tender swiftly paid it out. Hamaguchi felt the relief and the tide urged him forward. But again that strong pull back. Although his leaden feet rose up and down he stayed there being pulled back yet pressed forward—like the starfish and the oyster. In desperation he lifted his arm and grasping the tautened air-pipe pulled himself around and stared. The air-pipe was fouled around a coral block like a broken pillar. He felt himself being irresistibly dragged away by the weight of the lugger as it was being carried overhead by the tide, while against that awful pressure he was held back to the coral cup. As he frantically signalled the ship to go about, a gun crashed in his helmet and he knew the air-pipe had snapped. Instantly he closed his air-escape valve thinking:

"The life-line holds. They can haul me up." Then he felt a great strain on the line, a drag on his chest as if he were being pulled in half. The life-line was entangled too!

He slung there gasping, awaiting the last wrench. It came. The life-line snapped. He thrust out helpless arms to guard against the coral cup. He was a prisoner, bound to a coral cup on the bottom of the sea. No more came the faint cluk-clok, cluk-clok of the air-pump, the taint of engine oil. In an awful silence, Hamaguchi the diver awaited the end. He could breathe, for air was imprisoned with him in the suit. But with every breath he inhaled he would breathe out carbon dioxide-poison air. And in breathing again this carbonic acid gas it would slowly smother him.

With the all-conquering fatalism of his race Hamaguchi did not even think, he did not want to think, he did not even stare out of the face-glass. Inquisitive fish looked through it and passed by. As the thumping of his heart dimmed he refused to listen even to his own breathing—the one whisper now in the whole great world for him. Pressed away by the tide to the short length of the broken air-pipe he waited, his mind a blank.

Time passed but Hamaguchi had no idea of time. Time was a feeling now in which he was breathing slowly, deeply. Presently he laboured with a throaty catch; then he was panting. He felt his eyes slowly growing hard and large; his cheeks twitched before they gradually tightened; his mouth was opening wide, his lips swelling. A throaty rumbling was his lungs fighting for air; his scalp with the thick bristly hair stretched very tight. He had to raise his head up and fight to draw down thinning air—to draw it right down to his very belt so hungry were his straining lungs. His arms hung numbly. Something was squeezing in his chest and squeezing out his eyes; they felt like horses' eyes, but hard as marbles; and all they could see was blackness. Aching pain pierced his lungs. He was sagging in the dress; he felt his head nodding and knew the end was near. Only partly conscious, but just because he was a man he tried to hold his head up, to stand upright to the last. But his head nodded lower still. It was slowly growing larger while turning into lead; it leaned down towards his toes. His arms hung from the shoulders like lumps of lead. As Hamaguchi's head nodded lower so the fouling air forced up the back of the dress. Presently, the man was forced right down double, his dying fingers and the toes of his boots just touching the sea floor, suspended there by the foul air that has taken complete possession of what was now the highest portion of the dress. With his big eyes pressing hard against the helmet Hamaguchi lost consciousness.

When the air-pipe had snapped out over the sea the tender yelled "Let go anchor!" but before it could grip bottom the weight of the drifting vessel had snapped the life-line also. Still, that quick dropping of the anchor held the ship somewhere near the man lost below. Shigetaro ran up a flag at half-mast. The *Bintang* hoisted all sail and came with foam at her bows. Captain Talboys sent his diver below immediately but without success. What hope was there of finding a man lost on the bottom of the sea! Eighteen fathoms deep! The *Douglas* came sailing up and diver Akaro Yokeziro immediately went below. And the gods of old Japan guided him to within twenty yards of Hamaguchi—put him down there on the right side of the tide. He groped forward and fate took him straight to Hamaguchi.

Akaro unwound the remnant of the air-pipe from around the coral cup, working with the slow care that is fast at eighteen fathoms deep. Then he did a brave thing, he undid his own life-line and fastened it to Hamaguchi. Then tugged "Haul up!"

On the lugger *Douglas* they were amazed when a shapeless, apparently dead diver came up on Akaro's life-line.

Down below, Akaro calmly shut his air-escape valve. As the imprisoned air was fast pressed into his suit it began to inflate, slowly then quickly it began to rise, to end in a rush up to the surface.

Swept along by the tide while wallowing helplessly in the waves Akaro caught a glimpse of the lugger crews throwing overboard the rescuing dinghies.

CHAPTER XX
Black Magic

Broome seemed strangely quiet now. Of the boisterous spirits that had made the town so lively few remained. War activities had scattered them. Pearl-shell and pearls were of no use to the world now, articles of utility and beauty were useless for killing and maiming men, useless for burning down cities and gassing women and children. So for a period, most of the peaceful fleets were laid up. But even a world war does not stop the private affairs of the individual; these will carry on while there is humanity left on earth.

Con Gill the one-time bosun crouched behind his lattice work, staring towards his enemy's house. Some dark deed was being brewed there. A dark night too, breathlessly still, silent but for the vicious squeal of a flying fox. A wisp of vapour coiled around Con's head. His eyes were glowing; his face tautly lined. The pungent odour of incense smouldered from a brazier. A large frog squatted before this dark-visaged man, gazing up at him from round, black eyes, its greenish-yellow sides gently pulsing. The cottage was silent as the tomb.

Within the house opposite, black magic was being worked. For Puppa Lorenzo swore it was a spell cast by Con that had stiffened his leg, while a more subtle spell showed signs of affecting his wife mentally. That bosun was in league with the Black Powers, swore Lorenzo, not only was he a worker of malicious magic, but he could call Black Powers to aid him from the Pit. He could see into the future and the past. All Asiatic town was now whispering of that occurrence of yesterday! A man had come to Conard Gill to have his future told. Con had stared at him with those creepy eyes of his:

"You are going to have an accident!" he said impressively. "Very soon." And stared at the man.

The man drove away. His horse bolted in the street; he was thrown out; the wheel ran over his legs and broke them.

A conviction was growing upon Lorenzo that he was being charmed to die. In desperation he had engaged Upi, a hoodoo doctor among the Koepangers, a reputable caster of spells, to hoodoo Con. Upi was black but the tips of his jet-black hair had a reddish tinge as is occasionally found among this people. Hence Upi-fire. Below that reddish tinge, his deep-lined, cruel, black face glared evilly. He had staked his dreaded reputation that he would cast a malignant spell upon Con. Numerous attempts had been made through the years to hoodoo Con, but all had failed. Upi swore he would not fail.

Now that Con had forsworn drink, the coloured people feared he was invulnerable. Excessive drinking had been Con's one weakness. In previous years, it had been hoped that one day while he was under the influence, an expert hoodoo doctor might have penetrated his unguarded system; for when a man sleeps the sleep of the inebriate his "inner self" is open to the machinations of evil.

But this Koepanger doctor swore he would hoodoo Con even if he remained as sober as an angel. So now in all secrecy a dozen men collected in Lorenzo's house. The doctor had brought a fowl. They squatted around this uneasy thing, crooning incantations while soothingly stroking its head by a slithery movement of the thumb, closing and opening its eyelids until by degree the head drooped, the eyelids closed heavily of their own accord. They crooned monotonously while the doctor decapitated the fowl, not sparing it one last feeble gurgle. In a brass bowl carefully he saved the blood, muttering "poison" into it as it drained drop by drop from the fowl's neck. This "poison" blood he warmed on a brazier, then absorbed it into a porous charm composed of nauseous material which he warmed also. As the charm took up the blood so did the doctor chant into it that malign influence which by attraction would enter into Con when his shadow stepped over it. As steel flies to the magnet, so was this evil poison to fly to the foot of Conard Gill.

Around the doctor were brass bowls from which charm incense smouldered, while strung from the walls were withered things which had been buried in a cemetery. With clawing hands the hoodoo man wafted the vaporous smoke, loaded with evil properties, into the charm. As he chanted, hatred shone from the contortions of his almost black face. The presence of evil seemed slowly to grow and be in that sinister room now so overwhelmingly oppressed by evil thoughts. And as the Koepanger willed into that charm the active spirit of evil which was to imbue it with the magic of evil powers, visitors were gossiping outside on the veranda, the glow of their cigarettes there as usual for Con to see.

In dead of night, naked and oiled and ochred with hoodoo signs, with the dyed grasses and feathers of various malignant symbols twisted around certain parts of his body, the charmer crept through Con's gate. With whispered mutterings he buried the charm, now at a blood warmth and wrapped to keep it so, where Con must step over or above it. He buried it hand deep. For such a charm must not be buried too deep or too shallow or in damp ground; otherwise its efficacy, burning to be at work, evaporates. As the steel must be at a certain distance to feel the draw of the magnet, so the charm must be at a correct distance for its magic to enter into the body of the victim.

Then the conspirators waited three days for Con to fall ill.

On the third evening Con was particularly well. They heard him humming a cheery chanty beside his lattice; smelt the frying of bacon and onions.

"Something has miscarried, Puppa," murmured the Koepanger uneasily. Old Lorenzo dolefully shook his head. "He is very wise this man," he murmured. "He is the devil. I doubt if your charms will defeat his. And I will die."

"Conard Gill shall die," hissed Upi.

In the small hours, the Koepanger crept out to dig up his charm and ascertain why it had failed. It was not there! The Koepanger and old Lorenzo and the conspirators received a nasty shock. For a buried charm to vanish like this, portends evil to those who have planted it.

"I will find it," swore the Koepanger. "And with black magic I will kill him, kill! kill! kill!" But Lorenzo shook his head in a frightened way.

The Koepanger had to find the missing charm before he could carry on, for the results of black magic and hoodoo operate only under unalterable rules. He located the charm that he suspected had been planted near his house. He smoked a few whiffs of incense plant, closed his eyes and with outstretched arms slowly walked around the house. Soon, his closed lids twitched, he visioned small spirals of ascending smoke. He opened his eyes and exactly where he gazed was where the charm lay hidden. So the Koepanger found the charm-planted beneath his own doorstep!

"I am a dead man!" gasped Puppa Lorenzo.

Con carried on his daily business with a grim laugh in his quick, roving eyes. When he returned to his cottage each evening he would walk along the veranda and within the lighted room cook and eat his evening meal. Then he would put the lights out, lock up, walk out of the house and along the street for a stroll in Asiatic town to mark a Chefah ticket. On the ticket, for luck, he would mark those symbols which signify good against evil magic. A stroll down the main street, into John Chi Lane and into Sheba Lane would follow, nodding the while to acquaintances with a joke and laugh here and there. He would go, as if for the night, to one of the gambling-dens, only to vanish in the shadows and quickly double back to the tree-shaded road behind his cottage. Slipping through the secret entrance to his yard, he would enter the house on bare feet and, from behind the lattice, spy on the doings next door. He was rewarded by seeing the black magicians plant the next charm in the path, just inside the gate. He would surely have to walk over it when opening the gate. And they squatted near by until dawn.

"I'll put the terror of Hades into these swine!" swore Con furiously.

He went out the back way that day, and thought deeply while at work. In the small hours next morning he dug up the charm. Gingerly he handled it with tongs, muttering prayers against evil as he held the tongs at arm's length. The charm was wrapped within dyed cottons and paper covered with Malay magic symbols. It was pierced through with needles pointing to every direction of the compass. Black twine wool moist from absorbed blood was woven in and out amongst the needles. These needles with the poisons were the material agents charged to direct the disease poisons through and through Con's body. It did not matter which way he stepped through that gate, one of those needles *must* have pointed directly to his foot.

Now, Con knew that in the room where Lorenzo slept there was a horse-bell hanging up on the wall. Upi, the Koepanger charm doctor, slept in the same room. In the dead of night Con, less than a shadow in his nakedness, crept into the house and room. By a thin wire he lightly attached the charm to the tongue of the bell. With fingers light as the touch of death he placed the bell on the end of the bed right at the feet of the sleeping Koepanger.

In the morning when the man awoke the bell clattered to the floor and the charm rolled out before the staring eyes of the men.

That night the Koepanger dreamed, and his dream was all of Con and his blazing eyes, Con coming at him with a knife and behind Con was a fearsome shadow, the outspread wings of the Bat of Death.

The Koepanger begged of Lorenzo to be excused of practising any more black magic against Con whose evil guide was more powerful than his.

Tragedy came to Lorenzo. For his son was accidentally killed when stepping through a fence with a loaded gun.

And Con got the blame through magic. Thus the bitter feud went on.

A half-caste woman Teresa and her husband fell upon hard times. Con offered them a home until the man should get work, the woman to be housekeeper in the little cottage. One evening Con could not sleep; he kept dreaming three little girls were romping on his bed.

"Teresa!" he called, "have people been playing on my bed?"

"Yes, Con," came the answer from the adjoining room, "Fanelle and Isabel and Celeste. I told them not to play on your bed and they went out on the veranda after a while."

"Ah!" said Con thoughtfully. "It's all right."

Celeste was the little half-caste step-daughter of old Puppa Lorenzo next door. Con carefully examined his pillow. He found a small tear with a wee bit of fluff showing. He threw the pillow from him. When the household was asleep he went out into the back yard, burned the pillow with the charm still inside it and went sound asleep.

Again and again the efforts of magic-workers who sought to cast their spells upon Con came to nought.

Francis Paddy was trudging along at the bottom of the sea. The sturdy old Koepanger was in a smouldering rage. Men of that race can keep their tempers smouldering for surprising periods. He was angry with those enemies that had so disorganised the activities of the pearling fleets and of the white men whom he loved as masterful brothers. Practically all the Malays, and all of the sturdier class among the Koepangers both respected and liked the Australian pearler. A kindly master though a hard one, he was regarded as "father" by many of the coloured seamen, numbers of whom had worked for him nearly all their lives. The Malays would have enlisted in a body if the white masters would only have taken them.

And so, in smouldering resentment against enemies he would never know, Francis Paddy was groping away down there at the bottom of the sea.

Hate is a queer thing, when it can be sent out in thought-waves from the bottom of the sea.

Francis Paddy trod warily for he was in dangerous "country", working over a portion of the sea bottom where every here and there lay masses of black boulders partly covered by rubbery-leaved sea-plants slimy to the touch. Picking his way cautiously among these rocks, Francis edged away from a shadowy grey-black wall forming at his right. That, he knew, was the foundation rock, the base, of an island. Up above, the lugger was drifting among a group of picturesque little islands while down on the sea floor were numerous rocks that had rolled from them in bygone convulsions of nature. Gloomy, indistinct shapes generally are big boulders on the bottom of the sea. Huge rocky reefs were there which long ago had probably been parts of the bases of these or vanished islands.

Pearl-shell was not thick where Paddy worked, but it was large, of excellent quality, and rich in baroque. The baroque, with the probable chance of a pearl, was recompense for the lesser haul of shell. Cautiously he made his way over this rough bottom, glancing up now and then to make sure that his life-line and air-pipe were taut. Should these slacken, there would be the danger of them entangling around ledges or those rocks that occasionally stood up like jagged pinnacles. An exceptionally nasty place this, for the tide came swirling and criss-crossing here in swift currents and more dangerous whirlpools that twisted among the island foundations.

Any diver foolhardy enough to work here during the inrush or outrush of the big tides took the double chance of being jammed away in some crevice or of the tide swerving his lines amongst the rocks. This was not the time of a dangerous tide but Paddy worked cautiously for all that. Only a few days previously, a diver had been lost on this very bottom. It was thought that his lines had become entangled amongst the rocks, and the friction, aided by the weight of the drifting lugger, had sawn them through, and the diver had stayed with the fishes.

That, however, was not correct. Killer whales, those wolves of the sea, had been indirectly responsible for the diver's death. While he was working, a pack were harrying a humpback miles away out at sea, tearing the frantic thing to pieces. No matter how often he sounded, no matter how long he remained submerged these ferocious devils were waiting to hurl themselves upon him again. In frantic despair the tortured leviathan sought sanctuary among the islands-and sealed its doom. In the shallower water the killers dived with it, rushing its jaws, seeking to tear out its tongue. Almost beaten, the whale sounded for the last time and the diver, suddenly jerked from his feet, was in the midst of a terrible fight with the rolling body of the whale thrashing between his lines while a score of ferocious beasts attacked it from all sides, their dreadful teeth snapping right and left.

Entangled in this fury the diver was hurled aside; then his lines were snapped through, and he sank to the bottom as the fight raged past.

Francis Paddy did not know this. He would not have worried if he had; he knew there was far greater chance of disaster merely by his lines entangling among the rocks. Such a fate as had overtaken his fellow diver might not occur again in many years. Prowling on, every now and then he found a large shell and put it in his open-work bag. Suddenly he stood perfectly still as a turtle sped past, swerving to right and left, its snake-like head outstretched, its flippers propelling it at great speed. At its tail, following its every move, was a shark snapping at where the turtle's flippers were a second before. The pair disappeared almost in a flash, the turtle desperately seeking some crevice into which it could vanish.

"I'm glad I'm not a turtle!" mused Paddy as he walked on. Then stood with his heart in his mouth, his hair on end, as a big black body rolled among the rocks ahead. It looked like the hump of a black camel. But this hump was doing something dreadful. The unseen body in slow, bulky movement was wrenching and tugging as a mastiff might tear the sawdust stuffing from a doll. Then part of a big grey tail appeared; then the hump rose higher, turning into blotchy grey, and revealed a glimpse of a monstrous head and thick leathery lips and a great eye of liquid green. Then the thing bent to its tugging again.

Francis Paddy instantly closed his air-escape valve while clinging to a rock to hold himself down until the last moment. He had seen that luminous glare in a giant groper's eye once before. When he could hold no longer he let go and the inflated suit shot him straight up.

As he sped up above the groper he saw that it was tearing a dead diver out of his dress.

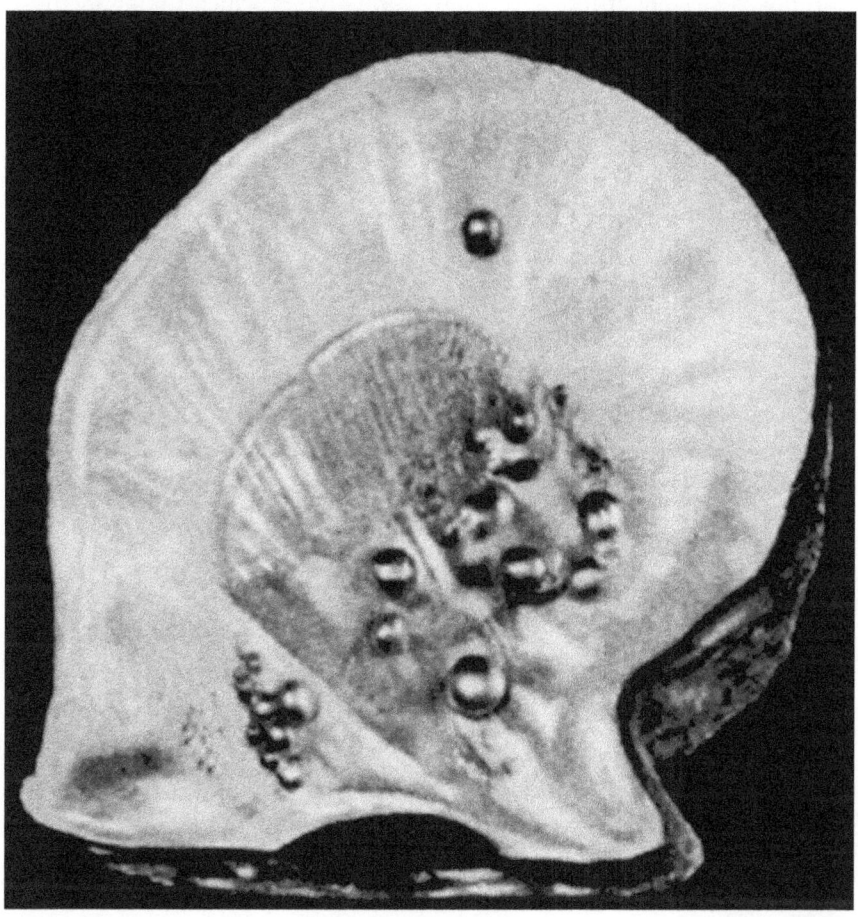

Cluster of pearls and baroque.

CHAPTER XXI
The Whale

In addition to the sentinel fish, some pearl-oysters have for sentry, and possibly as scavenger too, a very tiny red crayfish which finds sanctuary within the shell as does the sentinel fish. Another quaint "sentinel" is a soft-shelled crab hardly the size of a threepenny bit. In return for being the "eyes" of the oyster these small creatures receive a home, and protection from their own enemies.

Sometimes a diver sees a queer substance, somewhat resembling a gelatinous brick of honeycombed cheese, attached by strong threads to a pearl-shell oyster. This queer substance is a mass of shark's eggs which some cold, grey mother has anchored there.

The pearl-shell oyster gets many a thrill while living out its allotted span on the bottom of the sea. But not more than the diver who seeks it there. Nor has it more or greater dangers to face. The diver dreads the sting of the tiny fire-fish, no larger than a two-shilling piece. He dreads too the possibility of becoming entangled with a whale—perhaps larger than his own vessel. He may fall into a hole in the bottom of the sea. He may be caught, especially in the treacherous water of King Sound, in a whirlpool that suddenly forms beside him

When this calamity happens, the diver is sucked up and spun around ever faster, to be hurled away in a vortex which goes tearing across the ocean floor. The last spinning wrench is frightful; the life-line and air-pipe are strained to their limits while the vortex threatens to suck the flesh from the diver's very bones. Occasionally the frayed lines have broken under the strain and the diver drowned. But experience has taught divers to avoid the terrible passes in the Sound through which the water roars and foams and forms whirlpool after travelling whirlpool.

Life in the pearling fleets, however, is not all hard graft. There is relaxation and amusement now and then. Especially in the turtle season. The meat of the green turtle is relished, but because of the danger from sharks is strictly forbidden when a vessel is fishing. At other times the turtle is eagerly sought. His capture sometimes requires marvellous underwater skill that only certain islanders and experts among the pearling crews possess. Turtles are generally harpooned on the surface or caught on the beaches when ashore to lay their eggs. But there is no sport in this. Occasionally when below, a diver will come on a turtle asleep with its head under a rock so that a shark cannot bite it off. Perhaps it is only enjoying forty winks, for turtles breathe air and are often to be seen enjoying a long snooze on the warm sea surface. However, concerning this one with its head under a rock. No other vulnerable part is visible, the flippers being safely tucked under the huge shell that merges so well with the colour scheme of the bottom.

The diver signals and down to him comes a strong rope the end ready set in a running noose. He arranges this over the end of the shell then with one hand quickly tips up the shell while pressing hard as he whips the rope under and around the shell. It must be a sudden and strong movement. The partly "upended" turtle helps by surging forward under the stone, thus before it recovers from surprise the loop is around it and its flippers. No matter then how it backs out and struggles it is at the end of a rope attached to a lugger. That rope prevents the use of its flippers too and the diver stands aside and watches the grotesque struggles of the beast as it is hauled up through the water. Sometimes a cruising shark will attack the struggling turtle. The joke then may boomerang on the diver for a shark goes berserk once he tastes turtle blood.

Where skill and thrill comes in is during an underwater chase by skin divers, swimmers without diving-dress. Generally three men take part in the chase, all expert swimmers below water. On a calm, bright day a dinghy is put overboard and five men go paddling away. One man rows, the others stare overside. On such a day the bottom even sixty feet down may show pebbles clearly. The men quietly row over a "field" of sea-grass and spy a turtle down there nibbling at the grass. The dinghy is manoeuvred so that it comes up "behind" the turtle. One man noiselessly slips overboard, takes three deep, steady breaths, sinks with barely a ripple, turns over under water and shoots straight down. His comrades, their faces held right to the water surface, see him swim gracefully right atop of the turtle, then his legs sink down and he is astride it with his left hand gripping the shell behind the head, right hand gripping the tail of the shell.

With a startled swipe of his flippers the turtle is away. But the man on his back is the master by reason of leverage fore and aft. If he presses down while levering upwards at the tail the turtle must swim down; if he "hangs back in the saddle", that is, presses back on the tail while pulling upwards at the neck the turtle must rise. Likewise he can make the beast turn to right or left or keep on circling by the energetic sway of his body and the compelling pull of his arms at head and tail of shell.

The man's object is to force the turtle to circle as much as possible so that those above can follow his course with the dinghy. Up there, one man constantly shouts direction to the rower. In two minutes another man dives down and takes the ride of the man below. Imagine the skill required to swap seats on the back of that frantic turtle! Yet these experts do it—and gracefully. As the new-comer glides over the head of the rider his outstretched left hand grips the neck of the shell as the rider underneath slips from under him. In another two minutes the third man goes down.

So they tire the turtle out. The more frantically it swims; the sooner it exhausts itself; it wants to breathe all the quicker and yet cannot rise to breathe. Soon it begins to fret, for a turtle thus handicapped quickly loses heart, it wants to bury its head under a rock and just lie there. As it slows down, so the demon rider flogs it by jerking its shell, "see-sawing" it up and down and sideways until soon the turtle literally does not know whether it is standing on its head or its tail. It is a contest of reason understanding the laws of balance against blind strength.

When the turtle is tired out and gasping for want of air, the rider lifts at its neck shell while pressing down on its tail and the turtle comes to the surface to gasp and snort and blow like a grampus. Amid laughter it is turned on its back and a rope attached, or else it is manhandled into the dinghy. These turtles generally weigh two or three hundredweight. The shell may be four feet long and three feet broad.

Chosen men among the islanders of Torres Strait—the native skin divers—are particularly adept at thus riding a turtle under water. They can, like the experts among the Japanese divers, bring the turtle to the surface very quickly, should they secure their grip and seat. When the turtle plunges away the rider backs in the saddle with all his strength, and the turtle's frantic flippers swim it to the surface. Once there, the rider by leverage to right or left on the head and tail of the shell can steer it around and around the canoe or dinghy to the encouraging applause of his comrades. By pushing down the neck of the shell while holding up the tail he forces the turtle to dive again, makes it carry him a submarine trip under water until he himself wants breath, when he repeats the first manoeuvre.

But the divers who can accomplish this rather pride themselves upon tiring a turtle out under water.

Perhaps a diver when working below sees a browsing turtle. The crew are hungry for turtle meat, the diver is not getting much shell, a little fun with a chance of meat will not come amiss. He signals, and presently a swimmer comes down; wonderfully graceful is the human form when swimming deep below. The swimmers (they take it in turn to relieve one another) out of flashness swim astride the turtle around and around the diver until it is utterly exhausted, it is really "drowning". As the last swimmer glides off, the diver pulls on his life-line, make a running loop and slips it around the turtle; the crew haul on the life-line, and the diver comes up "on his air", that is, by inflating his suit.

Only the most expert underwater swimmers can thus man-handle a turtle. There are luggers in which not one of the crew can do it. Besides wonderful underwater swimming power and skill, knack is also needed; for several species of turtle have a sharp beak with which they would snap a man's fingers should he fumble that first instant grip; while the sharp shell edge of another species is liable to cut an inexperienced rider's legs. Further, these big creatures have great strength, and when they bolt they do so in no uncertain manner. Again, should the attacker not secure a quick grip his "ears are boxed" with terrific force, blows rain upon him from those powerful flippers, while the big body of the turtle heaves and plunges. Surprise and shock must be immediate, otherwise a large turtle would easily "get away" with a man. Even if he had secured a partial grip he could not guide it and would be forced to let go his hold. Though helpless and cumbersome while on land, the turtle in his native element is swift and graceful and surprisingly agile.

Once from a dinghy in the Coral Sea I watched three men capturing a turtle in the manner described. They were enjoying a glorious time when a shark came like a steely streak. The man on the turtle's back just seemed to slide off and disappear; but the next instant the turtle was being snapped to pieces.

There was no more turtle-hunting that day.

But let us back to the north-western Australian coast and another episode in a diver's life. It was a beautiful day in August 1916. The sea was lazily rolling in light blue waves suggestive of dreamy coolness. Except for the *Mina*, the *Sulituan*, under jib and mainsail, drifting along with the tide, seemed the only thing upon the ocean. One of Captain Gregory's fleet, she was as pretty a picture as a pearler could wish to see.

But Jitaro Naka the diver was not thinking about prettiness; his mind was upon the bottom of the sea and the shell he hoped to find there. For the bigger the take of shell the bigger is the diver's cheque when the lay-up season comes. And the Tables of Chance love the diver with money.

A wideawake, determined looking diver this Jitaro Naka; his clean-cut features, jet-black hair and closely cropped moustache were sharply matched by restless, keen brown eyes. To-day he still is one of the best divers in Broome.

When Naka, dressed in heavy woollens, dragged the thick canvas diving-suit on, he sat on the hatch while the tender, after calling sharply to the Koepangers, busied himself with the fitting on and screwing down of the weighty corslet. The Koepangers had the life-line and air-pipe ready coiled; the pump-crew down below stood in murmurous gossip by the pump with a sullen glance now and then at the Japanese. For throughout all the fleets the devils of race hatred were whispering hate and murder.

"Whale!" shouted the look out forrard. From the deck they saw the whales rolling along a mile away; one lazily spouted, and sunlight sparkled through the water spray. When whales blow after rising from below to breathe, the vapours forced through their spouts blow up water from the surface. The leviathans came sporting on, giants of strength, tireless swimmers of the sea.

Naka stood up and walked heavily to the side. "They are too far away to do any harm," he decided. "Come, fit on the helmet!"

"More better we wait a while!" advised the tender uneasily.

But Naka stepped impatiently overside and climbed down the ladder, resting his corslet on the side. The tender swung out the heavy weights and, bending overside, fitted them on the chest and back of Naka, then screwed down the helmet. "Click-clack! Click-clack!" started the air-pump. A Koepanger stood alertly with the air-pipe ready to run through his hands, the crew off watch stood watching the whales, the tender turned questioningly towards Naka who frowned resolutely. The tender screwed on the face-glass and Naka, throwing himself backward, sank slowly to a swirl of bubbles.

Naka came to rest at eighteen fathoms (one hundred and eight feet) and stood in the gloom adjusting his air-pressure. Then signalling "O.K." moved slowly forward, pushed by the tide.

The tide is an awesome thing. It carries people out to sea, strands whales ashore and fouls divers' life-lines. It changes at times whole vistas of the ocean floor. But it also brings food to the things of the sea; carries trees and shrubs and grass-seeds to barren sand-banks that they may grow into fertile islands. It does other things we do not dream of. A vast power, remorseless and elusive, is the tide.

The fishing was good. As Naka saw a shell he signalled and the tender instantly paid out more line, calling the air-pipe attendant to do the same, while he swung the lugger into the wind to hold her nearly motionless. With slack line thus making movement easy Naka would squat by the shell, seize it, wrench it from its grip on reef or plan and place it in his netted bag. That rough, slimy, weedy thing might contain a pearl of great price, destined, perhaps, to bring pleasure or sorrow to many.

But Naka straightened himself up; he knew that the shell probably contained only the muscular shellfish, a billion animalculae, and a miniature crab-sentry for its host. Not one pearl-shell oyster in five hundred contains a pearl.

He signalled, felt the tender hauling in the slack of the lines, then plodded on his grotesque way, excess and used air escaping in bubbles of wondrous beauty from his air-escape valve. His domed helmet with the deep sockets forming the side-glasses looked like the skull of some nameless monster groping half blindly in a world of light. Came a quiver of the life-line; rapid signals in Morse: "Whales are sporting around the *Mina*; one is diving. Come up!"

Behind his face-glass Naka frowned, he had seen many whales in his years of diving and none had yet troubled him seriously, his hand grasped the life-line and its message quivered into the fingers of the tender above.

"No! Shell is good. The whales will play a while then go away. Shell!" To the answering slackness of the line Naka squatted down and reached out for this shell. Not a movement as on land: if he had stooped or leaned forward, his chest weight with the push of the tide would have overbalanced him on his nose. Groping forward there among the grassy sea-growth he looked like a bear with shadowy arms wide stretched to hug. As he drew closer and that magnified helmet took shape he looked so terrifying that the sea things sped in alarm. But not all. Some circled a while, then deliberately tried to bite him, as a mischievous pup might nip a mastiff. Again he signalled "Shell!" and side-stepped towards it then squatted down, his gropings reminiscent of some mammoth crab of prehistoric times. A sea-snake whipped out of the grass and fled. Sea things are constantly hunting or being hunted—when not fighting or feeding.

Naka felt a strong tug that was not a signal and glancing up saw a gigantic belly, like a whitish-bottomed submarine, gliding effortlessly above. Two flukes moved lazily as a huge tail beat up and down with powerful, sea-saw motion. Naka's heart choked as that great body turned to glide around his air-pipe and he again felt the powerful tug as the pipe slid off a beating fluke. He seized his air-pipe and with puny strength held back on it as it slid along the great body now only thirty feet above. The pipe slid down the narrowing girth of the tail and Naka pulled away in mad fear as it neared the spreading flukes. It caught! The already uneasy whale instantly felt the strange pull and lashed powerfully down and up with a sideways motion of its tail.

Instantly Naka was jerked into mid-water, whirled round and round and jerked up and down at the end of a maddened whale's tail: he was transformed into a Catherine-wheel. The whale was like an animal with a can tied to its tail. And Naka was the can. Both were mad with terror. That great tail see-sawed up and down with Naka's legs spread-eagled by the leaden weights of his boots, his brain shrieking under fast varying water-pressures, as the whale whirled round and round.

Naka kept a death's grip on his air-pipe, the only definite thing his bolting nerves could feel. But through his reeling brain he still heard the air-pump clucking, then felt air missing in grunting spurts as the air-pipe was squeezed and pinched around that mammoth tail. Then instinct harnessed the beast and it sped straight off with Naka spinning around like a propeller. He knew nothing except terror: his grip on the air-pipe paralysed his arm for three days afterwards. Up above, the lugger's crew stared with a scared yell as the drifting vessel shuddered, then rapidly forged ahead. A man leapt to the tiller as the tender hauled in the life-line expecting the air-pipe to snap. Then, just at breaking-point the whale slipped away; Naka dropped to the length of the life-line; and the lugger slackened speed.

Through the buzzings in his head Naka gradually became aware of the tender's frantic signals.

"I am all right," he signalled back. "Stage."

Slowly they pulled him up, a stage at a time to drive probable paralysis from his veins. For from the surface Naka had dropped suddenly to depth with no chance of adjusting air-pressures. This is conducive to diver's paralysis. It was half an hour before they hauled him to the ladder. Rapidly the tender unscrewed the face-glass to stare into the bulging eyes, the puffed cheeks, the bleeding lips of the supremely grateful Naka.

It was a year later that the fleet of the Pearl King of all the northern seas found the "Star of the West", a beautiful pearl of a hundred grains weight, pear-shaped, of perfect colour, shape, and lustre. It came from a shell fished by the lugger *Esse* off Willy Creek only fifteen miles north of Broome. The fleets for years had sailed over that water, many divers had trudged over the ocean floor there — and now the *Esse* had found the Star of the West. The luck of the game. The shell was opened aboard the mother schooner *Ruby;* no one aboard had ever seen such a gem.

H. Sussman, pearl-buyer, offered ten thousand pounds for it in Broome. The pearl later was placed on exhibition in Melbourne, and the interest it created was so great that police had to regulate the crowds. This gem of the seas was later sold in London.

The Star of the West was fished by James Clarke's fleet, under the direction of J. T. C. Mackenzie. Clarke grew to be a pearl king whose fleets fished over six thousands miles of Australian waters. He operated a huge fleet too at the Aru Islands, in Dutch waters.

Few men in Australia, and not many in the world, could boast such a life of romance and success as Clarke, the Australian Pearl King.

CHAPTER XXII
The Shell-Opener on the "Donna Matilda"

It was a beast of a day, that third of October 1919. Lowering skies, dull water; even the sea-gulls had abandoned the lugger. She rolled with a slow, sliding motion that gave Tom Pritchard a headache. And a heartache too. Not that he regretted having left the shore-life of Broome. He had gone out with the fleets before and knew something of the life outside; he reckoned a shell-opener's life was just what you made of it—hell, or a rough life holding much of interest.

This was his first signed-on job as a shell-opener working for Francis Rodriquez, owner of the *Donna Matilda*. "Owner of the big pub in town, too," thought Pritchard glumly. He thought longingly of that cool bar and the cool drinks there. Thought hazily too of Con Gill the West India handyman, the heathen with the queer eyes and the drawly voice and the knowing smile who had assured him he would have luck on this cruise. Pritchard shrugged. Luck! Why, this was a beast of a trip, an awful life.

Sitting hunched up on the hatch he gazed distastefully around the *Donna Matilda*. Cramped little thing! Her decks could do with a wash if only to get rid of the smell of stale shellfish. Just look at the rigging-festooned with drying shellfish like strings of onions. For those sun-dried muscles of the pearl-shell oyster the crew get thirty shillings a bag, landed in Singapore. Ugh! fancy eating the smelly stuff! These coloured men, too, looking so beastly healthy while trying to hide the fact that not a man of them nursed a headache. Look at that solemn Malay there like a Buddha! Bin Mahomet, the quiet Malay they called him, seeing all while apparently seeing nothing. What a life! Without even a white man to talk to! He grimaced, and stared out over the bows.

The *Donna Matilda* was north of Port Hedland drifting along to Condon, meanwhile working to fill in time. She was one of the three last of forty vessels that had already sailed to the shore creek rendezvous.

Peter, the Christian diver, stood at the tiller, gazing straight ahead as if unaware that the master had a headache. Peter was seeking a good "drift", trying to bring the lugger over a part of the ocean-bed that might contain good shell. He knew from experience down below that there was a likely looking place on the ocean floor here somewhere, if only he could locate it. The Malay crew were gossiping forrard, chuckling over some coloured joke. Pritchard intercepted a frowning glance at the bent back of the Japanese tender. Momentarily he remembered the rumour among all the fleets of big trouble brewing between the Japanese and Koepangers. He wondered whether it would ever break out into serious trouble. It might go hard with the few whites, if a bloodthirsty battle flared up at sea.

A plop! from the water, a silver bolt flying overhead, the thump! as it struck the mainsail and a thud! as it struck the deck chorused by a shout from leaping men as the big fish bounced in beautiful contortions of its firm body. They were striking at it with anything at hand, shouting and springing aside from the snap of its champing jaws. It was Bin Mahomet who threw a blanket over it and with the one movement tossed it down the hold. To the hollow thumpings of the big fish they danced in delight. A sixty-pounder kingfish brings pleasure to any crew.

Those big kingfish leap from the sea with a flip of the tail and go hurtling through the air sometimes a surprising distance, at a surprising height. A beautiful sight but, occasionally, slightly dangerous. For the speed with which they leave the water, backed up by their weight, gives a great impact made dangerous by their champing teeth. Pritchard remembered an unlucky man standing by the tiller some time ago, whom a hurtling kingfish had caught on the jugular. He bled to death in moments. That, of course, was a mischance in a million.

Noisily the crew trooped back to their places, retailing the latest kingfish joke on Bernard Bardwell's lugger. The fish had leapt in between the foremast rigging on the starboard side, landed on the cabin top, shot off, and struck the tender on the back knocking him overboard. Forgetting all about the life-line he clambered aboard roaring:

"Mutinous dogs! Who been do that? Who been hittem me! I break him head. I kill him!"

Pritchard wished a breeze would spring up. The ocean was like a stale river covered with scummy patches of red and yellow stuff like spilled paint. Fish eggs, possibly. The lugger was just drifting along with the tide and this smell of shellfish and Chinese sauce and onions and curry and rice. Ugh! Cockroaches crawled over a man while he slept, they chewed his toe-nails and nibbled the hair above his ears. What a life! He stood up; rolled down the scuttle; rolled into bunk, and forgot all about it.

Tom Pritchard slept the clock around. Then awoke and groaned; yawned and groaned again. He stretched, and bumped his arms on the cabin walls. "What a dog's box!" he growled. His head was better, but he felt he still had it. Turning out of bunk he climbed up the scuttle for a breath of fresh air. Near sunset! An oily sea under a lowering sky. The lugger drifting aimlessly, as if she had nowhere to go. "Click-clack! click-clack!"

went the air-pump with clear, maddening monotony. The two Malays working so rhythmically grimaced one at the other. Easy to see the white master still had a headache. A beauty!

The Japanese tender was giving all his attention to the life-line, Bin Mahomet was paying out the air-pipe. Pritchard envied Peter the diver away in the cool depths below. He turned distastefully from the hold where beside the pump the cook was bending over the fire pot.

A pile of shell lay on the deck, sent up from below by Peter during the day's drift. Pritchard frowned down at the big grey shells with the sea-growths, weeds and coral tubes and sea-plants withering upon them. The oysters inside were gasping too. Squatting by the heap were several of the crew, each with a tomahawk, chipping rough stuff from the shells, making them ready for the shell-opener's knife.

"May as well open a few," thought Pritchard dismally. "It will give me something to do before tea." In melancholy vein he sat on the deck, picked up his opener's knife and a shell. Holding the "heel" of the shell from him he worked the thin-bladed knife around to the right, and thus cut the tough muscle as close to the shell as possible to avoid damaging any pearl that might be in the fish. His chance of a pearl was one in a thousand; doing the job mechanically, he never thought of a pearl. As he cut the muscle the bivalve fell apart, only the gristly hinge holding the halves together. He sniffed at the dirty looking grey mass of fish in the centre with its edging of transparent flesh that magnifies a pearl on the rare occasion when it holds one. Distastefully, with groping fingers he went through the meat for any baroque that might be there. He hated the feel of the slimy, squashy stuff. If it had had a pearl or baroque hidden inside it he would have felt it like a piece of shot. He threw the meat overboard, glanced once at the glistening mother of pearl of the opened shell, and threw it to the deck. There was no pearl or blister or baroque fastened to the beautiful inner shell.

Copper-fish sped out from the lugger, to the bottom of which they had attached themselves by suction, and hungrily ate the oyster he had thrown overboard. Lazy, fat, and overfed are the copper-fish. Pritchard wished he could make a living as easily as they. Wearily he picked up another oyster. Big oysters these; their shells worth a hundred and ninety pounds per ton.

Tom Pritchard felt utterly miserable. He did not want to ever drink again. Wondered how ever white men could live this life. Fancy a man living in a greasy little boat, his only company Asiatic men! Tossing and pitching day and night; opening shell from daylight to dark; sleeping from dark to daylight ...

His heart thumped; he stared as if mesmerized; every nerve was tingling with a crescendo of unbelieving joy. He knew that every eye was on him: the tender standing aft so religiously minding the life-line, Bin Mahomet at the air-pipe, the Malays at the pump, the Koepangers squatting near by, chipping at their shells with the tomahawk. Every head bent over its work, but covertly watching the shell-opener too. Just as the crew *always* watch the shell-opener. Pritchard heaved a sickly sigh. He gazed vacantly into space while his fingers worked the pearl in between them, the beautiful pearl that had rolled in the flesh of the oyster at the touch of his knife. With a grimace he flung the shell aside and getting up went to the scuttle and disappeared below. The crew grinned broadly. The shell-opener was fed up.

In the cabin, Pritchard opened his hand. His heart was thumping; his face transfigured; he was trembling. The pearl was slightly larger than a pea, and perfectly round. It was beautiful—his heart was singing with joy. The pearl showed several tiny white spots as if lightly dipped in gravy. Otherwise, the moist sheen of its coat gleamed upon his hand. To get rid of those spots would require but a delicate skinning. So far as careful examination by the eye could tell, it was a gem. Pritchard felt the happiest man in the world; he laughed silently at the cabin walls. He wanted every one to be happy too.

The *Donna Matilda* sailed in over the Condon Banks that night. Forty little mast-head lights were riding at the anchorage; voices and snatches of song made the night musical. Early next morning a dinghy came from Morry Lyons's lugger with an invitation for breakfast. Pritchard accepted with alacrity. Down in the cabin, he showed the pearl. Lyons drew a deep breath.

"A beauty, Tom," he murmured. "Some men are born lucky. By Jove, won't Rodriquez be pleased! This will put him right on his feet. He needs a godsend like this; needs it badly." He weighed the pearl carefully. "Forty-one and a half grains," he murmured. "And only a few grains must come off; it will take very little cleaning. It's a beauty, Tom."

The fleets sailed for Broome, for half the crews were down with influenza. In Broome, seventy vessels lay at anchor, the crews helpless. North along the coast, over two hundred other vessels were fishing in misery or laid up beside islands or in tidal creeks.

Pritchard took the pearl to Rodriquez who went wild with delight. Mrs Rodriquez's hands trembled as she laughed over the pearl. Con Gill looked on with shining eyes.

"I tell you true!" he murmured.

They took the pearl straight to Elles to be cleaned. That dusky expert smiled with the pleasure of a connoisseur as he examined this thing that awaited but the magic of his fingers to flower into beauty.

"You has the luck," he murmured. "Mine will be the pleasure to clean."

With delicate instruments he took several skins off it, lessening its weight by one and a half grains. When polished it weighed forty grains, a perfect "round": perfect in shape, colour, and lustre.

"Worth a hundred pounds a grain!" Elles murmured.

It was sold through the bank to Habib the pearl-buyer for four thousand pounds.

Pritchard's commission was two hundred pounds and a three months' trip to Perth.

"A shell-opener's life has its moments!" declared Tom as friends farewelled him on his holiday south.

Elles the Cingalee was on the highway to becoming rich, cleaning pearls on commission, buying and selling. He might make ten—two hundred—pounds in a few hours' work.

He chuckled now as he picked up a pearl he was about to clean. Slowly he turned the pearl in his fingers, for he wanted to enjoy his inner mirth to the full. He would work on no pearl unless he could give it full concentration.

He was chuckling at a memory of a well-known buyer. Elles had bought a pearl from him, a "drop", for forty pounds. Then the buyer laughed heartily, considering he had sold the famous pearl-cleaner a pearl that was hardly worth thirty-five pounds. So thoroughly did he enjoy having caught Elles that he shouted champagne to his friends.

But the dark-skinned man took the joke in good part, then took the pearl to his den. And as he bent over it his eyes saw things that no other man could see in a pearl, his finger-tips felt a hidden sheen that no other fingers could feel.

He cleaned that pearl. And when it was finished he leaned back and smiled at it in silence. Lucky man to love his work and smile like that. Several days later he took the pearl to that buyer.

"For sale," he said with a smile.

"Ah, ha, ha! Want to get back some of that good cash you lost on that drop the other day, eh! Well, this certainly is an improvement."

He bought back for three hundred and thirty pounds the drop he had sold for forty.

Elles sighed; he had had his laugh. He bent over his table and concentrated upon this pearl. It was a drop, too, a better one than he had resold to the buyer, a very nice twenty-grain drop. Sitting cross-legged, pipe in mouth, the owner watched as Elles deftly worked at the pearl with his delicately sharpened, little three-cornered file. It was going to be a quick job. No two pearls are alike, and each skin is different. Some have thick skins, some thin; some are dirty, perhaps spotted; perhaps there is a tiny crinkle or a ridge or pimple or pin-hole, in the skin. In twenty minutes Elles had peeled down to a good skin, a soft lustre. He worked carefully now, lest a mistake, a cut too deep, should lessen the value of the pearl.

Elles straightened up with a sigh, and laid down the tool. He took a silk handkerchief and while talking, with a hardly noticeable soft movement, kept polishing the pearl. Then he smiled:

"You has good luck; but not the *real* good luck. It is a nice pearl; but there is left a tiny blemish. Let the buyer take the risk. You will get a good price for it as it is. If I take off the blemish it may grow larger underneath and — you lose."

The owner nodded.

"Your opinion is the best in the world with me." He paid the commission and took the pearl straight to a French buyer. The Frenchman did not speak the best of English but he knew a pearl when he saw one. He weighed it ... twenty grains.

"How much?"

"Thirteen pounds per grain."

The buyer took his cheque book and without argument wrote out a cheque for six hundred pounds. He had thought the price asked was thirty pounds per grain. The owner took the cheque, nodded "So long", and walked out.

"Well," he reflected, "I've learnt something of the real value of pearls. He gave me thirty pounds a grain without bickering for what I thought was worth thirteen pounds. I believe I could have got fifty pounds per grain. The difference above the price I expected is going to mean a Ford car for me."

And it did.

While now ashore, at the time of the big tides the Japanese were remembering the price that is paid for pearls. The Tsuki Miro (Festival of the Lanterns), in remembrance of and in greeting to the spirits of the dead, was being celebrated. Beautiful lanterns fashioned by love and long labour hung from all the Japanese homes and business quarters. Under a dreamy night the cemetery to a thousand dead was like a handful of stars upon the land; tombstones and graves glowed with lanterns. Upon the carefully tended graves sat the silent mourners, while among the tombstones moved shadowy comrades. From bottles set in the cement work incense-sticks smouldered mistily. From tree branches lit lanterns gently swayed. Little women and children swathed in kimonos of lovely colours were there communing with the spirits of their dead. On the graves were plates and jars of rich foods, bottles of spirits of all kinds, offerings to the departed. For it is believed that at the full moon in August, as the sun goes down and the moon rises, the souls of the dead return to earth and mingle with their friends until midnight. For this sacred night the fleets return to Broome. Reverently but joyously the crews come to the trysting-place. Bunches of purple bougainvillaea and sweet-scented jasmine perfumed the night air. The massed flowers and lanterns vied with the beautiful silks of the kimonos.

Standing silently by in spotless white were the pearlers, business people, and officials of the town, guests every year at this Festival of the Lanterns. On a platform in the centre of the cemetery a Japanese chanted a dirge to solemn beat of drummers while young Japanese girls danced with fans and slow, stately movements of body and feet. The fans expressing sympathy with the relatives of those who had gone.

From a velvet sky a full moon shed a silvery radiance over all, brightening the slumbrous glow in the eyes of the black-haired girls. To a rumble of drums, a swaying of fans and bodies, a fluttering and a chanting, the dance suddenly ended.

The dancers faded away, and a circle was formed. Into this leapt a man stripped to the waist, the moonlight rippling over his muscular body. He stared straight ahead as he swung a sword that hissed and gleamed in circles to his hissing chant. Behind him danced children with fans whirling to the circling of the sword. When this dance ended, the elder Japanese gravely invited the Australians to dine. All then sat down to a rich table under the lanterns and the moon.

At long last, all trooped to the foreshore. Many luggers were out on the waterway, many were drawn up in trenches on the beaches. Along the foreshore came men carrying large models of luggers, exact to the tiniest detail. Their sails were marked in Japanese characters with directions to heaven. Reverently the tiny vessels were placed in the water. A spirit of a diver was supposed to sail each vessel, and if it glided safely out to sea, then all was well. But should any catastrophe wreck it then those ashore lamented, for the diver's spirit was in trouble.

Girls came forward with little lighted lanterns which they tied to the masts. Women had prepared many foods in tiny bundles; these and petals of flowers were loaded in the holds.

The tide was turning. All watched silently. A faintest breeze, it might have been a breath from heaven, gently swept over the land, and sighed away to sea.

Men gently pushed the little luggers away. Slowly the tiny sails filled; the vessels strained to the gathering strength of the tide. Under the vanishing moon, they made for the open sea. Tense eyes watched them. Little ladies in kimonos bowed a last farewell, while to the accompaniment of tiny hammers upon bells they sang, very softly, very sweetly, a song tremulous with sadness.

Straight and true the little fleet glided to clear Entrance Point, out where the big luggers sail.

"Ah!" Two of the tiny vessels had collided; slowly they began to sink. Another came drifting helplessly back, like a soul without a guiding star.

But the lights of the others gleaming like fire-flies vanished into the great unknown.

Japanese cemetery in Broome.

CHAPTER XXIII
Prospecting the Ocean Floor

Fortune smiled at last on Bernard Bardwell for, in October 1930, brother Beresford found a beautiful pearl during a lucky cruise in the *Raymond*. A full double button, ninety grains weight uncleaned, this big fellow gave them a wonderful thrill. Almost encircling it, however, was a dint in the skin as if some sea-imp had drawn heavily around it with a blunt lead-pencil. And equally placed around this indentation were seven distinct, apparent pin-pricks. Bardwell, with Robinson the bank manager, took it to Elles. Carefully the pearl magician examined it, turning it between his finger-tips as if it were a living thing. He put it down with a mingled sigh and smile.

"You may have thousands. You may have nothing. Impossible to tell whether that dint goes right into the gem. If not, it is worth thousands. If so, it is worth nothing. You can sell it as a gamble to a buyer, now, for hundreds. But if I clean it and the dint comes out, you make thousands. If the mark stays in, you lose everything."

Bardwell and his brother were experiencing a long-continued run of misfortune. They needed a few hundred pounds.

"Clean it," said Bardwell.

Elles smiled—almost sighed.

"They almost always take the gamble," he murmured. "I have seen high hopes and disappointments in this little room." He picked up the pearl and reached for a tiny tool. As he bent over the pearl he almost whispered: "I work on the hearts of men, as well as the hearts of pearls."

He held it in his left hand by forefinger and thumb, occasionally using the second finger. His right hand wielded that tiny three-cornered file, the tips of its three edges most carefully sharpened. He had a glass screwed over his eye; his face expressed intense concentration. Delicately he proceeded to shred its outer skin from the pearl. Quietness possessed the office. Somewhere, from far in the house, there came the busy ticking of a clock. After half an hour he laid down the pearl, sat back, took the glass from his eye, and smiled. That smile smoothed the tense face to normal.

"So far, it is well," he murmured. "Just one petal from the rose. But too early yet to see into its heart." For half an hour he talked softly of happenings in that little office; experiences when fortune hung on a hair; when the edges of his tool seemed cutting into the very breaths of men. As he talked, he gently massaged the muscles of his hands. Then he reached for the eyeglass, the pearl, and the tool. The clock could again be heard ticking within the house.

In another half-hour he laid aside his work, massaging his hands. "Come again to-morrow morning," he said. "I must not overstrain. One little nick too much, and you lose a thousand pounds. One tiny nick too little and you lose a thousand."

Towards the end of the following morning's sitting they saw the shadow of a flicker on the tense face, they watched his face as he was watching the pearl. At last he smiled:

"I think you will have luck!"

Bardwell sighed his relief.

"Congratulations!" said the bank manager heartily.

On a platter of mother of pearl were the tiny peelings from the pearl, little gleaming shreds of pearl-skin, four grains' weight of them. But the pearl itself glowed there now, a gem of moonlit loveliness tinged with the faintest pink.

"A beauty," exclaimed the bank manager. "Rosae too!"

Its loveliness was now only marred by a trace of one pin-prick.

"Come along the morning after to-morrow," said the Cingalee wearily. "I finish it then. I work for no one to-morrow."

"Why not work to-morrow, Mr Elles?" inquired the bank manager curiously.

"I massage my hands, bathe them in water. I think big commission in this."

They returned on the appointed day. Elles took up his tool. Bardwell shivered inwardly.

"Here goes another grain!" he thought. No, not quite half a grain. After long examination, with touches such as a fairy surgeon might have envied, tiny powdery flakes slid from the pearl down the point of the tool. The last pin-prick had vanished. Elles laid down the gem with a sigh.

"Five thousand pounds," he murmured.

The pearl, cleaned, weighed eighty-six and a half grains. The bank sold it for Bardwell for four thousand pounds. He tried for another two hundred to cover Elles's commission. The envelope came back marked:

"Four thousand pounds. Not a penny more."

Bardwell accepted. Next day came cable advice from London of the fall in the price of pearls.

Mark Rubin the Pearl King died, leaving a large fortune. Captain Gregory was busy building up his fleet. New pearl-beds were being found north up the coast right to the Timor Sea. The Broome fleets were all prospering, the little town still was growing. The *Gracie* still sailed the seas, an envied ship, for she had prospered exceedingly; the crew had now come to look on Tomumuki the ghost as the ship's mascot. To date the *Gracie* has lived out many a blow and seven willy-willys, and still takes the sea from the post of Cossack.

Occasionally there came a much better known visitor from another world—the "Bishop's Ghost." One night Bishop Trower sat up in bed and stared at the visitant beside him. He thought the man had come in a case of urgent sickness.

"What is it?" he inquired sleepily. On receiving no reply he asked irritably, "What is the matter with you? Can you not talk!"

Then he stared at the figure, attired apparently in rabbinical robes. With a shock he remembered other people having seen this figure. Slowly he swung his legs over the bed, shuffling for his slippers, staring hard.

"Just tell me who you are," he said, "and what do you want?"

He stood up and advanced towards the figure which backed away, then turned and glided through the wall. The bishop stood, staring. Then thoughtfully went back to bed.

Otto Blackman had described this figure when using this very room while the bishop was away in London; two bank managers had seen the visitant, other people, clear-headed people too.

The visitor was to come again until the bishop was familiar with it. He met the presence face to face at times when walking his veranda on moonlit evenings. At each meeting the bishop had momentarily to still the eerie shock to his nerves—overcome the "pins and needles" at his scalp. The feeling would quickly pass, then he would stare at his visitor, intensely interested to see that the figure appeared exactly a man, right to the moment when it would vanish through the wall.

Conard Gill was happy, experiencing adventures ashore. Hardly an intrigue in Asiatic town of which Conard Gill did not know the ins and outs; no scheme concocted by the big "coloured heads", the details of which he did not know at least something. His job had proved exactly what he made it, a congenial task for life. His evenings now were devoted to a new love-affair in which were thrills enough, for here again under the direct penalties he was forbidden to come near the girl.

The pleasure of outwitting certain strict guardians, however, was marred by the death of Bin Mahomet, the quiet Malay, to whom Con and Sebaro and Francis Paddy had been warmly attached for years. Bin Mahomet was employed as seaman by Alf Locke whose schooner was sailed north to Beagle Bay. While there, Bin Mahomet had arranged with an aboriginal woman ashore to do his washing and had promised her that within a week of the schooner's arrival in Broome he would bring her back a bag of flour. Believing, as all the crew did, that the schooner was sailing for Broome to return immediately with stores, Bin had made this promise under a solemn oath of death should he break faith.

The schooner returned to Broome, loaded up, and received orders to sail for new fishing-grounds. Bin Mahomet came to Locke in a great state.

"Master, woman do some washing for me at Beagle Bay! I promise I send her down a bag of flour."

"You can't now, Bin. All the boats have gone out; none will be going to Beagle Bay for a fortnight," explained Locke.

"Boss, supposem I can't send that woman bag of flour—I die."

"Nonsense. Don't be silly. A schooner will be sailing in a fortnight. Then you can send your bag of flour."

In three days Bin Mahomet was dead.

It is a queer trait, that fatalism of the coloured races dominant enough to cause death should the man wish it. Practically all coloured races, the Australian aboriginal included, possess this power of self-willed suicide. They will die, too, through being convinced that they are fated to die. Instances again and again occur among the pearling crews. Bin Mahomet was hardly dead when a mate of his stabbed a shell-opener on the seas. He thought he would be sentenced to be hanged. All he would say was, "I'll be dead before they try me!"

He was. But the shell-opener recovered.

When working at the bottom of the sea several reassuring sounds come down to the diver, distinctness apparently depending on depth and on the direction in which the wind is blowing the sound against the air-pump; and, possibly, according to the manner in which currents are vibrating against that portion of the air-pipe under water. Actually, the air-pipe appears to be a sort of aerial. The distinct but muffled click-clack click-clack of the air-pump comes rhythmically into the helmet as the diver slowly sinks, with the noisy gurgling of air-bubbles escaping from his air-escape valve. While working in shallow water this sharp click-clack click-clack and quarrelling gurgle is constantly with him.

But as the diver glides into deeper water the click-clack softens distantly while the increasing pressure of water puts a brake on the speed of the escaping air-bubbles, compressing their size and muffling their expostulations. At great depth, their faintly whispering murmur is distinguishable only to listening ears. He is then truly in a great silence;

imprisoned in a terrifying loneliness; moving uncertainly in a dim waterlight.

If working in the clearer light at moderate depth, and a steamer passes by, even though some distance away, the diver may hear the throbbing of the propeller quite distinctly. Probably the vibration carries the sound towards the diver, particularly when the tide is running from the propeller towards him, somewhat as the wind carries sound on the earth. He may hear, too, his own vessel lifting anchor should the anchor have been down. Strangely enough, many sounds occur on deck that he cannot hear. Only when the sounds take place in water, or are connected with the water, can he hear them, and but very few indeed of these.

Should a large fish charge close by he may hear the vicious "swish!" as the vibrations trill against his metal helmet. Should he kick coral or a stone with his heavy boot he "feels" the noise. Should a fish dart against his corslet or helmet he hears the "ping!" That is about all. He is encased within his dress like a grub within a cocoon. Should an accident happen—anything go wrong with his little man-made apparatus—then the laws regulating that underwater world rush in to destroy him.

The expert tender, who is regulating the ship while being responsible to the diver below, knows to a considerable extent what the diver is doing, provided depth, tide currents, and other conditions be favourable. He feels the signal tug that means "Slack away the life-line" when the diver wishes to reach for a shell. According to the tug of the signals which direct him how to manoeuvre the life-lines and the ship he knows to a large extent just in what position the diver is working, what obstacles probably are in his way, and what will be the best manoeuvre to help him. Ceaselessly his sympathetic fingers on the life-line should be in touch with the movements of the groping man below. Oddly enough, the diver can sometimes tell what is going on in the ordinary ship life above, by sense of smell.

"Start fire now!" he thinks as he sniffs the galley smoke. Later, as he bends to pick up a shell, "Huh! curry and rice for dinner!" He can smell the peeling of onions, and other little preparations for the meal. He can do this because these various scents have been sucked down the air-pipe by the air-currents from the pump. Movement vibrations from the sea bottom send messages to the man above, while air-currents and vibration report events to the man below.

In the latest of modern diving-apparatus this carrying of odours down the air-pipe is practically eliminated because of the danger accompanying these odours. Only cool, filtered, fresh air should reach the diver through the air-pipe. When the diver detects foreign smells through this modern apparatus, something probably is amiss. In it an engine is used and should any mechanical defect occur poisonous gases may be sent down to the diver, or he may not get a sufficient stream of pure air. In either case he is soon affected by breathing CO_2. This brings on asphyxia. He works on, feeling more and more drowsy; probably not realizing anything is wrong, he gradually lapses into unconsciousness. Death may follow from asphyxiation. Fumes from a leaky exhaust caused the deaths of two men within recent months.

The master pearlers work to British Admiralty requirements. With modern apparatus one cubic foot of free air per atmosphere per minute is pumped down to the diver. Thus a diver working in twenty fathoms is supplied with six cubic feet of air per minute; he would actually be using under two cubic feet, the other four cubic feet is "free air" flowing through his helmet. On double connection engine vessels the compressor has a capacity of fourteen cubic feet of air per minute and the air-containers hold a reserve of an hour's supply of air so that if anything should go wrong the diver has a large safety margin.

With our present knowledge of decompression and pressures, hygiene and fresh foods, currents and depths, tides, coastline, and atmospheric disturbances, fatalities are not common now on the pearling-grounds. But the diver's life still hangs upon his own and the tender's ceaseless vigilance. Two divers when they meet below may enjoy a *tête-à-tête*. They stand close together, their helmets touching if possible. Each shuts his air-escape valve, then they can talk and hear intelligibly. Conversation is limited though, for the dresses immediately begin to inflate and the divers begin to rise. By allowing air to escape they can come together again, and by shutting the air-escape valve may resume their conversation until they again begin to rise. But conversation is not only strictly limited; it is dangerous, too, for the tide may foul their life-lines. They draw apart again as they slowly sway up from the ocean floor; a strikingly white hand flutters up to each helmet valve; they sink down again; wave in farewell, then slowly drift away. The highly trained diver must know the ocean floor as a prospector knows country. As the prospector learns from experience among what rocks he may expect gold, so the diver must learn the "indicators" of pearl-shell, the type of bottom on which it lives, the "biology" of those areas of the sea floor favourable to its growth.

The diver must also be capable of sailing the ship while down below; that is, he must understand the manoeuvres he wishes to signal the master or tender above so that they can help him in his work. He must visualize the vessel above; remember the strength and direction of the wind, the changing conditions of tides and currents; be familiar with the elements above and below. He must know whether, under any given conditions operating both above and below, his signals can be carried out. If he masters these and numerous other problems in from four to six years he is a good man.

Should the diver as he drifts over the ocean floor come upon likely looking bottom he signals, descends on bottom, then walks about seeking the shell. If he is unable to locate any by sundown, the tender drops a buoy overboard with a red flag attached. Next morning the lugger sails back and the diver resumes his search for the shell-bed.

Romance and heartache are in this, as with the prospector on land. After long search the diver may find a reef not only rich in shell, but in baroque and with occasional pearls. That night, a storm drives the lugger away; or, if she has sought anchorage, tempestuous weather holds her to the coast for a week. Returning, the lugger cannot locate the buoy; it is washed away. The diver goes down in as near the correct locality as he can estimate. But to find that tiny reef on the vast sea floor, with no landmarks to guide him, is like looking for a needle in a haystack. He never finds that reef again.

On the other hand, luck and a thoughtful diver sometimes juggle successfully with fortune—as the goldseeker does on land. Mackenzie and Lyons's vessels by chance dropped on a patch of small and worm-eaten shell, but it carried a high percentage of baroque. Very quickly the vessels were filled with this acceptable shell. But they had no schooner or tender vessel on which to unload the shell, and so must sail to Broome. Could they locate this particular area of shell-bearing bottom again?

The shell occurred on a narrow strip of bottom upon which grew dwarf sea "trees," an ebony bush. Hamaguchi the diver had a brain-wave. On board one lugger was a lot of Turkey twill, red cloth. The divers tore this into thin strips; then, widely scattered, went down and every here and there tied a strip of red cloth to a bush, over a fairly considerable area. On return from Broome, the vessels spread out over the ocean opposite their nearest landmark. The divers went down and proceeded to "comb" the ocean floor. In a few days a diver came on a bush from which a red ribbon streamed out with the tide. He signalled his tender, the tender ran up his flag, and the other luggers came sailing to concentrate in search. The patch of shell was soon found.

As the experienced prospector rides over many miles of country and knows at a glance that it is useless seeking for mineral there, so the prospecting lugger sails over many miles of ocean. But neither diver nor tender can see the bottom from the deck. So, in cruising for new grounds, in an attempt to save time they endeavour to tell by the swing of the lead whether it is worth while sending the diver down. In the partly hollowed bottom of the lead is soap and as the lugger sails along a crew hand is continually swinging the lead. When it touches the ocean floor some fragment of the bottom adheres to the soap; perhaps it .is a blob of mud, the leaf of a weed, a splinter of coral, just sand, or gravel; whatever it is, the tender can tell at a glance whether the bottom there is a likely spot on which to find the pearl-shell oyster.

Only years of experience and keen observation, of course, enable a diver and tender to do that.

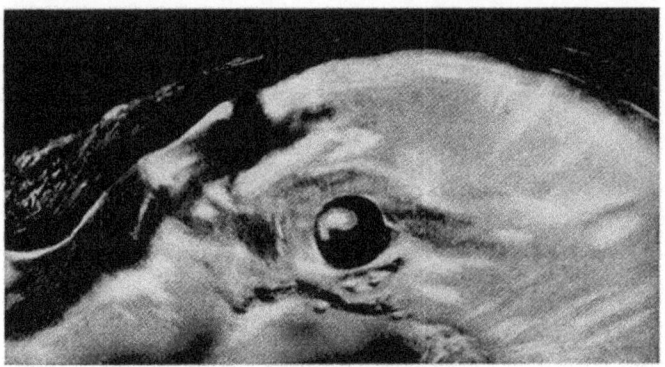

Williamson's £ 1600 pearl.

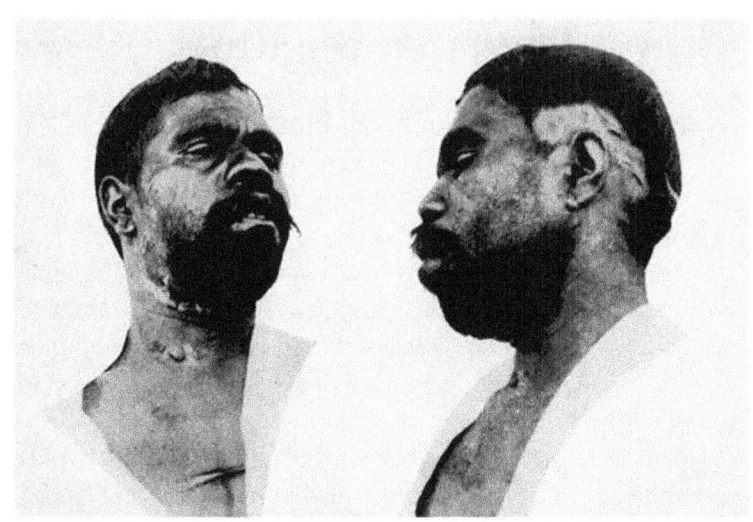

"Treacle"

Sail-fish. Note two baby sucker-fish.

CHAPTER XXIV
The Japanese Riots

It was December of 1920. All the fleets were snug in Broome or in sheltered coastal creeks, being reconditioned during the lay-up season. Christmas Day was near; all the whites were cheery.

But there was an ominous quiet over Asiatic town and among the big foreshore camps of the coloured seamen. Constant comings and goings too; concentrated movement at the Japanese Club; a threatening air among the sullen groups of men collecting in scattered rendezvous; a scared look in the faces of the women.

"Trouble is brewing," mused Conard Gill. "Some throats will be cut; bad blood will run. So long as it is not Con Gill's blood I don't care."

He was coming from work by the back way unexpectedly early one evening musing thus when he saw a Malay shrink away from the back fence. Con crouched down, his eyes flashing.

"He's wearing a red turban!" he thought. "Red for blood—Con Gill's blood!"

Creeping through his secret entrance he glanced expectantly around. The row of bottles that served as a border path, their necks buried deep in the soil, attracted his attention. Tentatively he felt a bottle—it was loose. He pulled it out and grinned at the charm down in the hole. In malicious relief he hooked it out with a piece of wire, replaced the bottle and walked softly down the path. His pet pigeons came to his feet. He crooned while feeding them, a gleam in his eyes. They were fine fat pigeons; he used their blood for charms.

Next afternoon while the Malay was at work Con planted the charm under the man's pillow and left—without leaving tracks. For when he walked from the charmer's cottage he dribbled wheat behind him and the fowls scratched his tracks away.

That night, the Malay dreamed fearsome things—and awoke next morning to find the charm under his pillow. He went livid with horror. So Con gradually won the sinister reputation of a doctor capable of transporting black magic through the air.

In the evening, chuckling to himself, he slipped out the back way: freshly bathed, every hair on his head sleekly combed, love-light in his eyes. A new love, with danger in the attaining. Somehow, the ex-bosun's sweethearts all brought trouble in their tantalizing trail.

A sudden hoarse, menacing roar made him pause. It came from the massed shadow of two hundred men running on bare feet. Con stepped into the shadows. With one concerted, savage shout the men raced by. All were armed with clubs, some were iron spiked.

"Skin and hair will be flying soon!" muttered Con as he hurried after them. "The signs are set for blood-plenty blood!"

Broome was at the pictures when the Japanese-Koepanger outbreak stormed through the town. Sergeant Spry and a constable jumped into a motor and raced to Mackay's foreshore camp as a hundred and fifty Japanese armed with clubs came shouting:

"Down with the Koepangers! The Koepangers are killing the ·Japanese!"

The sergeant and constable jumped amongst them, and after a hot ten minutes succeeded in pacifying them. Wiping hot brows they watched with relief the lowering of clubs as the excited men gradually returned towards the town. But a breathless runner came with tidings that other Japanese were swarming through the Asiatic quarter. The sergeant raced by motor but when passing the Japanese Club saw four hundred men arriving with clubs. He swerved the car and jumped out to harangue the excited men and was just getting them in hand when shouts in Japanese came from the town. The Japanese seized their clubs and rushed out into Napier Terrace pouring on as they mixed with other mobs racing into Dampier Terrace.

The unorganised Koepangers were taken in the flank and scattered, several groups cut off from their mobs were flying for protection into the bungalows and hotels. The Japanese Club was swarming with men, while fresh Koepangers came howling in from the foreshore camps through the town, mad with excitement as they rushed in mobs lacking the organization of the Japanese. In a laneway two antagonistic mobs clashed with an animal-like howl. Clubs swung to thuds and curses as panting men went down, until the beaten mob broke and fled, the victors howling after them. Dark shadows remained, some groaned, crawling weakly away. Others lay senseless. Sonuke Kusano would never see Japan again. Con gave a hand to Francis Paddy who with bloodied face was fighting back to the wall, snarling like an animal at bay.

Inspector Thomas had only half a dozen police at his command. He feared the fightable Malays might take sides. Should that happen, the police would find themselves up against three thousand coloured men run amuck. The whites then would, inevitably, be forced into it. What would follow among the scattered bungalows with their women and children, he dared not think.

Rapidly the inspector estimated he could put nearly three hundred whites under arms—if they had arms: In frightful anxiety, with scattered constables endeavouring to pacify fresh swarms of man-hunters, the inspector organized at fever pitch from the police station, into which were now running pursued Koepangers protected by a few whites who came hurrying to the station.

Town and foreshore burst into fresh uproar as a crowd of defeated Koepangers rushed into Sewell's shed, and succeeded in barricading the doors. The shed was instantly surrounded to a roar of voices swelling above the hail of rocks hurtling on the iron. The sergeant and two policemen backed up by six white men fought their way through the mob. Turning, the sergeant harangued the Japanese, and persuaded them to desist. Sullenly they began to melt away, into the lanes of the town and along the dark foreshore seeking other Koepangers.

A roar came from Dampier Terrace as Japanese met Koepangers; shrieks and blows and curses accompanied the rumble of bodies crashing against corrugated iron. The sergeant fought on into the crowd whose violent motions suddenly surged away as the Koepangers fled, leaving two prisoners to the Japanese. The sergeant claimed these and, as if on ordinary duty, commenced to escort the men away, Japanese gesticulating around him. He reached John Chi Lane as a further crowd came pouring down it and immediately attacked the prisoners, who clung to the sergeant. Jerking his head aside to dodge the rain of blows he tried to protect his prisoners, forcing their backs to the wall. But a Koepanger was pulled away. as Pearling Inspector Stuart came fighting through the crowd.

"Rescue the Koepanger, Stuart!" shouted the sergeant.

Stuart leapt to the Koepanger and immediately found he was fighting for his life. So was the sergeant, attacked furiously, as a little wedge of whites came grimly fighting their way up the lane. Stuart and his Koepanger, now severely injured, were got to Robinson and Norman's veranda and there protected by the rapidly organizing whites under Inspector Thomas, while the sergeant and his stricken man eventually reached the police station.

Two hundred white men, mostly returned soldiers, were fast enrolling under Bardwell as special constables. Patrols were being formed when word came that Ferguson's camp was being attacked in South Broome. Almost immediately word came that Captain Gregory's foreshore camp in the opposite direction was attacked, and Jock Hay had been felled from a blow on the head.

Things were serious. Wonderful control had so far been exercised by the police and by scattered white men all over the town and along the foreshore, who against tremendous odds had rescued and still were rescuing Koepangers. So far, not a man had been shot or knifed by either side. But fire-arms and the knife might be used at any moment. Then hell would break loose. The inspector warned all against the use of fire-arms except under the direst necessity. Hotels were shut; the sale of fire-arms forbidden.

But the Malays might burst forth at any moment.

These fighting men, second in numbers to the Japanese, had quietly congregated under a leader—waiting. For years antagonistic to the Japanese, grimly they thought their time had come. They were approached by white authority and asked to keep well away from the disturbances. They replied they were just waiting—waiting for their friends the Amboinese or themselves to be attacked. They asked to be allowed to join the fight immediately the whites were attacked. They were assured that it was no question of whites against Japanese: it was only Japanese against Koepangers. The whites wished, above all, that no other races should take sides in the dispute.

Instantly relieved by this temporary neutrality on the part of the Malays, Inspector Thomas hastened patrol after patrol into the fighting quarters of the town and to the foreshore camps that were being attacked. The Koepanger mobs were fleeing, unorganized and outnumbered. Along Dampier Terrace grew a murmuring that rapidly broke into the roars of a fresh tumult. The inspector, working at fever heat, was subconsciously awaiting the report of a gun that would signalize flowing blood instead of cracked heads.

Constable Howard, reinforced in the nick of time by a little squad of whites, just managed to prevent a howling mob from rushing a shed occupied by Manilamen, under the belief that they were Koepangers. Had one Manilaman been attacked, knives would have flashed and massacre started. A big crowd of Koepangers, eyes staring from their heads, came running along the foreshore to swerve suddenly, howling at sight of Japanese hurriedly congregating in front of Moss and Richardson's. In that furious charge the Japanese, greatly outnumbered, were swiftly clubbed or fled for life. Here Youmichi Kawana the diver was battered to death.

Two hundred Japanese attacked Owen's camp, the Koepangers there put up what fight they could, those that were not felled fled leaving prisoners who were bound and dragged away towards Streeter's store. But fresh mobs of Koepangers came howling to the rescue. This fight raged all the way to Streeter's where the mob were charged and dispersed by a detachment of whites. Hot work; swift, determined fighting by a compact, disciplined little patrol capably led against two hysterical fighting mobs. Numerous Koepanger heads were cracked here, numbers were hospital cases. Lefinas Maloki was killed.

Then the Continental and Roebuck hotels were rushed, for fleeing Koepangers had taken refuge there. But in both cases the aggressors were held off by white detachments. And still not a shot was fired.

At midnight town and foreshore were still in a furore. Fifteen hundred Japanese assembled in the open space fronting the police station and the Japanese Club, holding excited meetings to which runners came and went from the Japanese headquarters. Inspector Thomas addressed them, urging them to disperse quietly to their homes, promising full justice in the inquiry which would follow. They listened, while listening to their leaders; then rapidly forming into sections of a hundred men each, ran towards different points in the town shouting directions in Japanese.

The inspector wiped a streaming brow then hurried to form into patrols fresh whites arriving for service.

Armed white patrols were now marching through the town and along the foreshores hurrying the Koepangers into sanctuaries; preventing raids and rescuing men wherever a raid was actively taking place. In face of the last charge of the Japanese many Koepangers took to the bush, others fled into the mangrove swamps around Dampier Creek. Another large body fled through the bush towards Barred Creek twenty-five miles away, Mackenzie and Lyons and Jessop's lay-up camp, where many of their countrymen were among the crews.

At two in the morning a representative from the Japanese Club approached Inspector Thomas stating that five Japanese were at Barred Creek, and that immediately the trouble became known there the Koepangers in camp would murder them.

"Get a car and speed to Barred Creek," ordered the inspector to Constable Howard. "Bring back those five Japanese. Quick!"

It was a wild drive through the pindan along a sandy bush track where the headlights again and again picked out fleeting shadows that were Koepangers running for the creek. Howard arrived in time and quietly collected the Japanese. A score of Koepangers came from their bunks, sleepily curious as to what a police car could mean so early in the morning.

Returning just before dawn, Howard at full speed nearly ran into a black mass of Koepangers coming round a bend in the track.

At about five in the morning of the twenty-first a messenger dashed into the Japanese Club with news that Koepangers were sheltering aboard the *Gwendoline*. A body of Japanese rushed out and on past the Star Hotel to where near the foreshore the schooner was lying. They rushed her. But the Koepangers took to the water—all but one who was rescued by a following white patrol in the nick of time. In this skirmish several whites and Constable Lange· received nasty cracks on the head.

A menacing crowd quickly formed up by the police station, now sheltering hundreds of Koepangers, many bearing the blood-stained evidence of lively times. The Acting Resident Magistrate then read the Riot Act. The crowd gradually dispersed. But soon reassembled to again attack Gregory's and Alexander's camps. They met determined white squads here and roared their way back to the Continental Hotel where Koepangers were being protected by a few whites.

The Riot Act was again read here.

Those were three days of a terrible heat-wave. All through them crowds of excited men were rushing throughout the town and the length of the foreshore. Finally a line was drawn through the town, and armed patrols forbade the combatants to cross it. Under armed guard, Koepangers were continually being brought to the shelter of the police station and the public works enclosure.

Inspector Thomas conferred with the leaders of the Japanese who promised to do all they could to help quell the disturbance. Mounted patrols were now patrolling the streets. And still the Malays remained ominously quiet.

For three days and nights the danger was tense. The striking features of it all were: the forbearance of the whites in not using fire-arms, of the Japanese in not deliberately attacking the whites, and of the Malays in their waiting. The Malays were confident that the time must come when they would throw their weight into the melee.

Numbers of whites were knocked about, but not by individual attack; the blows were mainly received while endeavouring to protect Koepangers. The forbearance of the whites was notable; for besides being knocked about while protecting hunted men, they had the Japanese breaking through their ranks, slapping their chests, and challenging them to "Shoot! Shoot!"

The one white fatality was the man whose example, whose calmness and efficiency averted a truly terrible racial clash—Inspector Thomas. The extreme heat, the excitement and worry and continuous duty brought on heat apoplexy and heart trouble. He died suddenly, on the evening that all was over.

CHAPTER XXV
At the Bottom of the Sea

The fleets were ready for sea again, a heartening sight on a beautiful day. The vessels in line along the curving foreshore, the flag at the Residency mast-head. The beacon light clear cut on its sand-dune, Buccaneer Rock grey and grim—the old wreck upon it. Friends lining the foreshores, the fleets all newly painted, the unfurling sails white against the green mangroves, every lugger equipped for sea down to the last rivet. Lugger after lugger hoisted sail, slipped away with others side by side until in moments a fleet was racing for Entrance Point, the first fleet of the season to take the sea.

When their sails shone on the open ocean, again lugger after lugger slipped away from the foreshore, racing for the honour of leading its fleet out past Entrance Point. And over Cape Riddel a cloud of sea-gulls met the racing vessels, and shrieked a wild welcome, knowing well that another fishing-season had commenced.

On rounding the Point, the fleets cruised to north and south. The gulls, too, sorted themselves out and scattered as gracefully and in as good order as the fleets. To each fleet its own cloud of gulls. And in a week's time, or a month's, or whenever the vessels of each fleet separated, the gulls would scatter too, each following the lugger of its fancy. These gulls fared well upon the refuse of the pearling fleets. Venturesome vessels cruised along the wild, uninhabited coastline north of Derby, prospecting for new pearl-shell beds. And found them. And some paid the price of pioneers.

The lugger *Henry* was wrecked on a reef off rugged Cape Voltaire. Two of the castaways, Smith and Bass, fashioned a canvas canoe and sailed away, creeping north up that coastline walled by cliffs and frowning bastions of an impenetrable range. They landed, and living on kangaroos and fish, tried to walk overland. They were killed by natives, so, with other white adventurers, contributing to "the price we pay for pearls". On the north-western coast alone, hundreds of Australian pearling vessels have gone down since the first pioneers came creeping up the coast seventy years ago.

The fleets worked with slowly improving efficiency in vessels, methods, and equipment. Since the war, air-compressors and power have been fitted to vessel after vessel. Diving-dresses have been improved. Above all, a knowledge of decompression has enabled the divers to dive deeper, to stay under water longer, and, almost, to defy that terrible enemy, diver's paralysis. The divers' graveyards of our northern and north-western coasts are grim reminders of the price that has been paid. But the British naval authorities after long and scientific work discovered and recommended to the pearling men a method of prevention and of probable cure of caisson disease (diver's paralysis).

The deeper the diver descends, the greater the water-pressure he is subjected to, and the greater the pressure on the air that is forced down to him. Extreme working depth for commercial purposes, in the present individual apparatus, is approximately thirty-five fathoms (two hundred and ten feet). Men have worked at forty fathoms, but risked death every moment. At about two hundred feet depth men can only work a short time. The general working-depth varies between sixty and a hundred and thirty feet.

On the sea floor the water is always cold. Hence the diver within his dress is protected by heavy and warm clothing; otherwise he would soon get excruciating rheumatism, and then caisson disease. His thick, bulky canvas and rubber suit is inflated with air, just sufficient to withstand the pressure of water against the suit, while allowing him a constant stream of fresh air to breathe. When down below the diver is really moving in air, against water-pressure. He feels quite light himself; something like a caterpillar within a fairly roomy but cumbrous and weighty cocoon.

The air in the suit is pumped down the air-pipe under pressure from the lugger above, into the helmet through the inlet valve. On the outside of the diver's helmet is an air outlet or air-escape valve, the screw of which is manipulated by the diver's right hand. He adjusts the valve so that there is a constant stream of pure air coming into the suit to satisfy his breathing requirements, while keeping the suit just sufficiently inflated to withstand the outside water-pressure. As he descends or ascends and so comes under varying pressures he constantly adjusts his air-escape valve; closing it a turn or two if he needs more air within the suit; opening it a little if he wishes a greater volume of air to escape. The greater the depth at which he is working, the more air he requires.

The escape valve also allows the constant escape of used up air. Otherwise he would presently become asphyxiated. At ten fathoms (sixty feet), which is approximately two atmospheres of pressure, experienced divers become so used to their daily work that they stay below for long periods without coming up for a spell: With ordinary caution at that depth danger from paralysis is but slight. But at ten and a half fathoms and over the danger is always there for the incautious diver.

When working at great depths (which means working under great pressure) the diver's blood, as he breathes, absorbs nitrogen gas from the air. So that, presently, his blood-stream contains a quantity of foreign gas which is being pumped through his system by the heart. Under working conditions a few years ago, when tired and wishing to ascend, the diver would signal and come up quickly. As he rose the pressure would decrease much too fast to allow the nitrogen under pressure in his blood to escape. The diver would be quite all right until within sixty feet of the surface. Then, under the lessened pressure, the nitrogen would try violently to escape from his blood. It couldn't. Still the diver proceeded straight to the surface and into the open air to come under a totally different law of pressures.

And that nitrogen gas was still in his blood! In its attempts to escape, it was rapidly turning into many tiny bubbles of nitrogen gas. Draw a cork from a bottle of soda-water and observe the gas bubbles rapidly form. That is almost precisely what happens to the compressed nitrogen in the diver's blood when he comes rapidly to the surface from great depth. And that is mainly the cause of the terrible diver's paralysis which has filled the graveyards of the pearling-seas.

It was the Deep Water Diving Commission of the British Admiralty that at last solved the cause of diver's paralysis and found its prevention and cure. So simple, when after constant investigation and experiments all was found out.

But thousands of men died before the problem was solved. Since then the diver working at great depths ascends fairly rapidly to within sixty feet of the surface. There he "stages"; that is, the tender holds him at that depth for ten minutes, twenty minutes, half an hour; it all depends on the time and the depth at which he has been working. The deeper he has been and the longer he has been working at that depth, the greater the quantity of nitrogen gas in his blood. To free him of this means a longer time in stages. From a great depth, he will probably be staged several times before reaching sixty feet. He is then hauled up another fifteen feet or so and staged again, and so on to the surface. These stages allow the excess nitrogen in his blood time to escape from his system as he breathes. By the time he comes to the surface he should have breathed away all that nitrogen, and his blood-stream should be free of foreign gas, should be normal.

Those painstaking experiments and discoveries of a far-away Admiralty have been a romance of the pearling industry. They have saved hundreds of lives on the Australian pearling-grounds. Now, divers can work safely at much greater depths and for a longer time than they had dreamed possible.

Should the diver come to the surface in distress or pain or even apparently dead, he is sent back immediately to the depth at which he was working.

To ease the sick man below against the roll of the vessel rubber rings are sometimes tied to the rigging, and the life-line is attached to the rings, which act as springs. The rubber keeps stretching and so the diver remains stationary. Otherwise in the pitch and toss and roll of the vessel he would have an awful ride.

Like almost all changes in their life and mode of working, the crews at first viewed the staging method with distrust. Even the quick and intelligent Japanese had to be almost browbeaten into adopting the precaution. The diver, when finished below, was anxious to ascend to the surface as quickly as possible and could not understand that by staging he would avoid paralysis. Much less could he understand that by sending a crippled or apparently dead man below again he would probably recover. Such a procedure to their reasoning seemed not only childish but needlessly cruel.

Captain Gregory with his fleet at sea noticed a lugger run up a flag at half-mast. With all speed he hurried to the vessel. The diver lay on deck, his helmet off, apparently dead.

"Screw his helmet on and send him down again!" ordered Gregory to the tender. "Quickly now!"

"Oh, no, no, no, master," protested the companion diver. "He dead!"

"Send him down!" shouted Gregory. "Can't you hear what I'm saying? Put him down!" He advanced threateningly on the Japanese, he had to force the tender to screw on the helmet, force the companion diver to adjust the air-escape valve, then lower the unconscious man to twenty fathoms.

In an hour the life-line tugged feebly. Gregory ordered the tender to lift him six fathoms. Presently the life-line tugged more strongly. This meant that the recovering diver would soon become sufficiently conscious to close his air-escape valve and by thus inflating his suit come up on his own air.

"You go down," ordered Gregory to the companion diver, "and take a piece of cord. You regulate your sick mate's air-valve. Don't let him touch it. Above all, don't let him come up! Tie his hands with the cord if necessary."

"I don't like do that with man," objected the diver.

"Do as I tell you!"

Unwillingly the diver descended. Gregory kept them below for two hours at that depth, then gradually had them hauled up in shorter stages. When the sick diver came aboard he waved threatening arms at all and sundry. Immediately his face-glass was unscrewed he shrilled Japanese oaths demanding who was running the ship, shouting to know why he had not been hauled up on signal! To his stream of invective Gregory laughed at first, then shouted:

"Close up! You were a dead man a few hours ago! Now you keep quiet all the same dead man!"

And he proceeded to give all hands a thorough "roaring up" for not obeying standing orders to stage any diver who had been working at a given depth.

A diver may be only five minutes, perhaps half an hour, on deck before he feels the first sharp twinge of approaching paralysis; perhaps he suddenly sways and rolls over unconscious. One of Lou Marshall's divers was paralysed suddenly when down below and could not signal. When they brought him to the deck his eyes were out on his cheeks, a ghastly sight; his head swelled within the helmet. Sometimes a ball of wind accumulates in the stomach but gradually goes down when the diver is returned to the depth from which the air had accumulated. The awful paralysis takes divers in varying forms. Should a man come to the surface unconscious, the companion diver or tender adjusts his valve to half and quickly lowers him to the depth from which he came. When back at the same depth and pressure, the law of gases and pressure quickly gets to work. After half an hour the diver is hauled up a few fathoms and staged again. This gives the nitrogen bubbles their chance to begin leaving the blood-stream. The diver becomes partly conscious; feebly he signals; on deck they breathe a sigh of relief.[1]

Lou Marshall kept one badly paralysed man below for thirty-four hours. The diver was too far gone to be capable of regulating his air-valve even when he should regain consciousness, so the companion diver went down with him. A grim vigil that, all night long suspended above the bottom of the sea in a blackness of the pit slashed with livid green and orange as some monster of the deep sped by.

Down there, time seems to have no meaning. Only physical needs bring to the human body that sense of things we call Time.

To the diver clinging to his stricken mate there came an eerie phosphorescence that glowed supernaturally upon the helmet of the diver before him; trickled in liquid green upon the face-glass behind which with unearthly glow was a corpse-like face stricken by pain. With his own hair on end the companion diver peered through the glass, straining to note the ghastly roll of those other eyes that should tell of pain or relief or death. For long stage after stage those grotesque figures clung together, the normal man constantly regulating the valve of the unconscious man before him,

---

[1] It is thought to bring bad luck to a vessel should a man die at sea.

staring into his face-glass when sudden phosphorus turned the inky world green.

Thirty-four hours! In a silence as of death made earthly only by the far-away click-clack, click-clack of an air-pump and the whispering hiss of air. The joy as blackness faded to dull greyish-green, then into green, then the swift, almost transparent greenness, then the sight of a moving fish!

Every pearler had similar experiences with his divers. But once it was proved to them that staging was both a prevention of and a cure for paralysis, they adopted the method. But excitement, greed, and rivalry urge them still to defy even death. When a new shell-bed is found, there is a rush by the luggers; a rush by the rival divers; keen competition to reap the cream of the shell-bed. The diver works until exhausted. Should a white master not be aboard, the diver may come straight up, defying all laws of staging and depth, intent on returning below immediately he is physically able.

That was the direct cause of a number of deaths in 1935, and more in 1936. For numbers of vessels take the sea now without a white man aboard, and so there is no firm hand to insist on staging. The Japanese diver is a fatalist. He smiles as he dons the helmet in readiness to go below:

"I cannot die unless it is my day to die."

When the prize of a new and rich shell-bed lies within reach, our western science is not infrequently overruled by eastern fatalism.

Few gold-rushes on land are more exciting than a pearl-shell rush at sea. The news of the first finding gets noised abroad on the wings of the wind. From far and wide the luggers come like gulls that from afar have spied a shoal of fish.

Another problem experienced by the pearlers in dealing with their crews has been the explaining of the strongest end of the air-pipe. Air-pressure within an air-pipe is necessarily greater than the pressure of the water. The pipe under water is really "protected", somewhat as a motor-tyre protects a tube. Hence the length of pipe nearest to the diver (being enclosed by the strongest water-pressure) is safer from bursting than the length in the open air. So, the white man tries to impress upon his divers always to attach the weakest end (if there is a weak end) of the pipe to the diver's helmet.

The diver cannot see reason in this, explain it ever so carefully. He contends that the weakest end should be attached to the air-container on the deck above. His argument is that the diver cannot tell until too late when the tube bursts, but the tender will see and will haul him up immediately. There is something in the contention too; it is a case of the eye against reason.

In a modern dress, should an air-pipe burst, the inlet valve in the helmet automatically shuts off the rush of water. The diver immediately shuts his air-escape valve and the imprisoned air within his suit lasts him until the tender hauls him up. But both diver and tender must act quickly. Occasionally the diver is doubly unfortunate, as when both air-pipe and life-line become fouled around a coral cup (as happened to Hamaguchi and others), a ledge or crevice of rock, or other entanglement on the sea floor. The sawing against jagged coral, shell, or rock may cause the air-pipe to burst and also sever the life-line.

That happened when Jock D'Castilleau was shell-opening from his schooner off Wallal. It was a fine day and Blackman's, Streeter's, and several other fleets were fishing the same shell-bed. Suddenly a Malay shouted:

"Oh, master! Something terrible aboard that lugger! They lose diver!"

D'Castilleau stared at a flag wavering up to half-mast on one of his own luggers; little men waving frantically from the deck. Within minutes every vessel was bearing down on the distressed lugger. Every diver went overboard; sixty grotesque figures groping down there for a man lost on the bottom of the sea. They found him, but he was dead. He had "panicked" or had not had time to close his air-escape valve and so conserve his air. He was found so quickly that he might have been saved.

Only in exceptional circumstances does such a fatality happen, and then very rarely is the lost diver recovered. When both air-pipe and life-line are severed he is truly lost on the bottom of the sea.

But, like the wanderer who perishes in the far interior, his bones may be found at long last. As when one of J. T. C. Mackenzie's divers found what is believed to be the last of Bill Ward's diver. It may have been another; no one could be certain. Mackenzie's diver was walking the sea bottom, ready to rise again, when he found a diving-helmet weed-encrusted and covered with barnacles. As a curio, he lifted it under his arm and signalled "Heave up." Half-way up he glanced at the face-glass and saw a skull grinning at him. He dropped that helmet and signalled "Haul quickly!"

The diver, especially when working at depth, must be constantly alert against the "squeeze". This is a dreaded pressure following an accident. He may be walking along the ocean floor with his pressure regulated, his air just sufficient to withstand the water-pressure. He falls down a hole, he is gone before he has a chance to regulate his air-valve to the suddenly increased water-pressure which, now that it is stronger than the air-pressure, squeezes him in his suit; if he falls far enough, squeezes him right up into his corslet and helmet.

Occasionally a careless tender is at fault. Through not having proper control of the life-line he lets the diver fall, and down he goes carried by his own and the suit's weight. He is thus squeezed before he has had time to regulate his air-filled suit against the pressure.

Some of the holes in the sea floor are really craters. The diver generally sees these death-traps; but others are narrow crevasses, probably hidden by weird plant life and queer leafed things growing out from the edges. The diver steps out and goes straight down. The sudden weight drags the life-line through the tender's fingers and the diver is under pressure before it can be checked. The same thing can happen when the diver underestimates the depth of the bottom he is descending to and drops down too suddenly. Just as a man stepping out of a doorway in the dark thinks a step is there when it isn't.

When descending, an experienced diver generally regulates the speed of his descent by the amount of air he allows within the suit. But accidents or carelessness will happen.

A squeezed diver, if not killed, comes up bleeding at the nose, mouth, and ears, and with his eyes bulging. Some divers have had their eyes actually squeezed from their sockets. In very bad cases they have been squeezed right up into corslet and helmet. The helmet has had to be cut away to free the body.

A slight knowledge of medicine is valuable to a master pearler or white shell-opener. The craft with a white man aboard who is a "doctor" is a favoured vessel with the coloured seamen; they feel a sense of security should anything go wrong aboard. Some startling cures with medicine, plus the coloured patient's faith, have been recorded at sea. Some grisly operations, too.

The white "doctor" aboard has been called upon to stitch up knife and tomahawk wounds; to cut out spear-barbs deep buried in the flesh, and cleanse and heal the wound. Nasty wounds from the teeth of fish, gunshot accidents, poisoned limbs from stings, headaches, and "pains belonga belly, master!" must all be cured from the white man's scanty but magic medicine-chest.

An occasional master pearler acquires an uncanny efficiency in the treatment of these mixed ills. But Captain Goldie felt uneasy when he was suddenly called upon to perform a surgical operation upon a white man. In 1922 he was with his fleet in Admiralty Gulf in the Bonaparte Archipelago—a wild maze of cliff-lined waterways almost at the extreme north-western corner of the continent. The little party kept in touch with Broome, four hundred miles south, by means of the fourteen-ton ketch *Antepolo*, which acted as tender. Willie McBryde was master. Shelling was good and soon the *Antepolo* loaded up with shell and sailed for Broome,

Braham Barker and Lewis and Captain Goldie sailing as "working passengers".

McBryde complained of a sore throat; antiphlogistin was applied but the trouble developed to a severe attack of quinsy. Three days later he was struggling for breath and it became apparent that if the quinsy was not quickly lanced, he would die. The three men held gloomy conference. They were still four days' sail from Broome. It was decided that Goldie must operate. But all his "tools" were in Admiralty Gulf aboard his own vessel. There were no antiseptics aboard the *Antepolo*, while the only "surgical" instruments were a pocket-knife and a sail-needle.

They sailed in towards the land; entered the quandary in the ship's log, and solemnly signed it. Goldie sharpened his pocket-knife to a razor edge on both sides, and wrapped cotton around it to within half an inch of the point, thus making a lance; sharpened the sail-needle, and sterilized both by boiling them in water. Then they ran into an uncharted bay and anchored in calm water. Carrying the gasping McBryde up on deck they stretched him out. Barker held his arms, Lewis his legs, Goldie sat astride his. chest. But the nearly delirious patient could not keep his head still. Waiting his chance, Goldie knocked his patient unconscious by a blow on the jaw; quickly inserted a cleat to keep his mouth open; put the sail-needle through the tongue to keep it out of the way, and lanced the quinsy.

Four days later, when they reached Broome, McBryde was able to walk half-way to the hospital.

Broome: European quarter.

CHAPTER XXVI
The Monkey-Fish

It takes from four to six years to train a diver. Even then, many never reach that prized status, "a good diver". And no wonder. The ocean world is one we know very little about; a world regulated by grim laws; beset with pitfalls for the panicky, the inexperienced, and the unfortunate. The diver has to learn these laws; then has to learn many things about the conditions under which pearl-shell thrives. Some men learn quickly; others never master the "bushmanship" of the sea floor.

The bottom of the sea is always interesting; often fascinating. It has its seasons, just as on land. Seasons of abundance and of scarcity in plant and fish and shell and microscopic life. Hills and valleys are there; plains and grasslands and "deserts"; mud-flats and gravels, gullies and unplumbable depths, rockeries and weedy fields, even "forests". There, the tides govern everything; bring air and light and life to everything; and, at times, local devastation and death—as a cyclone will on land.

The tides are "winds" under the sea that prevent the water from going stale. Occasionally "underwater storms" alter the whole appearance of parts of the sea floor, tearing up vast acreages of sea-grass life, flattening hillocks, covering prolific areas with debris, until it is unrecognizable by the diver who has walked over it but a few days before. Rich patches of pearl-shell bearing ground have at times been buried under detritus and mud. More often a storm below "clears the air" by tearing away square miles of weeds that choke the small life on the ocean floor. Very interesting are such places as the bottom of King Sound where are the underwater whirlpools and the soundless volumes of water that tear through subterranean channels. Weird noises may resound down there and fill the new diver with superstitious terror; such as the huge round rock, poised upon others under water, that booms like the submarine report of a gun as changing currents sway it against its fellows. To be down in the depths and hear that uncanny boom vibrating against the helmet, is an experience indeed. Divers have been caught in these weird places, engulfed by invisible arms and whirled into eternity by forces they could neither hear nor see, let alone control.

That is but a dim picture of the world in which the pearl-shell oyster lives, and where the diver seeks the pearl.

"A beautiful thing of the sea!" exclaimed Claude Hawkes one day in April 1923. He smiled at the gem in the palm of his hand; the diver smiled, too, for this meant rich commission, and honour in the winning. Claude Hawkes was now in partnership with Arthur Male, and he thought of his partner's face when he should see this pearl.

It proved a gem needing hardly any cleaning, a "stringer" pearl of perfect colour and lustre and shape weighing one hundred and ten grains. It was later sold in London for five thousand pounds. What these pearls realize when sold as jewels in the great markets of the world, no one knows. Gems such as these are rare indeed. The master pearler and the diver fish for the pearl-shell, if a good pearl is found it is only when "dreams come true".

To a limited extent, fish share the diver's life much as animals, reptiles, birds, and insects enter into our life on land. The diver's world is in its primitive state, probably as it was before man appeared on the earth. We have conquered the land, the ocean surface and the air; but man is still a crawling babe on the shallow edges of the sea floor. What awaits him in the vast depths he has yet to learn.

And the diver at work is always alert for the tigers of the sea: the sharks, the crocodile (when working close inshore along a tropical coastline), the giant groper, the octopus (when in octopus waters), the giant devil-ray whose bat-like wings will grow to a spread of twenty feet and whose weight is up to two thousand pounds; that hideous thing the monster sawfish, the playful whale, and that titan of shellfish, the giant clam. These and several others are in his subconscious mind what lions and tigers, elephants and buffaloes are to a traveller in darkest Africa. But, like the traveller, the diver seldom suffers fatally from their attacks.

This, however, is only because of his unceasing watchfulness, because of his armour of apparent frightfulness, of his experience, of the help of the tender and crew above; and by reason of the things he can do with the compressed air within his suit. The great fish, like primitive man, have a dread of strange things. As the Stone Age man fears anything to which he is not accustomed, so the giant fish fears the grotesque form of the diver, fears his shadowy life-lines which may be great tentacles stretching away to envelop it, fear the brilliant burst of bubbles which he can spray from cuff or helmet. Is uneasy too about the squat, solid ugliness of the domed helmet and the deep round sockets of the face and side-glasses; is apprehensive at the slow, menacing movement of this strange being's approach. But for this dread of the unknown which big fish feel at the approach of the diver, there would be very few divers.

Of the vast majority of fish the diver takes little more notice than we would of a passing bird. These fish may be large or small, cruising in shoals, or in groups, or singly, but nearly all, swiftly or slowly, pass the diver with apparently not a glance. Curious ones will come and want to nibble at him; others simply flee. Others again soon become familiar to him: the timid ones, the curious ones, the shy ones, the bold ones, the fish that fly from him as if he were a demon, the fish that hide in the sea-gardens or frantically disappear into a hole in the sand or a cranny in the rock.

There are the fish both large and small that are all bluff, like a little dog that raises every hair on its body and barks with the fury of a lion's roar. These fish retreat foot by foot before the diver, blowing their bodies into grotesque ugliness.

A few fish, small ones too, are filled with their own importance as a fighting bull-terrier. These charge straight at the intruder. Their dismay on colliding with metal breast-plate or helmet has given many a diver a laugh. When they smack into the suit itself they simply rebound, for the tough canvas and rubber, under its pressure of air, presents the resistance of an anchored football.

Then there is the friendly fish that swims benignly up to "kiss" the diver, "twittering" at the face-glass with gentle licks of rubbery lips. Occasionally the man becomes quite annoyed with an extra affectionate one of these, being compelled again and again to brush it away. Many fish the diver likes or dislikes, feels friendly or antagonistic to, dreads or simply ignores.

The curious ones are a bit of a nuisance occasionally, for they combine curiosity and cheek with all the precociousness of a naughty child. These will come staring in at the face- or side-glasses, their quaint, marbly eyes and waggling tails plainly saying, "My! What in the sea is this? Just come and look at what dropped down in the last shower!"

There are a number of fish that occasionally are able to do him harm. As on land, we sometimes overturn a stone and find a scorpion or centipede curled there, or rest on the grass and may be bitten by a trapdoor spider, or reach for a flower and are stung by an insect, so the diver down below has to be aware of the stinging things of the sea. Such as the fire-fish, a tiny though beautiful thing that plays among the coral, sometimes hides behind a pearl-shell and stings the diver's groping hand. Immediate swelling is accompanied by excruciating pain. Ammonia gives the only partial relief. The skin diver suffers terribly; the poison goes all through his body, whereas the tight sleeve-cuffs upon the wrists of the dress diver prevents the poison from spreading.

Among coral reefs there lives a pretty little shellfish (luckily rare) possessing a poisonous sting. The little beastie stabs the diver's groping hand, injecting poison. Severe pain, then paralysis, ensues. In several cases among skin divers in the Coral Sea, death actually followed.

The stone-fish too is an awful thing for the skin diver to tread upon, or the dress diver to touch with his hand. Its hideous little head is armed with lancet spikes which eject a terrible poison. Men have lost a leg through this ugly fish. As with so many fish, the markings of its body resemble the weeds or rock or sands upon which it lies motionless for hours.

The sea also has its centipedes and scorpions; its stinging-plants and "itchy" weeds; its slightly poisonous shell-fish and corals.

And among its mysterious partly animal, partly fish, partly plant life there are things that squirt irritating matter. Then there are the "spike" fish, furies that are liable to charge and try to spike a hole in the diving-suit.

Despite these little risks, a diver may work a whole season down below and not receive a single thrill. He may work several seasons and nothing untoward happen. A season may come, however, when he will have enough adventure to turn his hair grey.

There is one fish whose company the diver really likes, towards which he feels a good-humoured comradeship. That is the "monkey" fish. Monkey is only about eighteen inches long with a thick but tapering tail and ferocious, ugly head quite out of proportion to his body. Goggle-eyed, he is nearly all head and mouth, and though ready for flight if imperative, is also ready to fight at the flip of a tail.

The monkey-fish, his big round eyes and leathery jaw warning all and sundry to mind their own business; builds a home and a castle. He selects a secluded sandy allotment around which are stray blocks of stone or clumps of coral rock, the tiny patch well screened by weeds of the sea or the giant sea-cabbage. The last thing Monkey wishes is to advertise his future home. He flips up his tail and bores head downward into the sand, twisting his leathery snout as a scoop, energetically tail-kicking while his bull neck bores deeper. Then he shoves his weight into it and his body bores round and round until the sand spurts up and around. He bobs up for a quick breather, then dives head down and tail up again until his bullet head disappears. At his last gasp for want of air (for fish breathe in oxygen from the water) he nose-heaves the loosened sand aside and catapults out, literally panting.

While he gets his second wind he circles just above the hole, his side fins and tail gently pulsing, as he eyes the hole with all the calculating thoughtfulness of a foreman examining a difficult excavation job. Then he dives into work again. Soon, half his body is buried in the sand which convulses up around him as loam does from the burrowing snout of a pig. Fish do not sweat, but Monkey works hard for all that while bending double like a spring, twisting, turning, writhing, until presently only his energetic tail is visible above the sand. When he has loosened the sand down to sufficient depth he again scoops it all out, using tail and wriggling body and shoving snout.

If deeply in love, he makes a good job of it, for this is but the preliminary toil necessary to scooping out a deep, roomy home. With his snub nose and tail he pats the heaped-up sand all nice and smooth around the top of the hole. But if he is one of those lazy lovers he will rest content with just making the hole sufficiently roomy.

A sympathetic and interested onlooker at all this is his friend and ally, the "Binghi" fish (a blue parrot-fish), swimming busily above him with beautiful body shimmering in opalescent colours, his anxious eyes staring everywhere as he does sentry duty lest voracious jaws catch his friend bending. One warning swish of Binghi's tail and he will have vanished. Monkey, too, disappears.

Here is Beauty and the Beast in a workaday alliance at the bottom of the sea. Few of the beautiful things of the sea could be more lovely than the living beauty of the parrot-fish; few could be uglier than Monkey. An unusual companionship, but a faithful one.

Like the land monkey, the monkey-fish's bark is worse than his bite; he bluffs many sea things with his ferocious aspect of being immediately about to tear something to pieces. Thus he bullies his own way with the timid and uncertain ones. Still, he is full of beans should it come to the point. Though he flies at the warning flip of Binghi's tail, soon he is back on the job again.

Presently, he has burrowed quite a hole; has ploughed upward with snout and shoulders and tail and pushed the loosened sand well out of the way in a fairly wide circle all around. He takes a breather, lying half-twisted there in his beginnings of a hole while his big eyes drink in the parrot-fish's approbation. Ceaselessly his sentry friend circles above him, anxiety apparent in the beautiful eyes, in the luminous scales of his gracefully gliding body. Monkey again burrows down and loosens yet more of the tight-packed sand. The deeper he excavates, the more preoccupied he becomes, the more vigilantly does the parrot-fish do sentry duty.

After much well-directed energy Monkey has scooped out a hole, a little deeper than a bucket, and wide at the bottom. The weight of that displaced sand is considerably more than the weight of the fish. He has now dug a decent basement apartment and has utilised the refuse by building it up as a castle wall above the cellar, a wall that, as it grows higher, begins to close in until it resembles a beehive. It is quite firm, for Monkey has selected a "cement" class of sand, and as he builds the dome higher he pats, pushes, and butts it with snout, fins, body, and tail into a compact domed roof. Very business-like he looks while balancing tail up, battering with his blunt snout, tapping here, tapping there. If you watch closely through the face-glass you will see he means every thump he makes, while every prod is in the right place. No master builder could be more scrupulously painstaking in building a modern mansion than Monkey is in building his castle in the sand.

Now that Monkey's work has reached the stage where his head is well clear of the hole, he is better able to look after himself; so the parrot-fish relaxes his watch and commences working too, darting away on scouting trips to return with a coral stone like a small twisted stick held in his mouth. He drops this chip on the wall and Monkey rams it into the sand which it binds just as we put wire and stone into the building of a cement wall. Again and again the parrot-fish darts away to return with his twig, appearing in a shimmer of green and blue, vanishing in a flash of orange.

At last the house requires only the finishing touches. It looks like a well-disguised beehive with a small, neatly rounded hole on top. And it merges perfectly into the colour scheme of the surrounding corals and vegetable growths.

With a quaint air of proprietorship Monkey noses around it seeing that all is perfect as perfect can be. He detects a white spot as large as a two-shilling piece that might attract a sharp eye. He noses it a while; appears to be slowly chewing at it with thick, leathery lips, and gradually it turns drab like its surroundings. The parrot-fish brings him several trailing pieces of sea-grass. These he lays carelessly over the domed roof until it is practically indistinguishable from the surrounding grasses, certainly indistinguishable to anything passing in a hurry. With the air of a job well done Monkey glides up to the entrance hole; his head dips down, his tail tips up, and he disappears. A second later his big, ferocious head is glaring from the hole. It perfectly frames his ugly menace.

The parrot-fish circles a while, gazing prettily down in admiration, then, signalling that all is perfect, it glides away.

CHAPTER XXVII
Monkey and the Diver

Monkey by now is ravenous, his eyes glare out from beside an ugly slit that can open into a mouth larger even than the hole. A crab, scenting freshly turned sand and anticipating sea insects, comes scuttling up the mound, the ball-like eyes of the ogre on top appear to swell. In a flash he pops out of the hole and circling back like a spring has disappeared down the hole from whence his head re-appears all in a breath. He twitches his leathery lips and, facing the oncoming tide, awaits another morsel.

Gently the tide flows over Monkey. His eyes see things our eyes cannot: countless infinitesimal things floating by in the tide, forms of active life so virile, so prolific, that the mind of man cannot grasp the reality. Vast quantities of invisible food ceaselessly flowing on to feed the life in the sea. After long waiting a little fish appears darting in and out amongst the weeds, nosing here and there as it seeks sea-bugs and crawly things upon the dreaming water-plants. Monkey's eyes protrude, you can almost see him gulping in anticipation as he notes that the course of the little fish will bring it directly over the hole should nothing frighten it, or prey not attract it away.

Turning from a frond of sea maid's hair the little fish comes on over the hole and a mouth shoots up and engulfs it and Monkey is back in his home with just half his ugly, camouflaged head framed in the invisible hole.

But now a big fish comes along. Ah, the menace of a big fish seeking something to tear and devour! Monkey's head sinks level with the hole so that his ugly, crinkled face disguises the fact that a hole is there. The big fish glides past, savagery in the gleam of its green, phosphorescent eyes. Monkey pops up again, making a face just as another big fish comes gliding around a coral block and charges. But Monkey has bobbed back, his raging mouth clashing needle-edged teeth on a level with the rim of the hole. The enemy tries to snap Monkey but cannot lest his own snout or fins or manoeuvring tail be sadly torn. And a wounded fish is doomed, for others may scent the blood and race to tear him to pieces. The big fish darts away, vowing vengeance on some future day. Monkey pokes up his head, grimacing horribly. You smile as you watch him through the face-glass, imagining the names he is calling the fleeing fish, urging it to return like a proper fish and take what is coming to it.

But Monkey freezes as an unarmed man would freeze if meeting a raging lion. A thick dark shape eight feet long comes hurtling through the water, its terrible head armed with fangs dreadful as the teeth of a crocodile: the barracuda, the ferocious sea pike, the Malays' "Curse of the Sea". This diabolical thing has disembowelled men; the skin diver, especially in tropic waters still farther north, fears it more than sharks. You cannot bluff the "Curse of the Sea". Be so foolish as to try, and he will come at you like a mad dog. Should he not instantly disembowel you or strip the flesh from your leg he will come again. No wonder the little monkey-fish freezes.

Time passes. Monkey watches, eats, fights, and sleeps with one eye open. Throughout the fierce ruthlessness of subaqueous life every living thing sleeps with its instinct awake. One day Monkey, somewhat bored, is waiting for something to come and be eaten when—by what instinctive vibrations he registers that electric approach we do not know—he vanishes as a blue flash comes and is below him while Monkey's head is back in the hole, his eyes flaming and his teeth gnashing at the face of the pursuing fish who somersaults upon himself and is gone in a terrible fright.

While, below Monkey, deep as he can hide in the little chambered sanctuary, trembles the blue parrot-fish, his eyes distended, his tail twitching convulsively, terror glinting from the changing lights on every beautiful scale.

So the monkey-fish repays his ally who had guarded his life while he was digging his home.

Monkey becomes quite bored with life; he even goes off his food; hardly responds sociably to Binghi's occasional visits. He takes to mooning about among the reefs and in the sea-gardens away from home. He returns more and more dejectedly until one day ...

With pride he shows his lady friend his home, humbly he asks her to be his wife. Disdainfully she circles the home; she does not think much of it nor of the Monkey either. In an agony of apprehension he circles around her, hardly daring to vibrate a word. Just as he has made up his mind that all is lost, she pops down into the hole and he is after her like a flash. Then his head stares from the doorway. He will fight anything now—even a shark.

The parrot-fish visits him; sees that "two is company", and sadly departs. But the divers say he is soon reconciled for about this time he rejoins his gay company who sport through the sea-gardens adorning the coral reefs. Doubtless he finds there some gay lady who reconciles him for the temporary loss of his friend.

Time passes very happily for Monkey. He willingly hunts for two now although the lady is quite capable of hunting for herself. Monkey's married bliss is but short-lived. One day she departs. He follows her imploringly.

She takes no notice; she has family affairs to attend to; she has eggs to deposit and knows of a snug rock cranny that she considers a safer bank than Monkey's hole in the sand.

Monkey soon recovers—especially after Binghi returns, and they compare notes.

But sometimes Monkey bites off more than he can chew although this particular bite is forced upon him. It is the "bro" fish. Quite an ordinary little fish is Bro, cussedly born with a mania to charge anything he sees. He has a fantastically inflated idea of his own size and strength and importance in the scheme of things. He will charge straight into the mouth of a rock cod.

Have you ever seen a rock cod, a groper particularly, with its gigantic mouth slowly opening and shutting at the bottom of the sea? That terrible mouth has been known to bite off a native diver's leg at one bite. Fish are ever ready to open their mouths down below but the largest shut it with a snap when they see a bro-fish coming.

Well, the bro-fish sees Monkey, and Monkey is in a predicament which must be instantly solved. If he vanishes down his hole the bro-fish comes too and the last thing Monkey wants is a bro-fish in his home. Bro charges straight at Monkey's mouth; his head goes in and is gripped. Monkey gulps fast as he can for even if the best happens he is going to imbibe a swelling pain. He tries hard to puncture his enforced meal with those sharp teeth of his, he lashes around in the chamber below trying to swallow and puncture at the same time. He knows what is going to happen if he cannot quickly deflate his visitor.

If Bro is very small, Monkey punctures and swallows. But if he is slightly larger and not punctured when swallowed, then Monkey circles his home to return to his look out with a drawn and expectant face. With a large bro-fish Monkey does the best he can, which is only to swallow the head. Before that goes down properly Bro begins to inflate; he blows himself up just as the diver inflates his suit when wishing to ascend to the surface. Bro balloons into a football until, despite his desperate struggles, Monkey is drawn with him and both go floating away with the current. Divers have great fun with them when locked in such unholy embrace. Often the fish, so locked, come floating past a working diver. He reaches out and tickles the ballooning Bro. All it can do is swell a trifle more; it looks as if it will go off pop at any second. Then the diver reaches out, and with his thumb-nail and third finger nips the tail of the monkey-fish and pulls the floating pair back to him. Monkey kicks convulsively, while his eyes threaten to pop out of his head. Helpless fury distorts his extended jaws. The diver laughs; walks after them as they drift away; reaches out again and pulls them back, stretching his arm behind him before letting them go. The tide floats them past his corslet again. He reaches out his left arm, draws them across to his right hand and reaches out behind and again lets them go. If two divers are working in company, they pass the helpless fish from one to the other. Then one flips a tail upward while the other flips a tail downward; in a moment they have the fish turning a complete circle which develops into a Catherine-wheel under the energized tail of the outraged Monkey. But soon it hangs limply in exhaustion again. The divers stand each fish in turn on its tail; practise all sorts of indignities upon them; flip with their finger-nails the distended belly of Bro, and if you were in a helmet beside them you would hear the sound just like finger-nailing a drum. Growing tired of the sport, the divers let the helpless ones float away at mercy of any voracious fish whose path they may cross. If both are not swallowed, or bitten in halves, or stranded on a beach, they must drift on thus until one dies—probably Bro. Then, at long last, if there is sufficient life left in Monkey he may be able to disgorge the dead one's head from his throat, recover partially, and wend his feeble and dangerous way home.

But there are fish that the monkey-fish cannot bluff, that he cannot flee from, and against which his home is no protection, once they see him. These simply rush him like a torpedo, his castle walls are shattered and he is pulled out and snapped to pieces.

With cheeky bravado Monkey treats that strange, bulky fish on legs, the human diver; even if his head does pop right down when the diver comes right up. The diver bends, picks up a stone and drops it down the hole, then, generally stands a little way off to watch. Very soon the stone appears wobbling at the mouth of the hole as it is pushed up by Monkey's snout. With a shouldering heave it is pushed out and over the side of the castle and Monkey's head is there, glaring his rage and disgust.

Sometimes the diver will pick up a large and weighty shell, place it over the hole, and again become the smiling spectator. Soon the shell begins to quiver and wobble as the fish below heaves to displace the trapdoor. It is beyond poor old Monkey's strength. Then he turns his snout into a battering ram and charges that shell until he must give himself a headache. But he can get no purchase, for his cellar is twice the depth of his own length. By some marvellous instinct the distant Binghi becomes aware that his friend and protector is in dire trouble. He appears like a blue flash that instantly circles round and round above the imprisoned Monkey. The diver watches the anxiety of the beautiful fish, knowing by its tail movements that it is vibrating a message to Monkey that it is there. But the body and snout of the parrot-fish is built for beauty and speed, and do what it will it cannot help its imprisoned friend. Sometimes Monkey, at long last, manoeuvres the shell so that it begins to over-balance. Then, with snub nose and big head, he pushes and pushes until the weight of the shell slides it away. Monkey gasps in total collapse upon his castle walls while Binghi tenderly noses his ugly head.

But should the shell prove entirely beyond Monkey's strength the diver as a rule will return and tip it off with his foot. It all depends on what manner of man he is, and whether the tide will allow him to return the few yards.

There is another fish who is a great lover. He and his wife always travel together; are never out of one another's sight. They are large, flat fish dressed in stripes across the back. And from their big, kind eyes is entirely missing the cruel gleam so common in the submarine world. Divers know this Romeo and Juliet very well. Occasionally they find time to pause and watch Romeo in solicitous attendance on the gliding Juliet. Perhaps Juliet comes to rest among the cool fronds of sea-ferns overhanging a coral ledge. Daintily he glides to rest beside her, caresses her gently with the end of his flipper; sidles up and rubs his nose on hers. If she responds he is very happy; if she wishes to rest and dream a while, he glides protectingly above her and half hidden by the fernery keeps close watch against anything that might disturb her peace.

After a while, Romeo glides down to quietly nuzzle Juliet; receiving no response he takes her fin in gentle lips and gives a little pull. Perhaps she trembles slightly; but if she shrugs her tail, he glides above to keep watch again. Though leading him a dance sometimes, even to hide and seek, with a little touch of the sulks at times, she never really lets him out of her sight. Apparently they share the same worries and joys, and live a fish life all their own.

CHAPTER XXVIII
Depths of the Sea

Fortune dashes the cup from the pearler's lips at times. J. T. C. Mackenzie and Morry Lyons one fine day located the tip of a rich reef, on which good quality shell, carrying good baroque, was large and plentiful. As the excited diver sent up bag after bag the partners eagerly looked forward to a pearl.

That reef was queerly shaped. It formed a peak the tip of which came up to shallow water. From this tip the main body sloped sharply down into deeper water on either side.

It was boisterous weather; anxiously the partners watched wind and sky. Unfortunately, their main fleet was some distance away. That evening it came on to blow with almost hurricane strength, and the lonely lugger was forced to slip away to safety. Before doing so, the partners buoyed the reef. When the weather cleared, the whole fleet came sailing back eager to load with shell.

But that reef was never found again. The buoys had been washed away or sunk. The vessels in line slowly combed the sea above the approximate position, all their divers suspended below straining their eyes to catch a glimpse of the lost reef. From every point of the compass the vessels manoeuvred for days; a rich prize was offered the diver who should first locate the reef. All in vain.

The coast is dotted with records of fortunes thus won and lost. But fate brings occasional recompense: perhaps with a season's record of good shell, perhaps with a big pearl. Or she brings welcome grist to the mill in some quite unexpected way. As when a lugger of Mackenzie and Lyons's fleet was working off Cape Leveque with barely moderate success. She sailed back to Broome with a light cargo of merely average shell.

"We won't make a fortune at this rate!" sighed Mackenzie as he supervised the sorting of the shell.

"No," answered Lyons, "if we do no better than this we will have difficulty in fitting the fleet for sea next season."

Some hundredweights of the shell were so small and brittle as to be valueless. While coloured labourers were dumping it away on the rubbish heap Mackenzie broke a shell, curious to see what thickness of nacre it contained ... Several small baroque pearls were embedded within the shell.

"Look at this!" he called to Lyons.

"Might be more where these came from!" said Lyons incredulously.

They broke all the shell and gleaned a harvest of small pearls—none of much value but still worth many times more than all the shell, even had it been of the best quality. These little pearls instead of being upon the shell were embedded within it.

Mackenzie stared thoughtfully down the path that led from their camp to the road. It had been paved with similarly discarded shell for years past.

"There's a lot of Cape Leveque shell in that path; Morry," he said speculatively.

"Yes," answered Lyons. "And I'm ordering the crew to gather it right away. We've been walking over pearls."

Much of the discarded shell contained nothing, but some held enough small pearls to pay handsomely. As Syd Prior was fond of saying:

"It's the luck of the game."

Harry Macnee, now of Macnee and Hunter, had his turn in the *Claudius* off the lighthouse on Gantheaume Point. A glorious day; Macnee and the crew in fine fettle; work a pleasure. The diver sent up one bag in which was a shell with a pearl worth a hundred pounds and also an intriguing black lump that might have been some curio of the sea. But when the horny black skins were cleaned from it, it was found to be a forty-grain round pearl which sold for two thousand five hundred pounds.

That adventurous seaman J. W. Tilly experienced for years luck that might have broken a man's heart. He fished the "father of all pearls", two hundred and sixty-four grains weight! If it had been the pearl it looked, it would have been worth a king's ransom. Elles cleaned it, but had almost to "chop lumps" off it to get at the pearl below. Then he removed skin after skin; each skin was discoloured, or marred by spots, unevenness or indentation; each skin promised a better skin below. But the whole great pearl peeled away until there was nothing left.

Then one day he fished a blister pearl that looked a beauty. Hunter offered him five hundred pounds for a half-share uncleaned. Tilly refused. Skin after skin of this pearl was blemished too. Then another pearl was found, a monster round of ninety-six grains. This cleaned down to a little eighteen-grain pearl. It would have meant a fortune had it cleaned as it looked. Then a ninety-nine grain drop was found. It cleaned down to a thirty-two grain pearl. Even then, when polished, it had a small black band right around it which lessened its value.

When vessels are fishing very close in company, a diver down below will sometimes see the magnified form of another diver working just ahead If that shadowy form happens to be a "learner", a practical joke immediately forms in the mind behind. Stealthily he advances, careful that his leaden-soled boots do not kick a stone. The joker is soon towering behind the unconscious man, looking like a clumsy grizzly as he waits for his victim to squat to pick up a shell. When he does so a magnified hand reaches out and with one twist opens full the air-escape valve. Escaping in one great rush, a thousand bubbles bathe him in a scintillating vision of marvellous beauty. The crouching diver feels his suit collapsing; water-pressure squeezes his body. He staggers upright, his heart shocked as the brain flashes, "What monster has pierced my suit!" His hand wavers to his helmet where his trembling fingers shut the air-escape valve. He is crouching again, pressed down by the sea, his straining ears singing hysterically to the reassuring click-clack, click-clack from the vessel above, the steady hiss of air flowing into the helmet. The suit begins to swell out again and slowly force back that living wall threatening to crush him in. He breathes again, a long, tremulous sigh. Straightens upright as his suit fills to normal. Then, feeling the inflating suit beginning to lift him from his feet, he timidly opens the valve—just a bit. Bubbles escape with a sibilant hiss. Fearfully, he closes the valve. Soon, he feels himself being softly lifted upward. Thankfully reassured, but still shocked, he regulates the valve to normal as he slowly sinks back to the ocean floor. The valve is quite all right; working perfectly; but he is tempted to close it and rise to the surface. Yet how his shipmates would laugh! How the despised Koepangers would sneer if he arose and nothing was the matter!

Yet, what had happened? Mentally he cautions himself that he must be extremely careful when "sitting" down to pick up a shell; he must then keep his hand on the valve and be ready to close it instantly. At last he lowers his hand and prepares to step carefully onward—then stands aghast, his heart choking as his hand flies to his helmet and closes on human fingers! Horror-stricken, his trembling fingers creep up and feel a wrist, creep farther and feel the cuff of a diving-sleeve! Slowly he turns and stares into the face-glass of a grinning compatriot.

Perhaps (due to carelessness of the tender) the life-line hangs in a long loop behind the diver, within reach of a fellow coming behind. He grasps it, and pulls. The man in front instantly thinks, "Life-line entangled! My God!" His lips frame a prayer to Mohammed or Buddha. He probably immediately signals the lugger "Stop!" wondering dismally if the signal can get around the supposed encumbrance. Then he fearfully turns to see what danger holds him prisoner at the bottom of the sea ...

Or sometimes a joker comes up behind a diver and gives him a kick in the pants. How would you feel, all alone at the bottom of the sea, if a fourteen-pound boot kicked you where you least expected it?

Some of these submarine jokers are clever; they can take the very shell from a man as he gathers it. The diver generally carries a little open-work cord bag at his waist or chest in which he puts the shell. When full the bag is generally hauled up the life-line by a ring with cord attached. While the diver is squatting an expert joker from behind may succeed in taking each shell from the bag as it is put in. The tales told on deck at evening yarn-time of a young diver looking for a "hole in his bag" on the bottom of the sea cause many a laugh.

Little old Solo the hermit Malay would never dive when another sail was in sight because he swore that divers thus stole his shell. They did not, of course. Water-pressure had affected the old man's brain until he imagined all sorts of things, the sea women and sea men and sea ghosts he constantly met were all living identities to him.

To a "learner" diver, another diver looks monstrously big and magnified down below, as do all objects. Experience brings them, subconsciously as it were, back nearer the reality. If the water is inclined to be "foggy", any object develops an unusually monstrous shape—and uncertainty. For cross movements of invisible currents and swaying influences of tides make things "move" that should not move. Small ledges loom big, large ones mighty and puzzling; some appear as leaning battlements swaying amongst drifting clouds. Holes in the ocean floor appear as gloomy craters with a horrible depth. Little wonder that an occasional diver will swear he has seen the face of a sea giant leering up at him from such a place—has even escaped the clutch of mighty claws. Sea-plants from ledge and reef and crevice stretch out slowly moving arms while among dim sea-gardens weird things take nightmare shape.

No wonder that the diver whose brain has already been touched by the phantasies of paralysis should be convinced that the sea ghosts are gliding past him through the water; that strange men nod to him and he religiously returns the nod; that mysterious women beckon to him from the mazes of the underwater gardens. Many a sea bower is known to the divers where reposes some beautiful form, a ghostly siren whose alluring whisper coaxes from among the fronds and trailing ferneries that drape it.

Along that unparalleled wonder of the world, the Great Barrier Reef, as nowhere else, are the fantastic grottoes of the sea, the water-lit caverns of mystery, the tasselled walls of enchantment, the coral lanes leading to sea-gardens with wonders of form and life that beggar description. On the north-western Australian coast the coral patches are few and comparatively small.

Down to the diver in his faintly luminous, elusive, shadow world come, strangely enough, distinct shadows from the world above: shadows of drifting clouds, of a passing ship. Shadows that he welcomes are the darting shadows of a shoal of white fish, each with his big lip constantly moving as he noses along the sand, suggesting a rooting pig gobbling up soup. The diver quickly signals. Instantly the tender shouts "White fish!" and down come the lines with their bright bait of tin or rag all jerking in anticipation. The diver watches the shoal gobbling, gobbling; their fins and tails moving; their scales and brilliant eyes gleaming. One big fellow glides up and kisses the diver's face-glass; another opens its mouth and grabs the bait, to be instantly jerked up fighting for its life. A line becomes entangled in a bush, the line jerks as the fisher above strives to free it. The diver steps forward—as a lean grey shadow comes and the white fish scurry away.

Divers detest sharks when they frighten away the succulent white fish. But when the bonito are about and a shark comes, they rave at him. Kingfish and bonito are caught generally on a tow-line. The Japanese eat the bonito raw, cutting it into thin slices and eating it with *soi* (Chinese sauce) and raw onions. The dish is called *sassene*. A shriek of joy signals a bonito landed on deck.

The diver, peering about for the pearl-shell oyster, sees groups of rock-fish resting like rabbits under a bush near a fan-shaped weed which always turns its edges to the tide. This peculiarity is a rough and ready "tide compass" to the diver, as is the magnetic ant-hill to bushmen, occasionally, on land. From the gloom come wedge-shaped China fish electrically brilliant in their gold, blue and green.

The eyes of some fish are very lovely down below; some times they change colour in bright metallic shades.

The diver signals for the fish-lines again as a Hong Kong China fish comes along in his beautiful deep purple coat, and with a tail somewhat resembling a long curved quill. This luscious beauty must have been chased up from deeper water. Malay people say that rainbows first put the colour into fish. If so, then the Supreme Artist must have breathed all his colours into his favourite fish, and left the rainbows faded indeed.

The diver stands motionless as a huge shape looms up, and a giant sawfish (possibly half a ton in weight) glides by, its eyes malevolently luminous, its broad saw with its spiky teeth jutting out seven feet from its snout. Perhaps this diver saw one of these monsters in a titanic struggle against a crocodile when the lugger was anchored in Barred Creek; heard the hoarse, grunting coughs of the saurian, the lashing of that terrible tail, the crashing of the mangrove roots as they fought there with the tide swirling in. The diver stays motionless until the grim thing has vanished.

Possibly from the water-light behind the big fish will emerge a swarm of little "snorters", these have a ridge down their back and a busy yellow tail. They may circle the diver before passing on. They have seen many divers, for often in a thick shoal they cling beside a sailing lugger for protection against kingfish. When sheltering so, their speed and distance never vary a fraction. The bait is a fluffed-out wax match upon a tiny hook, the crew tremble this across the water and soon hook a bucketful. Their sweetness is recompense for their lack of size. The coloured diner does not always eat fish as we do. He simply passes the fish across his mouth: the flesh disappears down his throat while the bones pass on over the side.

Perhaps the diver is passing over a patch of "winy-winy" country, where giant furrows, fourteen feet apart, appear to have been ploughed across this plain on the ocean floor. He pulls down on the life-line, coils a loop in it, sits in the loop, then goes comfortably drifting over the plain to alight on the other side and trudge across a field of Pee-sung (Malay for banana) each about eighteen inches high and resembling an enormous banana. In places they grow thick as mushrooms. In Carnot Bay between Broome and Beagle Bay they sometimes grow on and entirely cover the pearl-oyster. When the diver sends up shell on which Pee-sung are growing, the crew squeeze the heads at one another and laugh when the squirt of water flops a friend in the eye.

Sometimes the diver receives a nasty surprise. In an instant his world may go black; he appears to be enveloped in ink. If a young diver, he may stand panic-stricken ... Has he gone blind? Is a subterranean volcano about to belch around him? The hiss of air, the soft murmur of pumps far above is reassuring. Slowly the blackness fades to brown, then to grey, then disappears.

Only a cuttle-fish.

Poking about among tangled tufts of weed with petals like tentacles, seeking the pearl-oyster that could be so well disguised here, he startled a cuttle-fish and it squirted a cloud of sepia at him as it shot away. He passes on warily, and so, in an eerie place, notices what he would hardly have glanced at before: thin sticks like stubble two feet long, emitting a green phosphoric glow. Stepping among them, they glow brighter as if the vibration had set off a faint electric current. These sticks are tube-worms and each closes its tube with a piece of shell resembling the door of a trapdoor spider.

Other tubes too are there out of which come beautiful blooms; some indeed appear to be ravishing flowers. At his slightest movement they shoot back into the tubes disappearing as fast as the cuttle-fish. His late fright having given him the eyes that see, he notices a queer mass of glutinous looking shark eggs, anchored by silky threads to a tuft of sea-grass. Something moves at his very feet—a little ball of seaweed. It is a crab that has bitten off fronds of a certain sea-growth and planted them in the joints of its legs so that they may grow and disguise it from enemies.

Then the diver becomes suddenly aware of a surprising visibility, a weird radiance; the water all around has lightened to almost a phosphoric glow. It may keep so for an hour before imperceptibly dimming to green twilight. Perhaps this ghostly luminosity is caused by the passing of vast quantities of invisible microscopic things that glowed, through some law, just as the vibration of the diver's foot had made the tube-worms glow.

A little farther on the diver sees miniature fish dart into the centre of a giant anemone, and sees the petals of the lovely flower close upon them.

Then he sees what divers often pause to watch, a baby octopus sizing up a pearl-shell oyster; a large oyster this, almost as large as a dinner-plate. The diver has not seen the oyster, but the octopus has. As yet, it is only a squirmy thing with tentacles little more than a foot long but already it is becoming expert in battling for its living. Its colour is changing, it has made itself practically invisible, it merges with the gravel upon which it stealthily crawls, all hunched· up as it pulls itself along. Small though it is, it has large, staring, horrid luminous eyes. Its gravelly "shape" now approaches green weed and its wriggly little tentacles change imperceptibly to green. It passes over the green and reaches out towards a broad sea-plant of saffron and russet and as it does so its colour blends with that of the plant. The diver keeps his gaze directly upon it or he will lose it. The thing is crouching; its eyes grow bigger with a baleful glare. When the oyster opens its shell for food it dives its tentacles straight in and then starts the fight, the octopus to squeeze right into the shell and seize a vital muscle, the oyster to close its shell and cut those slimy tentacles in halves or paralyse them with pressure. Tiny puffs of "smoke" arise that is fine sand stirred up by the struggle to drift away in the current. Sea-plant tendrils touched in the tussle sway dreamily. The struggle may last for quite a time. Two divers standing by and watching the struggle will almost certainly "finger-talk," and bet on the result. It is surprising the fight that a large and powerful bivalve can put up, for the tough muscle that hinges the two parts of its shell is really a powerful spring.

Shellfish are really wonderful. Among them are those that can live on the bottom of the ocean under great pressures or on the shore edges under hardly any. Others can live on land and up in the branches of trees. One queer shellfish whose wobbly antics intrigue the diver looks like a hollow stick some eight inches long. The fish inside this queerly shaped shell burrows surprising depths into the bottom. If he has relatives who can live out in the air and on land, then to be contrary he can live down in the earth below the bottom of the sea.

A nasty fish that the diver is wary of is a large ray. The sting in its tail is capable of piercing a diving-dress. A diver may be trudging along when he notices before him little puffs rising from the bottom like smoke. It is fine sand, that fades away in the tide as quickly as it rises. A big ray is there, nosing along the sandy bottom, seeking shell-fish. These brutes often lie almost covered by the sand.

When Archer's lugger *Peggy* was fishing in Port Hedland waters Yama descended and saw the great ray below him—too late. He signalled to the tender as the ray lashed around him piercing his dress and leg, frantically winding its "wings" around him and dragging him along the bottom. When they hauled Yama to the surface he was foaming at the mouth, imploring for a knife to cut his throat.

Young Stainton thought instantly of Yama as one day he was drifting over a grassy bottom and saw on clear sand ahead a huge ray. Drifting with the tide Stainton would be over him in a moment, he could see the malicious glare in the thing's magnified eyes. Stainton was an amateur diver but thought and acted immediately. He signalled "Lower!" and instantly closed his air-escape valve; then signalled "Haul up quickly!" He thus touched bottom but as the life-line tautened from the drifting lugger above he was jerked up and his inflated suit lifted him high above the danger below.

The "Divers' Graveyard", Broome.

CHAPTER XXIX
Tigers of the Sea

The diver, though cautious, does not worry about sharks. But if a big fellow appears and means business the man ascends without arguing. "Shark he too much humbug!" he explains, at which the crew philosophically cease work or sail away on a new tack.

These men have been taught the ways of shark; have listened to their fathers and brothers and mates describing the habits of and encounters with sharks. They learn the practical risks in their daily work. Occasionally sharks may drive divers away from a good pearling-ground.

In 1935 a willy-willy wrecked twenty-four vessels and drowned a hundred and forty-two men among the Lacepede Islands. During the 1936 season when the divers went down they found the bottom in possession of countless sharks so ferocious that the divers were driven away. The fleets had to sail elsewhere.

There have been instances, under certain conditions, of a number of divers beating sharks less numerous and determined than those. Should vessels be fishing in company and the divers be on particularly rich shell they may descend again with thick, short sticks and in turn drive the sharks away. Dangerous work; but the men are experts, and the sharks are cowardly when a number of divers get amongst them. Even so, only experts among the divers themselves are capable of dealing with sharks in that way. The point of a shark's nose is tender and a solid blow on it causes him to see "stars".

Occasionally when below, a diver may see a shark chasing a fish so tired that it begins a frantic circling around the diver and at last swims to him for protection. If the shark rushes on a "low table" the diver will, if he can, kick it on the snout tip with his heavy boot, and then can easily capture the fish. Under terror like that a fish will sometimes "glue" itself between the diver's legs or squeeze under his armpit. A blow on a shark's snout tip, correctly delivered, spoils its appetite. Should the shark charge from behind him, the diver loosens a stream of bubbles from cuff or air-escape valve and the brilliant scintillation invariably scares the terror.

Determined attacks by a shark on a dress diver are unusual. Nagato, though, will never take liberties with a shark. He was working on a good patch of shell. Instinct more than the grey streak warned him to straighten just as a cavernous mouth closed on his helmet. In instant darkness the copper was ringing from the frantic crash of those terrible teeth. Nagato fell backwards, and the thing vanished. Utterly unnerved, Nagato pulled the signal cord: he reached the surface with his helmet deeply dented.

"I thought I eaten that time," he murmured, and collapsed on deck. The shock necessitated two weeks' rest.

Although Nagato's adventure was frightening enough, it was little compared to the almost unbelievable experience of Treacle, an aboriginal skin diver in the Coral Sea. Naked, he dived head-first straight into the mouth of a tiger shark. Instantly his thumbs found and gouged deep into the eyes of the shark which violently ejected his head. Treacle reached the surface, and his fearful wounds were attended to at Thursday Island hospital. He lived to become the admired of steamer passengers for whose cameras he posed on the wharf.

A large shark is cold and maliciously cunning. A small one is more like a terrier, less cautious, more likely to chase an ascending diver to the surface. It is not the big, wary tiger of the sea that causes most trouble, it is the partly grown shark that has not yet learnt to temper ferocity with caution. Those partly grown brutes, when really hungry, are liable to tackle anything at sight, and on occasion to return to the attack.

While one of Mackenzie and Lyons's luggers was off the Lacepedes, noted for turtle and shark, Yokichi Nishi went below and a small shark came nosing around him. He kicked it aside, but it instantly attacked his legs and arms regardless of the stream of bubbles he released from his cuff. He kicked out while facing it, his unprotected hands pressed well up under his armpits. But the little beast charged like a snapping dog, growing madder and madder. As it circled and charged and snapped Nishi waited his chance to kick viciously, alarmed now lest a snap tear through his dress and let in the sea. He had released almost all his spare air, too, in an attempt to frighten it off. Thoroughly alarmed, he shut tight his air-escape valve and wheeled to kick off a new attack, then signalled "Haul up quickly!"

But the brute followed his escape undeterred by his kicking legs. Now that he was rising through the water Nishi could not kick so surely; he had to throw out his arms to aid him. He was fighting all out when the inflating dress began to shoot him up faster. When just at the surface, that shark went berserk. Despite the shouts and blows of the crew it ripped long strips out of the dress as they hauled the now frantic Nishi aboard.

Practically every diver has gone through similar experiences, numbers have risen to the surface with the fear of death in their hearts but suffered no more than a wet behind.

A small shark fought one of Captain Gregory's divers similarly, starting the fight at depth and making it the more bitter the closer they came to the surface. As the diver was reaching for the lugger the shark seized sleeve and hand. Instantly the diver flung his arm and the shark across the deck screaming within his helmet:

"Chop it off! Chop it off!"

Yet another of Gregory's men came swiftly to the surface, a small shark frenziedly trying to eat him alive. As they were hauling the man aboard the shark snapped his boot off, an unappetizing morsel in return for such determination and energy.

It is the diver's menacing appearance when below that saves him from sharks, and also the fact that a shark is invariably careful of its teeth, liking to make sure on this point before it bites. The unfamiliar appearance of a diver, especially with the life-line and air-pipe looking so much like dangerous tentacles, and the dazzling spray of bubbles he can release from his air-escape valve or sleeve make the calculating tiger of the sea very wary. Sharks sometimes follow luggers; when one particular monster follows persistently day and night, it evokes uneasy glances and murmuring in certain races among the coloured seamen: "Shark is following—someone must dive overboard!"

This may have preyed on the mind of Cosumatz the diver, for one night he fell overboard and screamed in the dark. But he came up safely over the side as if shot from a gun.

Sazaki is a young diver in Captain Goldie's lugger *Rosef*. Sazaki dined one morning on crayfish and wiped his hands on his diving-dress before going below. When Sazaki finished his drift he inflated his dress and signalled the tender "Haul up". Then the shark came at him. The crew toiled hard for they were lifting a struggling weight. He shot up fast when near the surface and there the shark, coming behind, made a frenzied rush and snap. Bubbles like the swish of a comet doused that shark's snout. It fled.

But Sazaki felt icy fear with the rush of water into his suit, the men above felt the sudden dead weight as water clutched up over Sazaki's chest; pressed to squeeze his throat. But the air-pressure hissing down into the helmet fought back the water-pressure, and Sazaki reached the *Rosef* with a bad fright and a wet behind.

But it cost Goldie a new diving-dress. Sadly he made this entry in the log: "Dress 2633 torn by shark. Off Sand Point in twelve fathoms."

Love of turtle meat often gets the diver into trouble, despite the strict orders throughout the fleets that no turtle shall be killed on deck while a vessel is fishing. For both shark and diver love turtle meat. Sharks have not the keenest of eyesight but their sense of smell is extraordinarily acute. One spot of blood on a diver's dress, one stain on the life-line, is sufficient to bring a shark which will attack in a fury. From being timid and cowardly the smell of blood turns it into a beast maniac.

Tojiro is another of Captain Goldie's divers. One day Tojiro's appetite proved stronger than his caution. Hurriedly he ate his surreptitious share of turtle while the master was below, wiped his hands on his dress then stepped slowly down on the ladder overside. The tender winked as he leaned over and screwed on Tojiro's helmet. Tojiro winked back. Then the tender screwed on the face-glass and Tojiro flopped into the sea. As his right hand groped helmetwards to adjust his air-escape valve he winked again from behind the face-glass, then to a gurgling of bubbles slowly sank.

A distant shark smelt the taint of turtle meat, and came straight at Tojiro, to swerve violently at the hissing bubbles from his sleeve. He closed his air-escape valve; signalled "Up quickly!" and came fighting to the surface a badly scared man. As the tender unscrewed the face-glass Goldie angrily accused the diver:

"You fool! You have been eating turtle! Haven't I often told you not to do that?"

"Yes, master. Me fool; very sorry," answered Tojiro weakly. "I been forget him."

Several days later Tojiro met another shark. Under below he saw diamonds winking and blinking and darting among the fronds in a sea-garden that overgrew a reef. Now, those diamonds were the eyes of crayfish: glistening little beads which grow on long stalks that the cray can twist to all points of the compass. In the greenish twilight those tiny eyes sparkle like polished glass. The crays have their home in such a reef as rabbits do in a burrow, and they pop in and out of the vegetation much as rabbits pop in and out of a burrow.

These sea crayfish, nearly the size of a lobster, are quaint and agile denizens of the sea with brightly coloured shells. All along the back of their shells they grow spikes "the wrong way". For to swim, they gave a powerful "under" flip of the tail and this propels them backward like a squid. Should a man grip them then, the spikes tear the skin from his hand. That is why Tojiro was advancing so very cautiously. He wanted to grasp two of those long, twig-like feelers that were poking everywhere from among the grasses; once he secured a grip on these antennae, he could hold the cray as a child might hold a kitten by its whiskers.

As Tojiro hovered amongst the grasses, the little diamonds were peeping out and popping back all around him. Presently, with a cunning movement, he secured a surprise grip on a pair of "whiskers" and held them while his hand crept down and gripped the cray in a way that defies the spikes, just as you can hold a snake harmlessly by a certain finger pressure behind the jaws. But you have to know that grip! As Tojiro lifted the protesting cray from its home it tail-kicked violently and almost slipped away. As it was it broke a "whisker" in Tojiro's grasp.

Now, when a cray kicks like that it makes an underwater vibration like the clap of a hand. And this clap speeds instantly through the water; sharks hear or feel it a surprising distance. Sharks, like humans, are very fond of the sweet flesh of the cray and on this day a cruising shark came like a streak. Probably also it smelt the emanation from the broken antennae, for it came straight at Tojiro who flung the cray at it and signalled "Up quickly!" They were just hauling him aboard when, at a swirl below, Tojiro shrieked as teeth clashed within an inch of his drawn-up legs.

But the grand ogre of the diver is the giant groper. This monster awaits in the coral caverns along the northern Queensland coast, and in the rock caverns along the north Western Australian coast. No mere bubbles can scare this bulk of bovine pugnacity, and no kick on the snout is possible. To attempt that would be merely to kick into an enormous maw. When the groper does charge he comes like a bull at a gate. Luckily, he minds his own business—almost invariably. Even when, on odd occasions, he cruises slowly around and around a diver it is merely from curiosity, like a good-humoured bull that is harmless so long as he is not interfered with. As a rule, he remains at home in a cavern among the coral or rock; his great head with its magnified eyes merely glares at the diver groping past.

The mouth of a four-hundredweight groper could bite a man's leg off at a snap. It is all mouth; when that slowly opens, the great head almost disappears, while a fleshy cavern appears gleaming with rows of teeth.

Unlike the swiftly cruising shark, this sluggard likes to choose his gloomy home and there reign overlord of all the locals. So long as a diver does not venture too near its home when the groper is wooing a lady friend it rarely attacks, apparently being merely somnolently curious about this squat, ugly thing vaguely resembling itself.

When Bernard Bardwell went below to inspect the wreck of the *Lilian* he adjusted his valve on the bottom and stared around to get his bearings. The ship loomed up hazily. A pathetic thing is a broken ship upon the bottom of the sea. Bardwell started to walk towards it and soon myriads of tiny fish came. into view swarming the wreck like flies, attracted by the dead man in the cabin. Suddenly he halted: an enormous thing was floating in the tideless water only yards away.

Bardwell's hair tingled as the apparently saucer-large eyes focused directly at him, rolled slowly down, then slowly up with the awe-inspiring roll of the body. Motionless, Bardwell stared at those beautiful hazel eyes with their deep, black iris brightened by a greenish luminosity. As if suspended, the body rolled over to the right, then slowly back to the left, then to dead centre again. As it rolled, so its enormous mouth slowly gaped as if to eclipse the whole body, then leisurely closed. The bulk of the thing resembled two dinghies inverted one on top of the other. Its colour a dirty grey, with black mottles grey with age; now and then a slight movement of two big whitish fins just behind the gills. As slowly its mouth rolled open, again Bardwell stared at the leathery lips, the thick blob of tongue, the rows of gleaming, needle-pointed teeth. The thing surveyed him with a calm detachment, caring neither whether it annihilated him nor let him be.

Bardwell turned slightly aside and proceeded towards the wreck, he dared not ascend. The thing stayed there in mid-water, slowly pivoting to keep him in vision, but it did not advance. Hovering around the wreck were small rock-fish displaying the same leisurely manner as their colossal uncle, with smaller fish still darting busily among them. The wreck was lying on her port side and everything seemed fairly intact; Bardwell climbed up and examined the cabin top. A shower of tiny fish sped from here as chickens from a hawk. Bardwell was fearful lest the scurry should bring the monster at him. The hatches were still on, Bardwell walked to the starboard side, all was sound, he decided she could be lifted. There was no use in staying down any longer; the groper could outlast him anyway. He closed his air-escape valve while he stared back through the gloom at those big, rolling eyes. When Bardwell felt his inflated suit rising he signalled "Up quickly", let go his hold, and shot up with pins and needles shooting along his spine. As they hauled him aboard he saw their pointing arms, he knew they were shouting. The groper had followed slowly up, it was surveying the lugger in leisurely manner from just below the surface.

CHAPTER XXX
The Baby Devil-Fish

The *Mina* under jib and mainsail was drifting just off Entrance Point. The crew were casting longing eyes towards where Broome lay hidden, with romantic asides concerning particularly lovely coloured maids languishing there awaiting the sailor boys' return. The rhythmic click-clack, click-clack of the pump kept perfect time to the tap, tap, tap of the pump-crew's swinging feet. Squatting upon the greasy deck around a litter of shell the Koepangers joked to the scraping of their knives as they cleaned the shell of sea-growths ready for the shell-opener's knife. The tender stood by the stern with his hands grasping the life-line, the nerves of his practised fingers interpreting every movement of the diver below.

Jitaro Naka was drifting along over the sea bottom, the life-line suspending him so taut that his boots were barely inches above the ocean floor. Like some great spider on the end of a cobweb he drifted, a silent shadow. Through his face-glass he gazed at the shadowy bottom slowly passing beneath.

Though his helmet did not move, his keen brown face within did, peering through the side-glasses to left and right, then ahead through the face-glass and down past his big, leaden-soled boots. All that told he was human were his hands, the palms ghostly white and magnified. Dangerous hands, the bare flesh tempting to shark and sea-snake. At first sign of danger from either, Jitaro would hide those tempting hands up under the armpits of his dress.

Fish darted away, though several came curiously swimming around this drifting ogre; one dived viciously at his face-glass. To the sharp "ping!" of the contact Naka grinned sarcastically. A large crab sat back on its tail and champed enormous claws; as the monster drifted overhead it reached up and fastened on to a leaden sole. Idly, Naka lifted his heavy boot. The crab clung, those claws could have crushed a man's hand. Naka dropped his foot and the solid weight crumpled the crab and left it crippled.

"Shell!" signalled Naka. He stood on the sea bottom as the life-line and air-pipe came slackening down like loosening coils of snake. Naka had caught a gleam of nacre amongst a clump of sponges. With slow movement and eyes fixed on it he slouched towards that glint of mother of pearl. The nacre vanished. The oyster had closed its lips, warned either by its sentinel fish or the vibration of the diver's foot. But Naka's eyes had marked its indistinct grey mass among the sponges. With a crab-like movement he half squatted down, his white hand floated out and wrenched the shell off, placing it in his network bag. That pearl-shell oyster was doomed. Strange, that even a shellfish is not safe from man though hiding on the bottom of the sea!

Naka could see a surprising distance ahead. From a cloudless sky the sun's rays pierced this shallow water. Seven fathoms deep (forty-two feet) with no strong tide or current to stir up a veil of sand-drift, is play to the diver.

A shoal of tiny fish swam like a silvered shawl into the gloom ahead; a sea-snake edged sinuously away. Above him, his air-pipe and life-line stretched up to the lugger whose coppered bottom was eerily distinct with a "halo" around it formed by the open air and sky. Naka signalled and felt the tightening of the life-line as in answer he was gently lifted and again went drifting over the sea bottom. Here he was gliding over a field of grass stretching away as a field does on land. Vision of course was not like that, for though he was working in very shallow water with bright sunlight above, vision here was somewhat like gliding over a grassy field in misty moonlight.

Intent upon his work, Naka was not aware of the baby diamond-fish nosing the bottom of the lugger, obsessed by the curiosity of its kind: Luckily it was only a small diamond-fish, about a third of a ton weight and as broad as a spread-out blanket; it was not yet grown into the tremendous bulk which seafarers call the devil-fish.

Baby was enjoying itself. This smooth, rounded thing, along which it glided with a lazy rubbing of broad, cape-like "wings" was a new thing and good to rub upon. Its pig-like eyes glared up at the lugger's keel as, twisting in a lithe, flapping movement it turned and glided back to the stern, its flat snout and broad, slightly rounded back greasily gliding along the weed-encrusted copper sheathing. It turned again with lazy, upward wave of its wings and scratched its back on a sharp shell.

Its irritated twitch aside brought two long, slender things within its focus. It glided towards these new things that stretched intriguingly away down out of sight. It glided around them as they slowly drifted on. Baby had never seen a fish like this big whale-thing before, nor such long sea-snakes. It glided in between the lines and delicately nosed the life-line. That tentacle-like thing had no smell of living flesh but Baby felt its life-like quiver as it slowly moved on. With its snout tip to the line Baby slowly spun around and around it, its big mouth like a tight-shut gash.

It determined to see what kind of fish grew at the end of these long, unappetizing feelers. With its snout tip to the line it followed it down in a slow, undulating spiral.

There was something repulsively grim in the sinuous movement of that bat-like shape, something shuddersome as of a thing arisen from mud born in the gloom of primeval ages. Young as it was, there was awful danger in its playful curiosity, for as it spiralled down the line its curved horns were semicircled around it.

Baby saw the fish-thing when nearly on top of it, the fish-thing was crabbing down, rooting among the grasses with a feeler that gleamed white as it closed on a shellfish. Baby stayed there on its snout, glaring down from cold green eyes, its cape-like flippers barely swaying, its whip-like tail straight up along the life-line. In its short life it had not yet seen such a squat, hideous fish, had never watched a fish like this eating shellfish. Baby glared with uneasy interest, for it too ate shellfish. As the diver straightened up to place the oyster-shell in his bag Baby edged aside only to feel the strain against its opposite horn. Baby butted ahead with the life-line between its horns and the diver stared up, lifted off his feet by the tug.

Baby ran, that is, it flapped with a swirl that again brought the diver's weight hard against its snout, it saw two white feelers flash up to ward it off.

Baby went mad. Despite the jerking thrusts of its snout, it still felt that line between its horns; it felt it was caught. With frantic thrashings of flippers and whipping of tail it spun around and around with that line sawing between its horns, it plunged in twisting, wallowing movements that kept the diver jerking like a Jack-in-the-box. Naka, after one glance at that white belly thrashing above, prepared for a possible nasty fight. But this was a toy fish compared to the whales he had encountered. He clung to the life-line while with an arm warding off the blanketing brute. He could feel its power in the water-thrust that with propeller-like blows struck against and around his dress.

Then Naka was jerked up and forced through a water wall as the terrified fish took diver and line and all between its horns and bolted. A shout from the lugger's deck as fish and diver broke surface. In a thunder-clap of thrashing wings, amidst a welter of foam, the fish dived and the diver followed helmet first, his huge boots following. At the bottom Naka fought desperately while within his helmet was a turmoil of vibration as the entangled fish was drawn right up to him in a thrashing grey mass. Suddenly its black, cape-like wings enveloped him.

Frantically Naka pushed both hands straight out against that whitish thing as its wings battered him this side and that while spinning him dizzily round. He felt he was drawn into a vortex with swirling pressures of beating waters bruising him within those enclosing capes. Still the air came jerkily pumping down the air-pipe; but he was gasping now to the seasick hurry of his brain. Water-pressure takes quick toll when brain and heart suffer exertion down below. He could neither signal nor close his air-escape valve for his hands everywhere mauled slimy, struggling flesh. The fish swirled back lifting Naka high, then again rushed him with the weight of those enveloping wings and spun him around and around.

Then Naka's trained mind snatched at reason through the rush of primitive fear. Swaying his body to the struggling fish he got his hand in under a wing and pushed it solidly up between the fishy flesh and his helmet. His fingers gripped the air-escape valve and closed it tight to a warmth of reasoning joy as again he pushed and fell and pushed. The alarmed crew above were trying to pull up both fish and diver, but the fighting weight was too great.

But now the dress rapidly inflated and Baby, responding to its buoyant urge, in bovine instinct raced again to the surface. A shout greeted them as all hands hauled on the life-line—except one Koepanger, who rapidly hauled in the slack of the air-pipe. Baby, seeing the lugger with its moving, shouting beings, dived again but this time did not quite reach bottom for the strongly inflated suit was a buoy fighting to pull it surfacewards.

Again they hauled in the slack of the lines and Baby bolted across the surface, this time coming around like a veering torpedo at the end of the line. The tender had it all paid out, sixty-five fathoms (three hundred and ninety feet) of new, stout rope. Baby sped on, but could not haul the lugger as a whale could. Tiring at the fearful weight the fish wheeled and plunged back towards it with the crew rapidly hauling in the slack.

Again Baby wheeled when close to the lugger and sped straight out, towing Naka like an inflated buoy. And again the weight of the lugger brought Baby up with a round turn. It sped back once more; slower now. And so they tired it out while the dizzy brain of Naka was clamouring that the life-line would break.

It was like a dream to Naka when, the life-line slipping from between its horns, the tired fish slowly slid back to the depths. The crew hauled aboard the semi-conscious Naka.

Naka had every reason to be thankful. Had the diamond-fish been full grown, Naka almost certainly would not have been diving to-day. This fish ranges from the Coral Sea right round the entire northern coast of Australia. When full grown, the divers generally call it the devil-fish; it is known too as the giant sea-bat. It grows to a ton weight and probably more, with a spread of twenty feet across the back. One harpooned by a crew in H.M.A.S. *Fantome's* whale-boat towed the boat for four hours until the picket launch was sent out and the fish towed to the *Fantome* and hauled aboard. That fish weighed fifteen hundredweight, and was not full grown.

In the Coral Sea particularly, these monsters sometimes roam in little "mobs" of from a dozen to thirty. Such a mob is a thrilling sight under brilliant sunlight and in clear blue water. They sun themselves in bovine enjoyment, the tips of their wings curving up out of the water, the two horn-like mandibles that jut out from near the corners of their big mouths working to and fro, ever ready to scoop food into those hungry maws. Converging, then scattering, they wallow through the surface like active black blankets with occasional splash of white as huge wings rise playfully. Suddenly, the mob scatters in a flurry of foam, then a great flat shape rises high from the sea to fall with a thunder-clap audible a mile away. Another rises and falls to a spray of spume and again that astonishing clap. At dizzy speed the mob have formed a fast closing circle strangely reminiscent of horsemen galloping around a mob of stampeding bullocks. And this is almost precisely what the devil-rays are doing. They are closing in on a shoal of frenzied fish, herding them together by the encircling rush of their bodies and those terrifying thunder-claps until the "black horsemen" have encircled a silvery shoal of tightly jammed, frantic fish. Then the black blankets wallow with flapping wings through and through them while their path is specked by leaping points of silver. It is a great sight; especially when above the melee fly a screeching horde of gulls swooping down to snatch their fill.

I well remember the first night I heard this fish. The lugger was anchored in a quiet lagoon in Torres Strait. A perfect tropic night: sweet voices of singing islanders among the feathery palms; golden stars above; peace on the sea. Suddenly, right beside the lugger, a noise like an approaching train, then a deafening thunder-clap and the lugger drenched with spray as a devil-fish breached at close quarters. The next night another experience nearly ended in tragedy. While I was smoking on the lugger's deck, a canoe glided past with a statuesque spearman in the bows. Suddenly he launched a harpoon to a simultaneous warning cry. Too late he had noted that the black shape rising below was not a dugong. The water before the canoe seemed to erupt as all hands leapt overboard and a great black something crashed down on the canoe, sinking it immediately. Two men each had an arm broken against the canoe as they were diving over. Had they waited another second they would have been flattened by the giant ray.

Naka was lucky indeed that his adventure was only with a "baby".

CHAPTER XXXI
Leviathans of the Deep

When on the sea-bed, if moving amongst vegetable growth, the diver is wary of the snap of a startled sea-snake. Though timid and generally harmless, odd varieties are vicious and possibly poisonous. The pearl-shell oyster often fastens itself to a reef or sea-bush by a byssus of tough strings, and the diver has to wrench the shell to tear it away. It is when reaching out his hand amongst the fronds that he may disturb a snake which may instantly snap at his hand. Very rarely a bite proves fatal. But it killed Maso Fukami recently.

Fukami was on good shell. He had just sent up a full bag and was awaiting the empty return when a sea-snake swam straight out of the gloom and seized his wrist. Fukami frantically shook his wrist but the needle teeth bit deep. The agonized man tore the snake away, and signalled. He died very quickly.

The average length of the sea-snake is six feet, the most common in colour is yellow; but there are numerous colours and varieties, the banded sea-snake, for instance, is particularly nimble and vicious. At certain seasons of the year and in nice warm weather sea-snakes come in swarms to the surface to bask and breathe. In the Coral Sea I have seen them all around the lugger, a mass of squirming things with individuals occasionally apparently tying and untying themselves in knots. Away to starboard and port would be other yellow patches floating and wriggling and squirming upon the sea. What produces this particular activity I don't know, unless it is massed serpentine love.

Divers often watch the antics of sea-snakes. Perhaps a crayfish the size of a small lobster has ventured away out from the shelter of his home in the reef. A yellow band at surprising speed squirms through the water and whips around the cray which instantly kicks under with its tail, thus shooting backward like a squid. The coils of the snake tighten around it, trying hard to squeeze that propelling tail while its vicious head bites under at the mouth of the cray which wriggles and jerks in frantic attempts to spike the belly of the snake. Should the reptile fail to quieten the tail, the cray reaches the reef and struggles into a cranny thus breaking the snake's grip by pressure against the rock and its spikes.

Sea-snakes pick their marks of course. Once they coil around a fish it is generally doomed. Unable to use either fins or tail, the fish simply wallows in a helpless struggle. But the snake often takes a sporting chance. Then the diver watches an interesting fight, a pugnacious fish, its back fin with sharp spines erect, its jaws snapping, dives and charges and somersaults and Catherine-wheels in vicious attempts to beat the manoeuvres of the squirming, wriggling, snapping snake.

If both are evenly matched such a fight continues until both have had enough, or death comes to either or both. The snake is at a disadvantage if his first tactical rush fails. His aim in that rush is to whip his coils around the fish and flatten the back fin with its spines. For, immediately those spines are in fighting attitude the fish will do its best to shove the spines into the snake's body. And we all know how sharp are the spines of a fish. The snake finds them very formidable.

At times a sea-snake will hurtle straight at a diver to be hurled back by impact against his face-glass. Sometimes they twine around his leg or arm, viciously biting at the thick canvas suit. Quite often they will whip around his life-line or air-pipe; biting viciously. Sometimes they stay thus and are hauled to the surface to the dismay of the Koepangers, who dread them.

Jock D'Castilleau was fishing off the coast on a beautiful day when whales came playing around the lugger. One big old humpback in particular made "plenty humbug", circling the lugger in an effortless semi-roll to glide just under it, and then repeat the performance. At any moment they expected him to scrape the barnacles off his body against the keel. Sucker-fish were clinging to him like leeches to a pig. If he should decide to scrape those irritating pests off his hide by rubbing against the keel, then over might go the lugger. They could see his little eyes, the big knobbly lumps on his head and lips. He appeared most interested in the lugger and all on board.

The crew with bated breath, taking great care not to disturb the whale, began hauling up the diver. A little Koepanger was cautiously hauling in the air-pipe but his eyes were all for the whale. Slowly, foot by foot, inch by inch, the life-line and air-pipe came up, the Koepanger never for a second taking his eyes off the whale wallowing ominously close. Should pipe or line touch the whale it would become frantic at the unfamiliar touch and possibly that would mean the end of the diver. The crew watched breathlessly life-line and air-pipe and whale—most of all the whale. Up with the air-pipe came a sea-snake tightly coiled around it. No one noticed it: the diver was close to the surface now—so was the whale.

But the snake was already at the Koepanger's hands, in a flash it had twisted itself around his waist. With a shriek he dropped the air-pipe: in a trice he was up the mast.

In the whale season whales occasionally make life interesting for an hour or two to the scattered luggers. The leviathans come ploughing along in great numbers, a picture of mighty strength; happy monsters of the deep. They seem to congregate at times around the Lacepedes especially, as if it were a meeting-place preparatory to the school moving on. When a leviathan rises he announces the fact by a blast of "Whoof! Whoof!" invariably answered by his mate, "Whoof! Whoof!" They snort and blow a while, lazing and wallowing on the surface, blowing vaporous scintillating water-sprays in the air. But when a playful whale comes straight at the lugger to "humbug", the crew immediately haul up the diver (if not already up) and scamper for kerosene tins to beat them and dance and shriek to scare off the whale. As if in bovine disdain, sometimes a whale will rise right alongside, blow, and douse the crew with dirty water.

Last year Lou Marshall, aboard the *La Grange*, saw a sight seldom seen even by the sea-going pearlers. A whale that, evidently, had lost its school came cruising along, making for the lugger. Lou signalled the diver up immediately. A lonely whale will probably attach itself to a lugger for quite a time. For three hours this big old chap cruised slowly around and around the *La Grange*, until the crew became tired of beating kerosene tins. Gracefully the old chap would come towards the vessel, then when almost on top of it he would slowly dive, his huge slate-grey bulk just skimming the keel. Several times he gently scraped it, and both crew and lugger shivered. As he came up on the opposite side he would turn, massive head would emerge far out of the water, then his body, until practically standing on his tail he would momentarily gaze down upon the deck, then with a graceful upward beat of the tail come wallowing down, to glide again under the vessel, come up on the other side, and repeat his dreamy stare right down into the faces of the crew. Again and again he circled the lugger and repeated his diving and deck-gazing. Lou Marshall and his crew have seen many whales and numbers that rose straight up half out of the water, but this was the first to "stand on its tail", and gaze down on the deck.

When a school of whales come playing around a fleet all work must cease. The divers are hauled up to sit on deck and glare their disgust at the sporting monsters. It is a great sight, a fleet of pearling luggers with a large school of whales sporting and playing amongst them. Noisy too, with the occasional "Whoof! Whoof!" of the whales; the thunder as a leviathan surges from the waves to flop back with a gigantic shaking, the yelling of the crews, and the beating of kerosene tins. Perhaps some irate captain at last tries to sneak away. In vain; whales detach themselves from the school and joyfully follow the absconding lugger. It is followed too by the jeers and laughter of the remaining crews.

Sennosuke Yano, one of Captain Goldie's divers, felt particularly aggrieved once when the whales appeared a month before their time. One companionable old cow attached herself to Goldie's lugger and plainly showed that the yells and kerosene-tin beating intrigued her to such an extent that she almost tried to climb aboard. That whales should come in seasonal routine was bad enough, but to come a month before their time! ... Sennosuke shrieked to a crew-boy to bring his almanac from down below. He snatched the almanac and, leaping· to the side, yelled down at the whale: "You are here a month too soon, take a look at this if you doubt me, you stupid creature! Now go away!" And he flung the almanac at the whale!

In September of 1934 the fleets enjoyed a day-long laugh at the expense of one of Streeter and Male's luggers. A solitary old cow whale appeared, leisurely threaded her way through the fleets, and attached herself to the lugger. The diver was hurriedly brought aboard; kerosene tins and yells in vain tried to scare the lady away. At last the diver ordered the tender to sail the lugger down among the other vessels. Straightway the lady followed; the lugger moved on—so did the whale. Nothing could shake her off. Meanwhile, every other diver was working. All day long ribald jests were shouted across to the unfortunate lugger as the vessels passed by on their drifts.

Fortunately for the whales, they are never shot at. The crews believe that ill luck dogs the ship that kills a whale. The attempt would be dangerous whether or no; for if a maddened leviathan turned on a lugger the little vessel might be sent to keep her diver company. Still, the crews enjoy many a laugh over their quaint antics.

A whale will occasionally make an organ-like sound. When Jock Harver in the *Muriel* first heard this he was amazed, the sound fairly filled the cabin. He went on deck and the crew mutely pointed to a large whale just rising astern. It was playfully following the lugger which was trying to dodge its company. The weather blowing a bit, they were running with mainsail and jibs. They luffed and sailed north, but the whale effortlessly followed. There would be no sending the diver down again if this kept up. They paid off and ran out to sea. The whale disappeared. Jock went below again and immediately the organ-notes vibrated through the cabin. He came on deck just as the whale rose, so close that they could see the scars and wounds and barnacles upon its corrugated body. It takes more than manoeuvring to shake off a sociable whale when it is determined to accompany a lugger.

The whimpering of a baby whale, within eight inches of a man's ear at night, is an eerie experience. Especially if the night be dark, the lugger anchored in a lonely place, and the white man aboard has never heard the sound before. When I turned over inquiringly, the diver's brown, grinning face was beaming from the bunk opposite. The hurricane lamp was turned very low.

"Baby whale, master," he murmured. "Baby he been losem mother."

A friend of mine had his own experience. He suffered from nightmares and had ordered the diver to wake him immediately, should he cry out in his sleep. One night the diver woke him; he mumbled thanks, rolled over, and was immediately asleep again. Again the diver woke him; and again. Frowning, he couldn't remember any nightmare; he rolled over once more ... then a wheezy, vast whimpering filled the cabin. He looked into the diver's startled eyes. They stared at one another. Again came that heavy, plaintive whimpering as of some vast thing in babyish misery. The thick bristly hair on the diver's head began to twitch erect. When the whimper came again they turned up the hurricane lamp and sneaked on deck. A distant "Whoof!" gave them an inkling. They looked over the side: there was a baby whale pressed close against the lugger, whimpering for its mother.

Whales are troubled at times by itchy parasites in the form of sea-lice, barnacles, and sucker-fish. Which explains why on occasions the pearling crews watch a surprising sight. A mammoth rising straight from the sea like a submarine rising with its bows pointed direct to the sky. The mighty bulk of the whale sheers straight up until it appears to be standing on its tail; poises a second, then with a twisting motion falls upon its back to a thunder of spray. This no doubt helps to kill the parasites. Occasionally a monster will rise straight from the sea and shake itself like a powerful dog emerging from a pool. At such times it shakes off a shower of sucker-fish, that fly out to smack the water in all directions.

Occasionally a whale sleeps on the surface. When the crew awake in the morning he may be so close that it seems only a step to his broad, glistening back. In the season when the whales are plentiful, the crews often wonder just what would happen should a sailing lugger hit a sleeping whale at night. Some whales are longer and bulkier than the smaller pearling vessels.

When the old chap is cruising along, the great spreading flukes of his tail beat lazily up and down. He seems to be going very slowly; yet his speed and strength if called upon is amazing. It is these great tail-flukes, the hooked looking dorsal fin and the flippers that really cause all the worry to the diver, for around these massive protuberances the life-line and air-pipe is liable to become entangled if the whale comes too playfully close.

Some divers may never have an adventure with a whale; others get more than their share. Jitaro Naka, already mentioned, has three times "mixed it" with a whale; Hamaguchi who was lost on the bottom of the sea twice had his lines entangled around the flukes of a whale's tail. Other divers have fared similarly. Captain Talboys's diver received a great fright; the maddened leviathan towed the lugger for two miles before it disentangled itself. One of Claude Hawkes's divers experienced a similar thrill.

Perhaps for quick thought, quick action, and devil-may-care gameness the action of Marab the Malay seaman may take some beating. The *Olive* was fishing on a beautiful day, off the Eighty Mile Beach. A school of whales suddenly appeared—the diver was down on the sea floor, luckily they were working with a very slack life-line. They sprang to haul in the lines but just then a whale rose right beside the lugger, the life-line loosely hanging over a fluke. They stared as if paralysed but Marab instantly dived overboard, a few strokes took him to the whale, he seized the life-line and jerked it off the fluke. The whale swam lazily on to glide around the lugger while Marab to cheers laughingly climbed aboard.

What saved trouble on this particular occasion was the slackness of the life-line. Had it been taut the whale would have felt the unaccustomed weight; would have lashed with its tail to shake the thing off; the line (almost certainly) would have become entangled around a fluke; then the whale would have bolted.

Diver Ishiguchi, aboard J. W. Tilly's *Mariana*, had a surprising escape. He was working below, when suddenly a big shadow loomed right on top of him—coming silently down. With fast-beating heart he stared up at the monstrous body of a whale. With his arm stretched above his head he could almost have touched it.

With dignified slowness the whale nosed his great head, then all his huge bulk, between the life-line and air-pipe. As the lines stretched out the tender screamed "Whale! Whale!" All stared aghast at the tautening lines, but dared do nothing while the whale was actually at them.

The leviathan seemed to like the soothing rub of the lines, for he turned and slowly cruised between them again, twisting gently to allow them to rub slowly along his body. That great bulk was encrusted by barnacles and the whale was scratching them off against the lines. The horrified diver was drawn up and down in the water as the whale played in between the lines and in between again. The horror was that with the weight of the suspended diver keeping the lines taut they would cling tighter as the whale's tail tapered, and then would come—the broad flukes.

But again and again as the whale felt the obstruction it gracefully thrashed its flukes up and downward with a sideways twisting motion and the lines slid away.

At last the lines caught on the flukes. The whale's tail lashed irritably;

the lines held; the whale went mad-bolted.

... But the lines slipped off.

When they hauled the diver aboard, both life-line and air-pipe were found to be so cut by barnacles that both had to be renewed.

Truly, Ishiguchi had had a wonderful escape.

This type of accident is brought about by playfulness on the part of the whale; he takes a friendly interest in the lugger the bottom of which under water looks surprisingly like a companion whale. Possibly the real whale comes ploughing along to inquire what the other fellow is doing with all those sticks and rags on top, just like a sail-fish. He dives under the lugger and sees two long tentacles stretching down. One of these glides along his sides; it is caught against a fluke; he feels the strange weight; lashes out; the life-line is then twisted around the fluke, and the whale goes mad. Mitsura, one of Captain Gregory's divers, had a hair-raising experience in that way. The whale came straight to the surface and the crew saw the diver turned right over its back thus making a complete turn of the life-line around the whale's body. The yelling crew rushed to tiller and sails lest the strain break the line as the whale bolted, in a frantic effort to free itself of the lugger's weight and the brand-new life-line that was cutting into its body. Imagine the feelings of the helpless diver, fastened to the body of a bolting whale. The diver's case seemed utterly hopeless when, suddenly, the whale dived and the looped line dragged back by the lugger's weight slipped down its body, squeezed the great tail-flukes together, and slipped right off. But it broke Mitsura's nerve.

As I write these lines (October 1936) old Sakai has taken his last dive. Old Sakai of the quiet ways and withered smile. Captain Gregory's fleet was fishing off the Eighty Mile Beach when two whales came sporting around the *Buntie*. Old Sakai, the head diver, with the second diver remained on deck while the whales departed. In late afternoon all was quiet. The two divers descended sixteen fathoms deep into green twilight. Suddenly the No. 2 diver was jerked off his feet; a tremendous tug on the life-line lifted him far up into the water. In horror he saw the great white belly of a whale and saw his life-line twisted around a fluke. The great tail thrashed down and up; the line slipped off, and the diver dropped straight to the bottom as the frightened whale plunged straight against Sakai's air-pipe. To the beat of that powerful tail the air-pipe was entangled around a fluke and instantly Sakai was lifted in the water. As the now maddened leviathan twisted and turned, Sakai was spun around those beating flukes. The No. 2 diver with horror in his heart signalled wildly, shut tight his air-escape valve and began to ascend. But Sakai, fast to the tail of a maddened whale, was being towed through the water at a terrific pace. Came a shuddering jerk as the air-pipe reached its limit; the coupling was torn out of the helmet; the leviathan raced away, and the sea rushed in upon Sakai.

Quickly he sank, then slowly began to ascend as the frantic crew hauled in on the life-line.

With flag at half-mast, they brought Sakai back to Roebuck Bay.

They gave him a great funeral, all the whites attended as well as the Japanese and Malays. Father Wurms read the service. Then came the Japanese service with all the quietly picturesque mourning of the Orient.

Poor old Sakai! One of the best divers out of Broome; one of the best liked by all men; a real sash-wearer. No more will he tell me wonderful stories under the poinciana-tree, looking out towards Buccaneer Rock.

Vale, old Sakai.

In a dead man's house. Each of the lanterns holds a prayer.

CHAPTER XXXII
The Rain-Maker

Captain L. J Goldie's fleet was fishing off Cape Leveque. Now, the luggers required water once a month and Goldie used to sail to Chile Creek to replenish the tanks. It was a bonny day that he up anchored and sailed for the creek. The glass promised well; everything was set for a good season. Chile Creek is a little over thirty miles north-west along the coast from Beagle Bay. There is a quaint little mission station by the creek which runs through a small peninsula. The mission is proud of its one fence twenty miles long which "cuts off" the peninsula from the mainland bush and so hems in the few mission cattle. Surrounded on three sides by the sea, the stock are easy to manage. The station is on fairly level country near some low hills. Fair sized timber lines the creek. It is a lonely place; rarely visited, except by low-browed blacks from the wild pindan beyond.

Immediately the luggers arrived and before they were properly moored, an aboriginal lad from the mission appeared on the beach and called to Goldie to come up to the mission as soon as possible as the Father was ill. Goldie set his crew to filling the water-tanks, then walked up a faintly trodden path to the mission headquarters. The little church is a frontier building, of large logs squared with adze and axe. Two Sisters have their quarters there under charge of Father August Spendenberg, a comparatively recent arrival from Europe. Virgin bush surrounds the tiny buildings.

Goldie walked up to the Father's quarters and knocked. A blackfellow came noiselessly to the door.

"Where is Father?" Goldie inquired.

"He stop inside. He sick. He lie down," mumbled the aboriginal.

Goldie walked in. The Father was on a rough bush bunk in a sparsely furnished, dully-lit room. In surprise he stared at the visitor. He looked lonely and depressed.

"Fever?" inquired Goldie.

The Father nodded hesitantly.

"We'll soon see," said Goldie cheerfully. He took the pulse, temperature, examined the sick man's tongue, then looked in a puzzled way at his eyes. Goldie had some small knowledge of medicine.

"There is nothing much wrong that I can see, Father; just a touch of fever of which the worst is over," he decided in a puzzled tone. "Are you sure it is not worry. Perhaps the blacks are troubling you?"

The sufferer shook his head. Goldie sat down beside him.

"Look here, Father, you are getting better, but you seem worried and depressed. Tell me; I might be able to help. In this lonely spot it may be months before a visitor comes again. Can I help you in any way at all?"

The Father shook his head.

"It is just a touch of fever; it will pass away," he murmured, and gazed at the rough logs that walled the room.

"I don't want to force a confidence, Father, but I think you have something on your mind," insisted Goldie earnestly. "Won't you tell me? It will do you good to discuss the trouble with someone."

The Father lay silent for some time, then suddenly rose on his elbow:

"I should like to tell you, but I am afraid you will laugh at me. I cannot tell the Sisters, I might alarm them. It is such a stupid little thing."

"It is the stupid little things that grow and grow in such a lonely place as this," encouraged Goldie. "Tell me."

"It is the rain-maker."

"The what?"

"The rain-maker: an old aboriginal we and the natives call the rain-maker."

"Oh, I understand–a witch-doctor man."

"Yes, but not quite. This man is the 'maker of rains'. He is not a curer of ills, nor the companion of spirits. He predicts it is going to rain next Wednesday! I had set the natives digging an irrigation channel from the well to water some young sweet potatoes. The work was cheerfully begun, and progressing satisfactorily, when the old rain-maker appeared and told them they were wasting their energy, as it was going to rain next Wednesday. At about the same time I went down with this attack of fever. The work ceased. I am unable to enforce my requirements; the crop of sweet potatoes may be lost. But most important of all is the fact that I fear they may revert to the spell of their old superstitions. And all the work I have been slowly building up since my arrival will be undermined! These people are so close to the primitive."

"Ridiculous! It won't rain for six months. The wet season is finished; it is a beautiful sky; fair weather glass ... Nonsense!"

"That is so," said the priest eagerly. "I know it! It is now June, well into the dry season. It should not rain at very earliest until next November. How is your glass, did you say?"

"Very high indeed, 30.20 at 9 this morning."

"Yes. So is mine."

"There. There *cannot* be any rain."

"Of course not. And yet ... the old rain-maker says he is going to make rain!"

"Nonsense. How can you listen to such tommy rot! An educated man, a Christian gentleman, letting his reason be obscured by the superstitious mumblings of a Stone Age savage!"

"You are right, Captain Goldie! I was foolish. I am so glad you prevailed upon me to discuss it with you."

Goldie was pleased to see by the Father's face that he was clearing the mental air. He did so to such good effect that in an hour or so the Father got up and gave orders for dinner. He was like a schoolboy who has been quite ill but is up and about again. Goldie kept talking cheerily, giving all the news he could of Broome, with news of the pearling fleets and of the outside world. It was a pleasure to see the sick man responding; to answer his eager questions; to hear, presently, his cheery laugh.

With the going out of the tide it was time for Goldie to take his leave.

"Call up this old heathen before I go," he suggested. "I'd like to have a look at him."

"Boy!" called the Father. An aboriginal boy came in answer.

"You tell the rain-maker come up here. I want see him!"

With a startled glance the boy disappeared. Moments later, and quite silently, the rain-maker appeared. Withered and skinny, a circlet of old bones around his neck, he stared from unblinking eyes.

"What you mean? You say makem rain! You no savvy makem rain!" challenged Goldie.

"Proper I savvy makem rain," growled the old man.

"Before Father came here you people all time hungry!" said Goldie. "Only then can eatem kangaroo, sugar-bag (wild honey), sometime spearem fish. Now Father makem garden. Give all fellow beef, flour, sugar, tea, tobacco, and fish net. Altogether plenty tucker this time. Father teachem children read and write, and all fellow church. What's matter you tellem all that nother fellow no digem trench? You old man, you must help new young Father, not makem worry sick time."

"Arright. You wait! You see by em by! Rain Wensdee; rain he come. Big feller rain!" and the rain-maker slunk away.

With a reassuring farewell Goldie went down to the waiting dinghy — the call of the tide was imperative.

Next dawn as Goldie came up on deck he looked at the sky. It was like bright moonlight; a beautiful clear blue with a pinkish line spreading into crimson at the east. When the sun rose, it promised a perfect day. It might never rain for a year. The glass, too, certified perfect weather.

"Strange," thought Goldie, "the effect of a savage mind upon a sick, lonely white man. I believe that old heathen has been worrying the Father a long time; looked like a deliberate challenge to me."

Wednesday morning came. Sleepily Goldie woke to the shouted "Master here, coffee ready!" Yawning, he climbed up out the scuttle and almost fell back at the surprised "Ame Aru! Ame Aru!" of the Japanese tender and diver.

It was raining! Goldie could hardly believe his senses. He stared at the drifting rain coming across the sea to obscure the land. With a clutch at his heart he watched it rolling on towards Chile Creek.

It rained heavily for two hours, then cleared off into beautiful weather which lasted for months.

Japanese pearl divers off Broome early 1920s.

CHAPTER XXXIII
Broome Days

Alas, Broome fell on evil days in common with all the world. The depression struck the pearling industry hard. Strangely enough, good fortune allied itself to misfortune for a huge new shell-bed was discovered towards Torres Strait. This bed alone increased the production of shell one thousand tons in one year. This great good fortune came at a time when the price of shell was steadily falling. Difficult to imagine the change in the town of Broome. Gone were the days of riotous prosperity, of brave fleets setting out each season racing for a good catch, confident of disposing of every ton of shell and of selling the pearls on a hungry market. Now curtailment of output was necessary. The master pearlers had actually to remove the air-compressors and engine pumps from the luggers and replace them by the hand pumps that had lain in the lumber sheds for fifteen years. A tribute to British workmanship, those pumps. When taken to pieces, cleaned, and installed, they worked as efficiently as on the day they had been discarded fifteen years ago.

But it seemed a shame. These splendid little vessels, swift, capable of riding out a cyclone, had been evolved through the experiences and tragedies, the heartaches and triumphs of seventy years. The fleets, too, represented the last word in "modernity"; the latest diving-gear, modern engines to drive modern air-compressors, condensers to filter and cool the air, containers to hold that cool filtered air till driven under pressure to the divers. Auxiliary engines too, to propel the vessel when necessary, in addition to working compressors. The pipe pressure gauge which tells without the diver's signals whether he is all right, whether he is coming up, whether some mishap has befallen him, or something is wrong with the apparatus. Modern launches too, by means of which one master could manage five vessels operating at sea. The industry has risen to an efficiency of which the handful of pearlers might well be proud. In the old days, a successful diver would bring up five tons of shell per year. Now, working in a modern vessel he would average seven and a half tons per year; in an exceptionally good season he might send up even ten tons. And with infinitely less risk, less labour, less cost. It seemed a shame that progress should be forced to take a backward step.

And all this developed into a smoothly working organization that covered all the pearl seas; had prospected vast areas of the ocean bed and learnt their secrets; had trained a little army of divers, tenders, and coloured seamen.

The price of pearls fell with the price of shell. Each lugger was now allowed to fish only a few tons per season, the master pearlers struggling to keep their fleets in commission. From one hundred and eighty pounds a ton the price of shell fell to one hundred and ten pounds a ton. And it cost more than that to raise a ton of shell.

As to pearls, a most curious thing has happened, especially within the last few years. Firstly though, the fall in price. Whereas little Broome alone for years cleared more than one hundred thousand pounds a year for pearls, the reward fell to below ten thousand. And now a remarkable thing has happened, for in the pearl-shell won over the last five or six years there have been hardly any pearls. What has happened? Some thousands of tons of shell have been won in that time, but where are the pearls? The shell has not produced them for the master pearlers have sailed their own vessels and opened their own shell.

Has the pearl oyster refused to fashion pearls in quantity? Or is it that conditions have changed on the sea bottom. Perhaps that condition which irritated and caused the oyster to fashion a pearl has changed, or is it, as some among the pearlers are inclined to believe, that the deep-water shell has come up from the depths on to the reefs, and that this deep-water shell does not carry pearls? But if so, what has happened to the pearl-shell that formerly lived amongst the reefs. It is a perplexing question, some mystery of nature on the bottom of the sea. Probably it will be righted in time and the pearl-shell oyster will again produce its usual proportion of "tears of the sea".

As to pearls in the Coral Sea, we know nothing of how they have fared for there the divers retain all pearls won.

At Broome, even the Japanese Club was feeling the pinch. The ever mounting terms, the shrewd bargaining of the Japanese received a check as severe as unexpected. With pearl-shell hardly saleable, the pearlers simply could not give the Japanese the money demanded. After various meetings, the parties compromised, the Japanese sensibly and philosophically accepting the situation for the time being.

This was lay-up time 1933—and Christmas. The days and nights often swelteringly hot, the mornings cool, the water like a blue sheet of glass. Mrs Locke as hostess at the Continental was very busy supervising Christmas festivities.

Alas! the wretched goats came in, climbed all over the tables and ate the cakes and flowers. Those goats were filled with a devilish cunning. Mrs Locke mixed up cement with bran and spread it out in the yard. The goats ate the bran, but sniffed away the cement.

Old Con was all smiles as he tended his precious electric-light engine.

In fact his body seems saturated with "magnetism". When he puts a watch on his wrist, it stops. I have seen him get into a car, and the engine refuse to go. Con would smilingly alight, then away would speed the car. Yet, when he is in charge of machinery, it never goes wrong.

A crowd of white-suited people breezed in to the cool, flowered verandas and the easy chairs. Long Jimmy James started on Christmases that had been. Down the broad, tree-lined street walked old "Pa" Norman, very upright, worried but determined. Fine old man, one of the sea pioneers; up against it now like the rest of them, but fighting hard. Some distance away the short, natty figure of Captain Owen, quiet, cool, cheery, and clear of eye, beside the tall form of the young Government Resident, Mr. Wallwork. A decidedly interesting job this of the Government Resident, holding numerous problems liable to keep him awake at nights.

I strolled up the road for a yarn with Elles the pearl-cleaner. And had for company one of Broome's feathered furies. A quaint character, the giant jabiru. Occasionally, when pictures are on, he strides majestically down the street and "regulates" the traffic. Standing higher than the hood of a car, he is some bird, and knows it. He loves chickens—tasty morsels. Cats fly at sight of him. He really belongs to the Continental, but he "owns" the town and none dare say him nay. He was now apparently *en route* to the Roebuck, half a mile away, strutting along on his great long legs, now and again throwing out his chest and straightening his neck to rise like a giraffe, then spread and flap his great wings. By way of diversion he would stride into a residential garden, advance to the veranda, and announce his presence in ear-splitting trumpetings. Nice ladies who advanced on him hysterically waving a towel and saying rude things, had difficulty in persuading him to retire. The gamest dog would not venture within twenty feet of him. That long bill on the end of that long neck when stretched from those broomstick legs could reach a staggering distance. To peck a hole through a dog was his delight. The afternoon before, during the latter part of the siesta hour, this devil on stilts strutted across a lawn and looked inside a window. All windows in Broome are kept open to any heaven-sent breeze. A man was in the room. He had just stepped from the bath and dropped the soap. As he was bending, the terrible beak shot out. The yells of that man woke the town while the bird retreated with triumphant trumpetings across the lawn.

But I am afraid the victory will cost the jabiru his life. That man vowed that when he could walk he would come bopping along with a gun.

I strolled slowly behind the jabiru up the road. We were approaching the dense buildings of Asiatic town. The jabiru deviated to a coloured man's cottage. A cockatoo was in a cage on the veranda, he screeched appallingly as he saw the jabiru step over the fence and come strutting towards him. The great bird stood off, thrust in his gigantic beak and pulled out a couple of feathers. To the blood-curdling screech of the cockatoo he souvenired several more feathers. Then calmly secured a beakful of tail as the cage crashed to the ground. With the tail between his beak he swung the cage high and hurled it across the garden, retaining the poor cockatoo's tail in his beak. A coloured man came rushing out with a long boathook which he thrust forward as a lance. For a moment I hoped the jabiru was going to tackle man and hook. However, he executed a series of gigantic hops, spread his big wings and make the welkin ring with trumpetings.

We strolled on up through the town, crowded now with Japanese, Malays, and Koepangers. They all gave the bird a wide berth as he strolled down the narrow lanes. He entered the Roebuck by the back way. The bathroom is down the yard, a girl in a bright dressing-gown was just coming out. She hesitated, half closed the door, and shooed the jabiru away with the towel. He did not seem particularly interested, just strolled around the back. The girl made a run for it. She shrieked on the last lap, just diving in through the kitchen door inches ahead of that awful beak.

The world's greatest pearl-cleaner sat discontented in his office, something plaintive about his smooth, round face.

"What fools men are," he complained. "Must have a war; must have depression. Never satisfied. They pay hundreds of millions for gunpowder, but they won't buy pearls. Rubin had the sense; he went in for wool." After a while he lapsed into talk of the years just gone.

In the last twenty years Elles had handled over two million pounds' worth of pearls, he had often made a hundred pounds commission in two hours' work, had often bought a blister for twenty or thirty pounds, and sold it for two hundred or three hundred pounds. Reputedly now the richest man in Broome he had built a temple in Ceylon for ten thousand pounds—a temple he had never seen. And now he was selling the biggest and cheapest lemon squashes in the north-west. No wonder he sighed for the glorious days of pearls.

But he has been a wonderfully lucky man. Despite heart-breaking reverses in earlier years, he has grown grey at a work he loved.

Murikama the Japanese business man had lost his fortune but he was very quiet about it, hoping, with the white pearlers, that the good days would come again.

Brahim Sa Maidin the Imman had grown more worry lines on his brow. A few years ago at a cost of a thousand pounds he had built a church for the Mohammedans. Now, when he went among them seeking a pound each to pay for it, they shook gloomy heads, declaring that times were too bad. Truly, the depression had much to answer for.

Perhaps old Con in his humble circumstances was one of the happiest men in Broome. Liking his job, his quiet smile and slow drawling voice ever ready for a cheery joke, seeing everything while saying little, he was as keen as ever in pursuit of love.

Old Lorenzo his enemy had died. But for several years before he died Con was his good friend, helping him in his long illness, bringing him good things from his scanty store.

Francis Paddy had left for Koepang to end his days there in the pretty little capital of Dutch Timor. But old Sebaro stayed on in Broome, surrounded by his family. That night we sat under the poincianas with the old man. The three-quarter moon was misty as the wisps of grey hair stuck up on his shining brown pate. Capitano, short and bulky and of indeterminate business, lounged by the garden gate. Women were in the house, coming and going on soft feet, as coloured people do. Sebaro sat with his back against a palm, speaking in a soft voice, his laugh all cynical humour. He had sailed Thursday Island waters in the days of the blackbirders and hell-ships, and the north-west coast in the days of the "Pirates". No Broome then, the shellers were just creeping up the coasts before the days of the fleets. Sebaro had seen high adventure; life and death in numerous forms; the opening up of six thousand miles of coastline, and of a thousand coral isles. Wonderful, how some men's lives are destined to be living pages of continuous adventure. We talked of many things, including the great pearl, and the "Bishop's Ghost". I wanted to see the ghost. White people in Broome swear they have seen it, and I was curious. If a bishop, and perfectly sober white citizens of both sexes, could, on a bright night, see the figure come from the Bishop's Palace, glide across the street and through the chained and padlocked gate of the -Residency, then why shouldn't I?

A few days later, rather diffidently, I approached John, Bishop of the North-West. It is not a usual request to make, to ask a bishop if you may sleep on his veranda in the hope of meeting a ghost.

However, the bishop smiled; he is a very approachable man. The ghost was well known to him by repute, though he had never personally met it. He had on various occasions been approached by persons — not desiring to see the ghost, but seeking permission to dig up the grounds and search for the supposed pearls. He invited me inside and showed me exactly where and how his predecessor, Bishop Trower, had on various occasions seen the ghost. Bishop Trower was firmly convinced of its reality.

Bishop Trower's brother, a medico in England, has a note-book half-filled with notes of the bishop's experiences.

The present bishop gave me permission to sleep on the veranda, in company with Con, while he was travelling his diocese. That diocese is possibly the largest in the world, with probably the smallest population. The bishop travels around his diocese visiting as many stations as he can once in every two years. He was preparing to visit the southern portion of his domain, for in the north the wet season was due. As soon as he left I was welcome to come and meet the ghost—if the ghost was willing.

Back at the Continental, the weather was still and sweltering; talk at table was all of "the glass", the one the mercury is in. Across a low sky ominous clouds were gathering and an occasional flash of lightning split the horizon. There was another storm brewing too: Inspector Tuohy and Sergeant Clements were very worried; seven hundred Koepangers were sullenly fashioning clubs, working up to a big fight against the Malays.

We watched the cock-eye bob approaching. Fleecy clouds steadily rolled up; the sky steadily came "lower and lower"; a hot breathlessness absorbed energy from every living thing. Towards evening the south-eastern sky was growing black; by nightfall the world was pitch dark, frightening with its continuous, vivid lightning as of many guns firing over a front of twenty miles. Far to right and left, in vivid crinkling across the front, those red splitting flashes seemed bursting to overcome the blackness that instantly swallowed them. In the small hours of the morning the cock-eye came with a rush and a roar that threatened to tear the town down. Wind howled over the roofs; ripped in under verandas and slammed windows and doors, blowing chairs and books and bedclothes out of the very hands of those who rushed to seize them. Rain came roaring down, in minutes the streets were running, thunder was crashing and rolling and vibrating the very earth. But it hardly lasted half an hour. It cleared away leaving brilliant stars, glorious cool air, refreshing sleep.

CHAPTER XXXIV
The "Bishop's Ghost"

The Koepanger-Malay trouble almost went "over the top", but not quite. At the critical moment Sergeant Clements with his half-dozen men strode right amongst the excited Koepangers and broke the gathering. But for three days afterwards things looked very nasty. With quick staff work Inspector Tuohy hurried the arrangement for hundreds of the aggrieved ones to take their leave to Koepang, after their two years' service. So the threatened fray petered out in the excitement of preparations for embarkation.

Quite a sight, the home-sailing of the indentured seamen. The quaint little tram packed with excited men and their belongings. Big trunks painted in blue and orange, yellow, green, and red. Hundreds of shiny new suit-cases, coloured cloths, shawls and blankets. Kerosene tins and Chinese baskets from which peeped handles of tools and pots and pans and the oddest assortment of articles they had gathered about the town during the last two lay-up seasons. Rice bags bulging with coloured and spotted cloths, guitars and mandolins and heaven knows what. When these sailor lads returned to Koepang they would be the envy of the stay at homes, especially the female ones.

The police on the long jetty guarded the train until every man had been identified. A busy day this for the customs officials. The *Centaur* down at the jetty end blowing off steam, with Chinese sailors in uniform on guard at the gangways. Groups of white-coated pearlers and officials. The Japanese who were returning, smartly dressed, efficient, embarked apart. Quick system throughout despite the excited, hilarious embarkation of these hundreds of Koepangers.

From lower down the wharf, a group of aboriginals watched the fiesta of departure. A very sophisticated little crowd, the local abos. They organize their own "lottery" and not only quietly defy authority but have kept the financial secrets of their Monte Carlo inviolate. Some business head among them goes around the little crowd every evening and collects the threepences and sixpences that their toil has garnered throughout the day. This wealth constitutes the "bank", and from each bank the "organizer" calmly collects a modest fifty per cent as his "commission". Then the "tickets" are made, scraps of paper pencil-marked. The organizer shuffles these in an old hat and the first prize is drawn for.

"The local abo is well and truly civilized in these parts," remarked

Stainton. He was classing a parcel of baroque in his bungalow. I was smoking. We had just been talking of the "abo lottery". Stainton examined a bead of baroque that with cleaning might be transformed into a small pearl.

"I was feeling my way across the flat last night," he said. "It was midnight and pitch dark. Suddenly: 'Aces!' 'Tens!' 'Fives!' came almost from my feet. I could just distinguish a number of abos sitting in a circle playing cards. They were too interested in their game to take any notice of me: they knew I wouldn't put them away anyway. If I only had their eyesight in the dark! You can be sailing outside at night with no sign of land and ask:

" 'Where Cape Lévêque?'

" 'Him there!' grunts the abo seaman with an upward thrust of his chin.

" 'You see him?'

" 'O ai! Him there.' And sure enough he takes the lugger straight to it."

Old Con was anxious that I should believe—should see the "Bishop's Ghost". The first night seemed propitious. Pitch dark, water pools here and there from the previous night's rain. Another cock-eye brewing; everything quiet and still on the big veranda; a breathless feeling over everything. We spread our blankets by the room where the bishop used to see the ghost, and stretched out. Con started yarning in a low, earnest voice. We discussed the great pearl, Castilla Toledo and Pablo, Simeon and Hagen. (Con had his opinion as to where they all were.) We spoke of other pearls and of killing individually and *en masse*, of mutiny and cyclones and intrigue and dead men in the sea, and other thrilling incidents that have all gone towards "the price we pay for pearls".

Then Con spoke of Lucifer, and surprised me with his knowledge of the Bible, the Koran, and books I had never even heard of. He seemed to have made a special study of the beliefs of men of many races concerning life after death. A padre would be stumped by some of his questions. Con's idea of Lucifer was not conducive to sound sleep. According to Con, he is a notorious chief, with power unbelievable, whirling through the universe leading flying armies of cavalry defying God, every now and then breaking through some gigantic heavenly cordon to stir up trouble in the hearts of men. At such times the earth is overrun with Lucifer's invisible flying cavalry whispering berserk thoughts into the minds of king and subjects, employer and employee; into all men of all colours and all creeds on all questions; stirring up the passions of men and woman while clouding their reason. This malign influence working through the minds of men caused the Great War, according to Con, as it causes all troubles upon earth.

However, we did not see the ghost that night, though Con dreamed of a nurse who used to live in the bungalow. She stood looking at us, frowned slightly, then walked on down the veranda.

Con believes in dreams, as do practically all coloured people. One night the nurse came to him again in a dream and asked him what we were doing there. He told her whom we wanted to meet; she frowned, shook her head and glided away. Another night quite a number of people came to him, one asked insistently for a needle, which he promised. Con could not understand why I did not dream. To ensure that I did, he brought some dream incense and burned it under my pillow. Well—it helped to keep the mosquitoes away.

In a Chinese store I bought a packet of needles—"Seagull" brand. Con was delighted; his dream woman had asked him especially for "Seagull" brand. That night Con crouched aside and mumbled over something; then reached across and put a little hard something into my hand. It was to make me dream. There are intricate laws regulating dreaming and bringing people in dreams, that he would not explain. These people have a queer dream-life impossible for the uninitiated to penetrate.

That particular night he dreamed a motor-truck and a cart came up to where we slept on the veranda; both were loaded with pillows and mattresses and beds. Strangely enough, a week later when we came to the veranda, we found that the cane chairs had been removed; and we nearly fell over a dismantled bed packed across our sleeping-place. A smell of wet paint explained the mystery. Evidently the bungalow was being renovated during the bishop's absence.

However, we did not see the ghost. I was too impatient, or else those veranda boards were too hard. Con wanted to work by the moon and the tides. The moon plays a surprising part in the lives of many coloured people. They regulate much of their business—especially their love-affairs—by the phases of the moon. Some will not even sail a cutter at sea by night unless under moonlight. From time immemorial the moon has influenced their lives. That is not to be wondered at in island people. The moon causes the tides that so intimately affect their livelihood. And the tides mean fish. The moon brings rain and sometimes winds. Through the tides it causes the seasons on the ocean floor. And these seasons affect pearl-shell and trochus, dugong and bêche-de-mer, and many fish.

But it is too intricate a subject for the uninitiated to fathom. And because Con would not, or because some obscure brotherhood forbade him to, explain to me fully why departed spirits should be more visible to humans under certain phases of the moon, I refused to continue to sleep on the bishop's veranda. The boards were too hard.

One night, under a bright full moon we were yarning at old Sebaro's. Con was strange, quicker and livelier in his movements, brighter of eye. He was almost startling. He led the conversation, brightly telling story after story with a shrewd, infectious laugh that was not the laugh of old Con of the Continental Hotel. The explanation lay in the slim young coloured girls who ever and anon came noiselessly through the gate and vanished in the house. Twice he vanished after some shadow in white. Old Sebaro kept talking; the others made no movement. Among Filipinos and Malays, with their ceaseless intrigues and jealousies, I had never seen any man so straight as Con; he scorned to be secretive where other men would be wily as the serpent.

After we left Sebaro's, I saw Con had business at another house, where though all lights were out the murmur of voices came from deep inside. But he insisted on seeing me home. We talked under the poincianas for another two hours.

Con talked rapidly and lucidly, and his head kept turning from side to side, his eyes shining. He seemed brighter and younger by years. I could not understand it. When I left him he was a vigorous man bound for adventure; I, more than twenty years younger, could hardly keep my eyes open. He had worked twelve hours that day, but went off with a laugh and a glance at the moon.

The master pearlers got their fleets to sea again. But it was a struggle; the limited tonnage of shell they could dispose of barely returned them enough to refit the fleets.

The pearl-shell industry is of peculiar importance to Australia, for it holds a tiny white population at three strategic points along our immense northern coastline. Take away the cattle and three tiny pearl towns, and the north would be empty.

Perhaps we can find some other use for pearl-shell. It is a strong and beautiful material and surely could be utilized in more ways than the very few for which it is bought at present. A greater consumption in bulk would not only expand the industry, but would help us populate the coast-line.

To make matters worse, the pearlers began to find themselves up against what has quickly developed into a ruinous competition. The Japanese have created a problem that has developed amazingly these last three years, fishing shell and putting it on the world's market at less than what it costs the Australian pearlers to land the shell from the luggers.

Nearly fifty years ago the first Japanese came as humble seamen to the pearling fleets. They were trained and employed as modern dress divers, tenders, and "captains". And how patiently, how efficiently they learnt their jobs to the minutest detail! During all those years they have sailed the six thousand miles of our coastline, the Coral Sea, and the Great Barrier Reef; have mastered the geography of the thousand islands, the thousand channels, the thousand thousand reefs, the sand-banks and anchorages, the pearl and trochus and bêche-de-mer beds and all the intricacies of navigation. They have mastered their jobs.

For years now, the complete fleets of one great pearling centre have been taken to sea entirely manned by these excellent seamen. Whites no longer go out with those particular fleets now, nor do they get any of the pearls.

Time-expired divers on returning to Japan explained to financial business compatriots, the pearl-shell wealth in Australian seas. And now Japanese, from bases in the mandated islands, are actively exploiting it. Modern vessels based on the type evolved through seventy years by the Australian pearlers have been built, powerful engines and modern living equipment have been installed, and the vessels have been manned by divers trained in the Australian pearling fleets. Larger, faster, and better equipped vessels than in the Australian fleets are the object worked for.

In 1935, the first large Japanese fleet fished successfully in the Arafura Sea, and not far off the Australian coast. While these vessels fish outside territorial waters they are of course perfectly free to do so. The Australian pearler does not mind fair competition, but he does resent the fact that he who founded and developed this industry is fast being threatened by a competition against which in a number of ways he is severely handicapped.

As this is being written (1936), word comes that a fleet of eighty Japanese vessels is to start operations immediately.[2] Before these lines meet the eye of the reader that fleet may have increased considerably.

The Australian pearler is up against it in more ways than one. He has to pay rates, taxes, customs dues, duties, tariffs, fuel, and licence fees—and much heavier food and gear bills. Since the start of the pearling industry the pearler in this way has spent millions in Australia, and a great deal in Great Britain for machines and various diving gear. So besides helping to settle the isolated northern coast, the industry has been of material benefit to Australian and British commerce, and labour both directly and indirectly concerned. Unfortunately, added costs and low price of shell in recent years have handicapped him in this sudden fight against highly organised

---

[2] Ninety vessels were reported operating before the end of 1936, while others were being built.

competition. It costs him one hundred pounds per annum to man even the old-fashioned, obsolete hand-pump boat, two hundred pounds per annum for modern vessels equipped with double-connexion engines and auxiliaries. Before he puts a single vessel to sea at the commencement of each season he must spend two hundred pounds on it. All this naturally increases the cost of raising each ton of shell. That is conservatively estimated in Broome waters at one hundred and thirty-eight pounds per ton (in the different centres local working conditions vary the cost somewhat.)

As it costs his Japanese competitors considerably less, the Australian pearler must put to sea each season handicapped to that extent.

When he loses the divers whom he has trained at considerable expense and years of time, he is handicapped still more.

If there was a wider market for the shell, Australian fleets could be quickly increased, larger and even better vessels equipped; and the added tonnage raised would be some recompense for the low price of shell.

But the market, apparently, is limited. Surely the world could make much greater use of this useful and beautiful article! Factories at Broome, Darwin, and Thursday Island, in which the shell could be turned into the completed article of commerce, would, probably, go a long way towards successfully meeting foreign competition. One thing appears certain; if our pearling fleets are not sent to sea under less expensive conditions, or if we cannot find a greater market for the shell, then the industry may be doomed.

At the close of the present shelling season the Japanese fleet had fished, approximately, two thousand five hundred tons of shell. This may prove to be more than the total haul of our Broome, Thursday Island, and Darwin fleets combined.

At the end of next season, with all fleets enlarged, production will be considerably more. If an enlarged market does not await all this extra shell, what will happen? Possibly a compromise. The Australian and Japanese fleets may come to some friendly marketing arrangement. It is a very interesting position, especially when one looks back to the beginning of the pearl-shelling industry seventy years ago.

To create a vastly enlarged market for pearl-shell would be the best solution. Any arrangement by which both fleets produced only so many tons of shell per year would merely keep both sides stationary. There would be neither development nor progress. A poor policy. In these days every industry should increase.

Much to-do has recently been made over an occasional sampan operating off our northern and north-eastern coasts. These stray sampans have visited our Great Barrier Reef on the north-eastern coast, the Northern Territory coastline, and the extreme north-west of Western Australia for many years past. Why the fuss now? Any damage that could be done has been done. In view of the fact that for forty years we have been training and paying Japanese seamen to sail six thousand miles of our own coastline in our own vessels, it seems inconsistent to become uneasy now over a stray shark-fishing sampan, or one seeking tortoise-shell, or trochus. Up-to-date poaching sampans are, of course, a different matter; they could be serious if they raided the long and lonely coastline in sufficient numbers. But poachers could be combated. It is the well organized, highly efficient and modern pearling fleets, operating lawfully at less cost than our own, that constitute the real danger to our own pearling industry.

It is high time we awoke to the real facts concerning our northern land, our northern coastline, and northern seas. We have done a marvellous work in settling the south, east, and west, but we must remember that just beyond our northern coastline are teeming islands and—Asia. An increasingly efficient, a hungry Asia.

Japanese All Souls' Day, September
Feast of lanterns, to send spirits out to sea.

CHAPTER XXXV
Sea Wealth

Our seas are a wondrous gift from the gods. Seas, and six thousand miles of northern coastline teeming with wealth. The time has come for us to work it.

How long it has taken us to realize the extent of our pearl-shell-beds! In 1861 Tays the Sailor found pearl-shell in Western Australia strewn in abundance all along the shore at Nickol Bay. That started a rush on the western side of the continent, and the dawn of seventy years of prosperity for the industry, the first fifty of which meant wealth and wild adventure.

On the north-eastern coast of the continent, in 1868, a black-bearded giant, Captain Banner, during a venturesome cruise in the brig *Julia Percy*, cast anchor off Warrior Island, the headquarters of the fiercest and ablest fighters in the Coral Sea. He made friends with the great chief Kebisu, and one night at the camp-fires saw the natives dining from the pearl-shell oyster; saw them throwing roasted pearls upon the sands. That started the first of the great pearl-shell rushes to the Coral Sea, and fifty years of adventure and romance.

But for many years, with the width of a continent between them, the men of the two great shell ventures thought that each new shell-bed would be the last, they feared that the sea would become exhausted of its pearls. But those on the western coast crept ever farther north and then east; while those on the east after exploiting the Coral Sea, and the Great Barrier Reef, turned west into the Arafura Sea. Then, midway between them, at Darwin, another pearl-shell port opened, to fish the Arafura and Timor seas.

Those tiny pearl-shell fleets, those wandering schooners and freelance luggers accomplished a marvellous work. They sought and found the pearl-shell with adventure, danger and (not seldom) death over thousands of miles of uncharted coral reefs, amid thousands of islands, many inhabited by fighting savages, and six thousand miles of uncharted coastline. That is the briefest outline of a chapter in our pioneering history that has not yet been written.

Only now are we grasping the significance to our nation of this sea heritage. The pearl-shell beds are inexhaustible—far above the wildest dreams of the early pearl-shell gatherers. On the north-eastern coast, bounded by the Great Barrier Reef, the shell waters stretch right to the Coral Sea. They cover all the Coral Sea right to Papua. In the Coral Sea we are extraordinarily lucky, for it is the richest, and all its waters and its island systems belong to Queensland, to Australia! From the Coral Sea west into the Arafura we have proved pearl-shell beds that stretch right to the Aru Islands in Dutch waters. Where the Timor Sea laps our coast the pearl-shell beds are found; and they extend right around our north-western corner into the Indian Ocean, and for a thousand miles down the Western Australian coast.

Our great need is to find but some universal use for this wonderful material, and thus supply a world market.

But we have found not only pearl-shell. For many years we have fished bêche-de-mer and trochus-shell on the eastern coast and in the Coral Sea. All three were big industries in our north, until the depression.

Another vast source of wealth, that some day will be envied by the world, is the Great Barrier Reef.

This twelve-hundred mile long wall of coral with its mighty sea-gardens is the feeding-ground for incredible numbers and varieties of food fish. There is no other reef like it in the world. And within that reef, between it and the coastline and stretching right across Torres Strait to New Guinea, are a thousand thousand smaller coral reefs, each breeding- and feeding-grounds for fish.

More than that, these waters are visited by great shoals of edible fish, migrating from other seas, from the herring to the tunny, from the sardine to the whale. I like the old whale, and hate to hear of him being slaughtered to oil the machines of man. But if he has got to go, then let our own whalers administer the *coup de grâce*. It is an ill wind ...

Along our northern, north-eastern, and north-western coastline we will establish, I hope soon, trawling enterprises that will, in the near future, create small towns which will be the ports of a fishing population such as sail out from British shores to fish the North Sea. Ports suited for bases are already established: Broome, Derby and Wyndham, for instance, on the north-western Australian coast, Darwin in the Territory, Thursday Island in Queensland's Coral Sea, Cooktown and Cairns down the Queensland north-eastern coast. There, trawling fleets and canning bases would soon build up a population born to the sea.

We have the brains and capital and labour. We want the experience—and the markets. Surely we could get the experience from the established trawling industries around the British Isles, and the experience there too that would know where to find the markets.

We learn of up-to-date nations utilizing brains, labour, and vast sums in the finding and mapping of new sea areas which in the near future can be fished on a great scale. Organized science is ready and willing to help these national prospectings for new fish beds. That the search is important to the nations concerned there can be no possible doubt.

British trawling interests are seeking fish as far away as Iceland and the Arctic Circle. And yet in our warm waters of the northern coast no British trawler has ever yet been seen. Could we not transplant, lock, stock and barrel, a branch of this sturdy trawling industry?

Nature here has been more than generous. Our northern seas are kindly for nine months of every year. There are none of the rigours that the fishing fleets of northern countries experience almost daily. And the fish are right at our doors—not hundreds of miles away as are some of the American fishing-grounds from the American coast.

If trawling fleets anxiously seek fish so far from their base and under rigorous conditions, and yet find their ventures profitable, it certainly seems reasonable to conclude that fish from northern Australian seas could be profitably transported to a market. Our northern cattle interests can send chilled beef ten thousand miles across the seas to European markets. Why cannot fish be sent too?

Probably there is a market much closer. The East is fast becoming westernized and will need our beef and fish as it needs our pearl-shell, bêche-de-mer, sandalwood, trochus-shell, and tortoise-shell. Let us give and take with the East; supply it as the demand grows and work in harmony with the Eastern nations to our mutual benefit.

We must grow continent-minded quickly. Inland from our northern seas is the cattle country capable of keeping lines of steamers busy shipping away beef canned in our own factories on our own coasts.

The strengthening of our pearling industry, the establishment of a trawling industry, would create coastal township life which would help the cattle industry immensely. That intelligent triple combination would solve the problem of the North.

With our small population we have done wonders in this great and largely inhospitable continent during the short time we have been in possession. It has been a struggle, but we have won out extraordinarily well. Now, we are no longer isolated from the world. Moreover, the world considers us a nation, and demands with increasing vehemence that we should shoulder the responsibilities of a nation.

Life, including national life, being a struggle, we should be glad to have such a big thing to struggle for. In the North, with its many, varied, and locally peculiar problems by land and sea, we have a great field for our energies, and life work for our sons.

Our national life in earnest is only just starting. There is high adventure for the individual and the nation in the development of the North and the holding of it in trust for those who will build up the Australia of our dreams.

GOLD-DUST AND ASHES

The Romantic Story of the New Guinea Goldfields

ION IDRIESS

The 26th illustrated edition now out from ETT Imprint, Exile Bay.

Brisbane Courier :-"His latest book is really the romance of the Edie Creek and Bulolo diggings, situated inland from Salamau; and with the discovery of the field are associated the names of diggers as "Shark Eye Bill" (William Park), Matt Crowe, Jim Preston, Arthur Dowling, Frank and Jim Pryke... men who in pre-war years, crept across the frontier, defying the Germans and dodging the head-hunters... These men endured terrible hardships, and frequently faced grim tragedy. Mr Idriess writes of it all, and writes of it as if he had been with them.. What a romance! What a story! It is packed with adventure, studded with splendid pen-pictures of pioneer prospectors, airmen, and patrol officers, and told with a fascinating simplicity that is borne from something very close to genius."

THE YELLOW JOSS

ION IDRIESS

With Foreword by Tony Grey. Illustrated.

Sydney Morning Herald :-"The Booya is a masterpiece of the weird and terrible. But of all the tales "The Castaway" has most power and surely merits a place with similar episodes in Conrad. Mr Idriess is adept in working up the feelings of his readers to a pitch of expectancy .... Here the excitement is terrific."

The Herald (Melbourne) :-"Every one of these tales bears the impress of truth. Anybody who lets unreasoned prejudice against short stories deter them from reading this book is missing a treat."

The Sun (Sydney) :-"Idriess tells a good story. These come from another world, a primitive and violent world, where things that seem fantastic and incredible to dwellers in the Australian cities are commonplaces of life."

Queensland Times :-"He has the happy knack of being able to blend truth and fiction in such a way that even commonplace things assume an important role and have definite and impelling force."

Woman's Budget (Sydney) :-"They give a clearer insight into his varied and adventurous life than anything he has previously written."

Honi Soit (University of Sydney) :-"Rich humour enlivens the book, particularly where the exploits of one 'Scandalous' Graham are concerned."

Producers' Review (Brisbane) :-"The name of Ion Idriess has become a household word ... as a maker of short stories he has lost none of his flair for tale-telling. Indeed we prefer this style."

Now in its 10th edition, 210 pages, available from ETT Imprint.

THE RED CHIEF

Told by the Last of his Tribe

ION IDRIESS

In times past there was an Aboriginal man
called Cumbo Gunnerah
His people called him The Red Kangaroo.
He was a clever chief and a mighty fighter
(this man from Gunnedah)
Later, the white people of this place
called him The Red Chief.

It would be hard to find a more satisfying hero than the young warrior Red Kangaroo, who by his mental and physical prowess became a chief of his tribe - the revered and powerful Red Chief of the Gunnedah district in northern New South Wales. His story is a first-rate tale of adventure but it is something more - a true story handed down from generation to generation by its hero s tribe and given by the last survivor, King Bungaree, to the white settlers of the district.

Now in its 18th edition, 214 pages, available from ETT Imprint.

www.ingramcontent.com/pod-product-compliance
Lightning Source LLC
Chambersburg PA
CBHW020752160426
43192CB00006B/313